LF

DEEP SURFACES

P H I L I P   E .   S I M M O N S

The University of Georgia Press   Athens and London

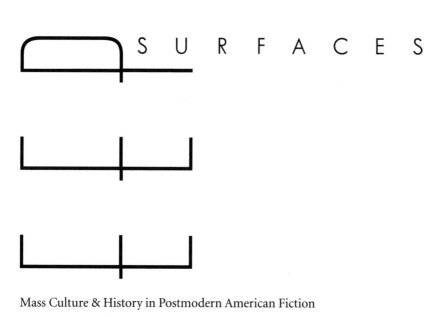

S U R F A C E S

Mass Culture & History in Postmodern American Fiction

©1997 by the University of Georgia Press
Athens, Georgia 30602
All rights reserved
Designed by Mary Mendell
Set in Minion by Books International, Inc.
Printed and bound by Braun-Brumfield, Inc.
The paper in this book meets the guidelines for permanence and
durability of the Committee on Production Guidelines
for Book Longevity of the Council on Library Resources.
Printed in the United States of America
01 00 99 98 97 C 5 4 3 2 1

Library of Congress Cataloging in Publication Data
Simmons, Philip E., 1957–
Deep surfaces : mass culture and history in postmodern
American fiction / Philip E. Simmons.
p.   cm.
Includes bibliographical references and index.
ISBN 0-8203-1843-4 (alk. paper).
1. American fiction—20th century—History and criticism.
2. Postmodernism (Literature)—United States. 3. Mass media and
literature—United States—History—20th century. 4. Literature and
history—United States—History—20th century. 5. Popular culture—
United States—History—20th century. 6. Popular culture in
literature. 7. History in literature. I. Title.
PS374. P6485 1997
813'.5409—dc20   95-52474
British Library Cataloging in Publication Data available

FOR KATHRYN

CONTENTS

ACKNOWLEDGMENTS

I would like to thank Bob Weisbuch, John Kucich, and especially Enoch Brater for their help in seeing me through the dissertation that was the first and crucial phase of this project. And thanks to Charles Newman for first sparking my interest in cultural criticism. My thanks to Richard Mallette and Judith Stone, not only for reading and commenting on parts of this book, but for their sound advice on the academic life in general. Thomas Schaub boosted my confidence in this project by publishing an earlier version of one of these chapters and has since provided timely advice and encouragement. Thanks to Gerald Graff for reading a portion of the manuscript and providing helpful response. My readers for the University of Georgia Press, David Cowart and Steven Weisenburger, read the manuscript in its entirety and provided invaluable commentary and suggestions for revision. Thanks to Geoff McNeil for his research assistance. Much of this work was supported with research funds provided by Lake Forest College, for which I am most grateful. And last, I must thank my wife, Kathryn, who has suffered this project and much else with grace and unswerving commitment.

An earlier version of chapter 4 appeared in *Genre* 24.1 (Spring 1991): 45–62. Chapter 1 appeared in *Contemporary Literature* 33.4 (Winter 1992): 601–24.

DEEP SURFACES

INTRODUCTION
A Postmodern Problem: Imagining History from
within Mass Culture

In thinking about the position of the postmodern novel in the larger scene of
American culture, one at some point confronts television, which seems at once
everywhere and nowhere, substance and shadow, defining our cultural moment
and distracting us from it. Together with popular film and advertising in all
media, television is one of the primary means by which the postmodern conditions of knowledge are established within everyday life. The task of this book
will be to examine how those conditions are registered in the work of a number
of postmodern American novelists, with particular attention to ways in which
mass culture informs historical thinking in their fiction. With the vertiginous
self-consciousness and skepticism that belong to the postmodern historical
imagination, writers as different in style and approach as Thomas Pynchon,
E. L. Doctorow, Ishmael Reed, Don DeLillo, Nicholson Baker, and Bobbie Ann
Mason not only write about the present while writing about the past but also
construct histories of their own novelistic methods, of the conditions of their
texts' production, and of their own approach to representing the past. In these

constructions, mass culture—particularly film, television, and the consumer culture built on advertising—shows up as a significant historical development in itself. Enabled by new technologies and multinational organizations of capital, mass culture has become the "cultural dominant"—the force field in which all forms of representation, including the novel, must operate.[1] In their vision of an American culture in which history and the self are unavoidably mediated, if not produced, by mass culture, these texts treat the history of mass culture as the history of an epistemology. By observing the relations between mass culture and these exemplary narratives, we may discern the shape of the postmodern historical imagination. That shape is a paradoxical one: a "deep surface" that both invokes and rejects traditional modes of historical understanding in "depth," as it reconfigures the human subject and ranges among local and contingent historical narratives organized at the mass-cultural "surface."

Postmodern culture has been characterized by its lack of belief in master narratives of history (Lyotard) and by its inability to think historically at all (Jameson). In searching for culprits for the supposed loss of historical consciousness in contemporary life, cultural critics from all regions of the political spectrum frequently choose mass culture for attack. The common view has it that mass culture, especially film and television, threatens "genuine" historical understanding, giving us an awareness of "surface" appearances only, and failing to penetrate to the "depth" of an authentic understanding of historical process. This attitude toward mass culture is of a piece with an attitude that sees postmodern fiction as having relinquished "authentic" historical inquiry in favor of an endlessly ironic play with cultural surfaces. In its complicity with a mass culture that entertains more than it informs and whose texts seem concerned more with their own processes than with any reference to an extratextual "real world," the postmodern historical novel, according to Fredric Jameson, "can no longer set out to represent the historical past; it can only 'represent' our ideas and stereotypes about that past (which thereby at once becomes 'pop history')" ("Postmodernism" 71).

In answering this charge, Linda Hutcheon has argued that Jameson has got the story half right. The postmodern historical novel, what Hutcheon calls "historiographic metafiction," simultaneously uses and abuses the conventions of historical discourse, in effect "doing history" while exposing the artifice and convention that all history writing entails. "The postmodern, then," writes Hutcheon, "effects two simultaneous moves. It reinstalls historical contexts as significant and even determining, but in so doing, it problematizes the entire notion of historical knowledge" (*A Poetics of Postmodernism* 89). One way to think of the deep surface is as a *rhetorical* strategy that relies on these two "simultaneous moves": one that attempts to offer some understanding of history in "depth" and one that reveals all such attempts to be a trick of surface effects. The effect is to stage a kind of drama in which the reader is lured into the depths of fiction's funhouse only to become lost among mirrored surfaces.

Considered as a rhetorical strategy, the deep surface bears comparison with the rhetoric of Jameson's theory of postmodernism itself. For while Jameson describes a postmodern culture characterized by "depthlessness" and an inability to achieve "genuine" historical consciousness, he seeks "the renewal of historical analysis itself" through a direct engagement with the concepts of postmodernism (*Postmodernism* 401).[2] Jameson's rhetoric enacts a drama in which we are saved from the depthlessness of postmodern culture by the tools of Marxist historical analysis. This is of course the essential drama of any interpretive act: to correct error, to get past immediate and superficial response, to get to some deeper meaning beneath the level of appearance.[3] Jameson is more sanguine about the efficacy of interpretive criticism than another important theorist of the postmodern, Jean Baudrillard, who writes that "*Every interpretive discourse (discours de sens) wants to get beyond appearances; this is its illusion and fraud. But getting beyond appearances is an impossible task*" (*Selected Writings* 150).[4] Jameson's rhetoric is commensurate with that of postmodern fiction—both invoke the paradox of the deep surface—but with the course of the drama reversed. For whereas postmodern historical fiction beckons with depth, only to scatter us among surfaces, Jameson's analysis threatens us with surfaces, only to lead us safely (so he claims) into depth.

That is, of course, putting the matter too simply. Postmodern fiction opens itself to the play of mass-cultural surfaces as a way of enacting a thoroughgoing skepticism regarding foundational modes of truth and representation. But it does not, as its detractors would have it, do merely that. In the fiction studied here, the presence of mass culture on both the thematic and formal levels does not occasion the loss or effacement of history but rather a vigorous investigation of the possibilities for historical understanding. In the process, these texts "do history" in perhaps the only way that is left to us under postmodern conditions. In much the same way, Jameson's theory of the postmodern is not merely a retrograde imposition of depth models of analysis on a contemporary culture seemingly resistant to such forms of critical "mastery." Rather, his is an attempt to work *through* the phenomena of contemporary culture to some comprehensive theory of a postmodernity that necessarily alters the critical methods with which it is described.

A metaphor becomes poetic by doing something "wrong" with language. Time does not *really* ride a winged chariot, and there is something distinctly awkward about trying to imagine it doing so. But it is through just this sort of determined awkwardness that metaphor blocks habitual understanding and forces us to "see" something fresh. I have something of that poetic intention for my metaphor of the deep surface, except that as a paradoxical figure it cannot be "seen" at all. By resisting the easy reduction to a thing seen, it makes us newly aware of the conventional nature of the depth/surface metaphor. Depth is good, surface is bad. We like our fictional characters to be "three-dimensional," not "flat." The good old days had a depth that the superficial present lacks. To Jean Baudrillard, modernist New York represents "the final fling of this baroque verticality" while postmodernist Los Angeles is an "extravaganza of undifferentiated surfaces" (*America* 21, 125). Like many metaphors for knowledge, the depth/surface metaphor would seem to have its basis in visual perception. We use the phrase "I see" as equivalent to "I know." To see only to the surface of things is to have one's vision stopped—by reflection from a window, say, or simply by the opacity of an object's surface—and to be denied a more comprehensive vision of the object of our scrutiny. We want to "see into" things, we want "insight," we "look deeply." One common understanding of postmodernism, then, is as the cultural condition in which all attempts to "see" beyond surface appearances are systematically blocked.

But I would hope that my unpresentable, unimaginable metaphor of the deep surface might tease us into some fresh thought on this question. This study proceeds by a successive unfolding of this metaphor, exploring the different ways in which the paradoxical shape of the postmodern historical imagination is realized in individual texts. From the undecidable choice between multiple historical schemes in Pynchon, to DeLillo's darkly ironic shifts between the visible, banal surfaces of culture and its terrifying, inexplicable depths, to Reed's playful deconstruction of historiographic conventions and master narratives, we see how engagement with mass culture has produced a rich field of inquiry into antifoundational modes of historical thinking. The metaphor of the "surface" can suggest by turns the nonhierarchical, decentered geometries of the network and the intertext, the refusal of the linguistic referent and of master historical narratives, and the two-dimensional surface of the video screen on which television organizes our perceptions. But the addition of the adjective *deep* is meant as a rejoinder to those who see in postmodern fiction a loss or refusal of historical consciousness. These "surfaces" indeed signal a problematic departure from earlier modes of historical understanding, but the "deep surfaces" found in postmodern fiction do not necessarily entail a loss for historical thinking.

Some Definitions

How one approaches the relations between novels and mass culture depends on how one defines "mass culture." Though film and television figure most prominently in its examination of contemporary image culture, this study extends the definition of mass culture beyond the technologies of communication to consumer culture generally (K-Mart, McDonald's, the contents of your medicine cabinet). Most broadly considered, mass culture is the culture of the products and services of corporations organized on a national or multinational basis. Such a definition argues for the aggressively inclusive nature of contemporary mass culture, which in its global and manifold reach into every cranny of our daily affairs promises to become *all* culture—a historically unprecedented situation that in part defines the postmodern moment.

What about novels? As commodities marketed and distributed by national and multinational corporations, commercially published novels are themselves mass-cultural artifacts. Therefore, this cannot be a study simply of the "effects" of mass culture on the contemporary novel.[5] The novels discussed here are neither the passive victims of a barbaric colonizing mass culture nor modernist icons of artistic purity, engaging mass culture from some privileged vantage point beyond its reach. The issue is not how to conceptualize a direct causal relationship between novel writing and the products of film and television but rather to understand how certain developments in fiction mark the novel's participation in a larger mass culture and can be seen as part of a shift to general conditions of knowledge and conventions of representation that may meaningfully be termed postmodern.

But what *can* meaningfully be called postmodern? One approaches a term as large and ungainly as "postmodernism" the way the blind men approached the elephant. Each took hold of a different part and described a different beast. Considering postmodernism narrowly within the American cultural context, certain postwar developments in literature, the visual arts, architecture, music, and performance coalesce into an image of a postmodernism whose shared obsessions with antifoundational modes of truth and representation are marked by a set of common procedures that sometimes extend but more often counter modernist ones: ontological disruption and play; an aggressive mixing of "high" and "popular" cultural styles; pastiche and parody of genres and of conventional forms of historical representation; a deconstructionist or otherwise interventionist approach to representational conventions generally. In the visual arts of the 1950s and early 1960s one finds Robert Rauschenberg, Jasper Johns, Claes Oldenberg, and, decisively, Andy Warhol rejecting the prevailing Greenbergian orthodoxy represented by Jackson Pollock and the abstract expressionists. In music, the work of such composers as Philip Glass, Steve Reich, Lukas Foss, Dominick Argento, and David Del Tredici announces variously a return to tonality, the recovery of historical styles, and a newfound concern for the listener in reaction to serialism, austerity, and abstraction in such composers as Babbitt, Berio, Stockhausen, and Boulez. The shift to postmodernist modes is perhaps most visible in architecture, where the work of Philip Johnson (from the AT&T building onward), Charles Moore, Robert Venturi, Frank Gehry, Michael Graves, and Peter Eisenman rejects the purified forms and utopian social pretensions of modernism in favor of an eclectic recovery of past styles, exposure of architectural conventions, populism, and contextual reference.[6]

The story of postmodernism in literature, as in the other disciplines mentioned, is one whose complexities and internal resistances make summary formulation difficult. Though Irving Howe and Leslie Fiedler used the term *postmodernism* to describe the weakening of the modernist impulse in literature in the 1950s, it was John Barth's influential 1967 essay "The Literature of Exhaustion" that first defined what later critics would call postmodernist fiction. In that essay, Barth describes the predicament of the self-conscious contemporary writer who laments the "used-upness" of certain literary forms and finds him- or herself unable to surpass the achievements of either modernism or nineteenth-century realism. Faced with these difficulties, the contemporary writer (Barth did not yet use the term *postmodernist*) can be original only by creating work that comments upon the impossibility of its being original. Barth's model is the fiction of Jorge Luis Borges, whose story "Pierre Menard, Author of the Quixote" is both a parable of the writer's predicament and a demonstration of Barth's preferred way out of it. Barth's own short story "Lost in the Funhouse," published in the same year, demonstrates the procedure brilliantly, and a number of the most influential of the postmodernists published important works in the late 1960s: William Gass, *Willie Masters' Lonesome Wife* (1968); Donald Barthelme, *Snow White* (1967); Thomas Pynchon, *The Crying of Lot 49* (1967); and Robert Coover, *Pricksongs and Descants* (1969).[7]

In the same year that Barth was publishing "The Literature of Exhaustion" and "Lost in the Funhouse," Jacques Derrida published *La Voix et le phénomène, De la grammatologie,* and *L'Écriture et la différence,* the three books that established him as a major new force in continental philosophy. Taking hold of the elephant here, postmodernism appears as a new phase of philosophical thought and critical theory identified with poststructuralism. On the American scene, poststructuralism's inaugural moment was Derrida's delivery of "Structure, Sign, and Play in the Discourse of the Human Sciences" at a Johns Hopkins Humanities Center symposium in October 1966.[8] In that well-known essay, Derrida argues that structuralism as exemplified by Claude Lévi-Strauss practices a sort of atavistic humanism in its efforts to identify and articulate "centered" linguistic and cultural structures. Using a radicalized Saussurian linguistics, Derrida undermines (or "deconstructs" as the process will later be called by Derrida's students) the concept of the "center." The antifoundational approach Derrida uses in his attack on structuralism will come to be one of the defining features of postmodernist critical theory and cultural practice. It is best characterized by two core attitudes or obsessions. One has to do with the impossibility of any center that would ground a system of thought or ensure that one is able to arrive at a disinterested position outside of the text, symbolic system, or culture that one is studying. As Frank Lentricchia puts it, "there is, in effect, no 'point,' no origin, no end, no place outside discourse from which to fix, make determinate, and establish metaphysical boundaries for the play of linguistic signifiers" (*After the New Criticism* 160–61). The second obsession is really a consequence of the first: the inability to find a stable center or the archimedean point outside of language means that one is forever bound within the process of signification. There is no escape from the systems of signs in which we are enmeshed and which can be said to constitute our very identity. And because the process of signification is always in flux, always in play, and never entirely within our control, there can be no fixed essences and no truths other than those that are local, contingent, and temporary.

One difficulty with using poststructuralist thought to define postmodernism is that the continental philosophical tradition out of which poststructuralist thought develops uses a different historical scheme than the more narrow American one described above. As Derrida's program becomes an attack on the "metaphysics of presence" of the entire Western philosophical tradition, and as Michel Foucault simultaneously exposes and unravels Enlightenment practices of knowledge and power, the postmodern moment becomes an epochal shift of much larger dimensions. Now more than a postwar cultural and artistic movement that succeeds the modernist period of roughly 1890 to 1945, postmodernism becomes the successor to 250 years of Enlightenment thought if not (in its most grandiose claims) to the entire Western philosophical tradition since Plato. In this larger sense, the cultural and intellectual developments of the recent decades become not simply post-modernist but post-Enlightenment and post- or anti-humanist.

The confusion of historical schemes can be seen clearly in the reception in the United States of the work of Jean-François Lyotard, who in *The Postmodern Condition* defined postmodernism as "incredulity toward metanarratives" (xxiv). In Lyotard's continental context, the primary metanarratives toward which we are said to be incredulous are the French narrative of national liberation originating with the Enlightenment and the French Revolution, and the German narrative of the progressive emancipation of the spirit, epitomized by Hegel's idealist, dialectical model of history. That these master narratives are the product of Enlightenment thought produces an important but too often overlooked difficulty in importing Lyotard's continental concept of postmodernism into an American or Anglo-American context. It is impossible, on the basis of incredulity toward these particular metanarratives, to distinguish between postmodernism and what in the Anglo-American context is termed *modernism.* The "modern" period against which Lyotard poses the "postmodern" is not the "modernist" period 1890–1945, but rather the period from the Enlightenment and French Revolution forward. The confusion is exemplified by Lyotard's invocation of Godel's theorem as an underpinning of "postmodernist" science, when Godel, like Einstein and Heisenberg, is preeminently a figure of what is normally called "modern" science. None of this lessens the validity and importance of Lyotard's insights into the pragmatics of the legitimation of knowledge by narrative, insights which have proved useful in this study and elsewhere. But his work has sown confusion among cultural critics who apply Lyotard's historical terms to an American postmodernism seen as beginning in the late 1950s or 1960s.[9] In much of the critical and theoretical discussion of recent years, there is an often unacknowledged slippage between postmodernism intended in the wider sense of "post-Enlightenment" and in the narrower sense of "post-modernist."

Which sends us to the elephant a third time. Certain developments within mass culture help us to define a postmodernism that belongs decidedly to the postwar period and yet has some of the larger philosophical consequences suggested by poststructuralism. Furthermore, certain features of our mass cultural environment correspond to the formal features of much postmodernist artistic and literary practice. The common procedures of postmodernist art, music, architecture, and literature described above are all found within contemporary film and television as well: ontological disruption, mixing of high and popular styles, pastiche and parody of genres and of methods of representing history, and a continual disruption of representational conventions (Fiske 84–128). The correspondences between postmodernist fiction and our mass-cultural environment prompt Brian McHale to remark that "what postmodernist fiction imitates, the object of its mimesis, is the pluralistic and anarchistic ontological landscape of advanced industrial cultures" (*Postmodernist Fiction* 38).

A clear advantage of tying our understanding of postmodernism to mass culture is that the development of contemporary mass culture is marked by particular technological developments and "real world" economic changes of the postwar period, providing a material basis for the distinction between modernist and postmodernist conditions. For despite the significance of film and radio in the earlier decades of this century, and the long and significant history of advertising in American life,[10] the beginning of what is variously known as the Postindustrial Era, the Information Age, or the Consumer Society is marked definitively by key postwar technological and commercial developments: the rapid diffusion of broadcast television in the 1950s; the development of the first commercial electronic digital computer (the UNIVAC I in 1951); and the initiation of satellite communications beginning in 1958 (with the first commercial communications satellite, the COMSAT Early Bird, launched in 1965). As the basis for global information networks, these and other information technologies enabled not only the global projection of military command and control for which most of them were initially developed but also the global integration of corporate structures and financial markets.

A further reason to see mass culture as central to our understanding of postmodernism is that our global, image-driven, electronic culture seems to be bringing about the larger epistemological shift that poststructuralist thought announces: the idea that there is no escape from representation is given special point by our experience of a mass consumer culture that surrounds and invades us with a ceaseless flow of images and information. One of the most striking developments in late twentieth-century American culture (if not in that of the remote Balinese village whose members gather nightly to watch videotapes of *Dallas)* is the extent to which television, film, radio, popular music, and consumer culture have become an inextricable part of our consciousness.[11] It is true that every age has told its own story of the threat to the distinction between reality and images. Not only the Western philosophical and religious traditions but the Hindu and Buddhist traditions as well have continuously articulated the possibility, if not the certainty, that the world as we experience it is nothing but shadow and illusion. From one perspective, then, contemporary mass culture has done nothing more than give new material manifestation to an ancient problem. But we are far from understanding just what it means that one billion people can watch the same football game, as they did Superbowl XXVI in 1992, or that 55 million people tuned in for the farewell episode of *The Tonight Show Starring Johnny Carson* (22 May 1992), or, perhaps more important, that millions tune in routinely to the regular offerings of prime-time television. At some point quantitative differences become qualitative ones. Global electronic mass culture has to an unprecedented extent saturated contemporary society and the contemporary psyche with images and newly imperils the distinctions between image and reality, self and world, inside and outside that have grounded claims to knowledge in the Western rational and empirical traditions.[12] Enabled by postwar developments in computing and telecommunications technologies and considered as part of a complex transformation of the global economy, today's mass consumer culture is not simply a rerun of the shadows flickering on the walls of Plato's cave, but a historically distinct phenomenon that defines the postmodern period.

Attitudes toward History

Everyone has his or her favorite precursor of the postmodern artist—Duchamp, Sterne, Cervantes.[13] However, the foregoing discussion suggests the importance of seeing how a text's formal and philosophical concerns are conjoined with material and social developments. The formal disruptions in Sterne's *Tristram Shandy* (1767) do resemble Ishmael Reed's use of pastiche in *Mumbo Jumbo* (1972). But as we shall see in chapter 3, Sterne's subversions belong to a particular moment in print culture's ascendance and consequent transformation of an older rhetorical culture. Reed's pastiche, on the other hand, engages a particular historical situation in which the novel is transformed by the conditions of its survival within an ascendant image culture. Nor does a marked concern with postwar mass culture by itself make a text postmodernist. In chapter 1 we find that mass consumer culture forms the central obsessions of the protagonists of both Walker Percy's *The Moviegoer* (1961) and Nicholson Baker's *The Mezzanine* (1988). Yet only by attending to the modes of social and economic organization represented in the two novels can we place Percy's and Baker's fiction historically within the cultural moments of late modernism and postmodernism, respectively, and see that the difference in how mass culture informs the historiographic enterprise of each novel marks the shift to the postmodern historical imagination.

To talk of a shift to postmodern modes of knowledge is to suggest the construction of precisely the sort of universal, linear history that postmodern historical thinking is said to reject. However much one insists that the story one tells is to be taken as only that—a constructed, contingent narrative, something to be resisted, argued with, qualified, and finally, no doubt, forgotten—one is seen as attempting to present some essential truth of a matter that lies "out there," independent of our conceptions of it. This predicament should be familiar to all those who work in the wake of poststructuralism. If in describing postmodernism one seems to adopt a disinterested position outside of the phenomena one is describing and uses a discourse that seems little concerned with the inherent instabilities in language described by poststructuralist theory, either of two things is the case: one has been terribly naive, or the claims one has made about postmodernism (that there is no getting "outside" of culture, language, and representation, no escape from the indeterminacy of meaning, etc.) are demonstrably untrue. There are a number of good reasons for viewing this as a false predicament.[14] Even if one did not think more apparent than real the contradiction of attempting to "master" a system premised on the refusal of mastery, as a practical matter one can do little more than make one's disclaimers and pass on, trying to achieve self-consciousness without self-paralysis. Brian McHale has gone so far as to put his disclaimer in the title of his book *Constructing Postmodernism* and has offered theorists of postmodernism the consolation that "postmodernism's failure to satisfy the criteria of objecthood is one it shares with other interesting and valuable cultural artifacts, such as, for example, 'the Renaissance' or 'American literature' or 'pastoral elegy' or 'Shakespeare.' Like these other artifacts, postmodernism exists discursively, in the discourses we produce *about* it and *using* it" (1). The experience of teaching undergraduates who are hungry for linear narratives of knowledge, and who want to leave the classroom with a tune they can whistle, reminds me daily that to the extent one values coherence over incoherence one risks engaging a totalizing rhetoric. In practice, however, one cannot go far as a critic (or a teacher) without being reminded, sometimes crushingly, that one's theories and ideas have only contingent and temporary value. Indeed, one of the best antidotes to critical hubris is to read postmodernist fiction, whose deep surfaces continually remind us of the dangers of mistaking our narratives of history for the real.

In trying to grasp the "real" forces of history, a critic such as Fredric Jameson tries to recover precisely the kind of depth that is rejected by the postmodern fiction studied here. A historical imagination characterized by "depth" would locate its representations of history, if only implicitly, within some ultimate framework or master narrative. For Jameson, the necessary framework remains the Marxist historical narrative of class struggle, however much he and other neo-Marxist critics, such as Louis Althusser, have refined and altered its classical formulations. From a broader perspective that includes Anglo-American traditions, we could add other frameworks, such as the Providentialist narrative of history as the unfolding of God's plan, the Whig narrative of the progressive realization of individual liberties, or the narrative of industrialization as material progress. These master narratives legitimate local representations of history by providing a ground of explanation beyond which one is presumably unable to go.

The most influential definitions of postmodernism speak directly out of an anxiety about the ability of such narratives to organize and legitimate historical knowledge. While Lyotard defines postmodernism as an "incredulity toward metanarratives," Jameson begins his book *Postmodernism* with the claim that "it is safest to grasp the concept of the postmodern as an attempt to think the present historically in an age that has forgotten how to think historically in the first place" (ix). Arguably, such formulations are merely the latest versions of a perennial anxiety about historical understanding. After all, those historians and thinkers who are supposed to have invoked so-called master narratives in the past rarely did so with the sort of sunny confidence that today's cultural critics seem to assume they did. But Jameson's lament for postmodernity's historical amnesia is more than simply another case of moaning for a lost golden age. Different periods, and different writers, produce characteristic attitudes toward depth among which it is important to distinguish. In making the following distinctions among classical, romantic, modern, and postmodern attitudes toward depth, I am not asserting that any given historical period was homogeneous in its historical attitudes. Rather, I am once again describing a "dominant" attitude that must be understood within a matrix of resistances and countervailing trends at any particular historical moment. Further, these attitudes toward depth, much like medieval humors, are to be found admixed in varying proportions within individual writers.

The attitude furthest from the postmodernist can be called the "classical," which holds that depth both exists and is knowable. This is the attitude of classical Marxism, and belongs as well to Enlightenment thought at its most confident (and least interesting). As exemplified in the movement from Locke's theory of language to that of Burke, the "classical" typically summons its opponent in the "romantic," an attitude which presumes that depth exists but cannot be known.[15] The romantic attitude toward the impossibility of knowing historical depth is found in Thomas Carlyle, who in his essay "On History" laments the fact that "Narrative is *linear,* Action is *solid*" and that "every event is the offspring not of one, but of all other events prior or contemporaneous" (221). This view of total history as a plenum makes the writing of any one "true" history impossible: "Alas, for our 'chains,' or chainlets, of 'causes and effects,' which we so assiduously track through certain handbreadths of years and square miles, when the whole is a broad, deep, Immensity, and each atom is 'chained' and complected with all!" (221). Carlyle's vision of the total connectedness of history partakes of what Kenneth Burke calls the "paradox of purity," for pure connectedness in this case is indistinguishable from pure disconnectedness and incoherence. This is the same observation we will make in chapter 5 in regard to *Gravity's Rainbow:* Slothrop's disintegration is simultaneously the means by which he grasps the essential connectedness of all things. In quailing before

"Immensity," Carlyle is willing to trade classical confidence for the energies of the romantic sublime, rejecting what he perceives to be the reductive certainties of Enlightenment historiographers, those "cause and effect speculators" who read "the inscrutable Book of Nature, as if it were a Merchant's Ledger" (222).

The classical attitude typically unfolds into the romantic—often within the work of a single writer—at that point where its explanations come to an end: the classical certitude evinced by today's religious fundamentalists stands ultimately on the mystery of revelation, just as Descartes's confidence in reason was founded on the belief in an undeceiving god. This moment occurs in the final section of Book I of David Hume's *Treatise Concerning Human Understanding*, where Hume confronts, with considerable anguish, the consequences of his skeptical demolition of reason and experience as a foundation for knowledge: "I am confounded with all these questions, and begin to fancy myself in the most deplorable condition imaginable, inviron'd with the deepest darkness, and utterly depriv'd of the use of every member and faculty" (269). Here Hume deploys a rhetoric of weakness, defect, and hesitation that we can locate in Rousseau as well, and which later, through Coleridge, will become an important feature of the romantic persona. It is not until his later *Enquiry Concerning the Principles of Morals,* where he reestablishes morality on what to him is the solid ground of *sentiment,* that Hume recovers fully his classical equanimity.

The "modernist" attitude, like the romantic, rejects classical certainties but makes the radical move of assuming that depth itself no longer exists. The modernist historical imagination then continues to struggle toward a depth that it knows to be illusory. This attitude informs Walker Percy's *The Moviegoer,* as we shall see in chapter 1. It also informs Faulkner's *Absalom, Absalom!:* though history is revealed to have a foundation no more solid than the breath of the various narrators who construct the history of the Sutpens, depth nonetheless remains the norm against which the depthlessness of the modern world is evaluated. Frost's narrator in "For Once, Then, Something" evinces the modernist attitude as he peers into the depths of the well. Wallace Stevens's idea of the "supreme fiction" that would replace religious structures is another example of the modernist effort to establish foundations despite their acknowledged fictionality. The characteristic tone of this effort is in Eliot's plaint at the end of *The Waste Land:* "These fragments I have shored against my ruins." To Terry Eagleton, modernism's doomed struggle for depth is what continues to make it interesting: "for this struggle continually drives it toward classical styles of sensemaking which are at once unacceptable and inescapable, traditional matrices of meaning which have become progressively empty but which nevertheless continue to exert their implacable force" ("Capitalism, Modernism and Postmodernism" 70). Modernism gains its sense of tragedy from its view that the loss of absolutes and the continued effort to reclaim them are equally necessary.

Finally, the "postmodernist" attitude toward history is one that both assumes that depth does not exist and also ceases to see this as a tragic loss.[16] Depth has ceased to be the norm against which contemporary depthlessness is measured, so that the terms *depth* and *surface* lose their ordinary meaning as value terms. The search for depth may persist, but it is no longer an ennobling, tragic enterprise. This search becomes in a curious way simply another "option" or "language game," one among many arrayed at the cultural surface. Though in postmodernism a certain poignancy may still attend the struggle for depth—as in the case of Don DeLillo's Lee Harvey Oswald—just as often this struggle is played for laughs. Samuel Beckett's work exemplifies how the modernist attitude unfolds into the postmodernist one at that point where, rather than being a noble failure that confers some meaning on the struggle, the search for depth is seen from the outset as pointless, even comic. In Baker's *The Mezzanine*, DeLillo's *Libra*, Mason's *In Country*, Reed's *Mumbo Jumbo*, and Pynchon's *Gravity's Rainbow* and *Vineland*, we have characters in quest of deeper understanding of self and history. In each case that quest not only fails but fails in a way that lacks the kinds of intensity we expect from modernist works. In these postmodernist novels, the search for depth provides a basic narrative form but one that is treated parodically as a literary convention and thus stripped of its mythic resonance.

One could argue that the sort of bleak comedy postmodern fiction often constructs out of the failed search for depth is found in modernist works as well. In Faulkner's *The Sound and the Fury*, Jason Compson's rabid self-delusions and his botched efforts to catch his niece in the act of fornication remind us that tragedy easily tips over into farce. And yet depth retains its hold on the imagination in Faulkner in a way it does not in postmodern fiction: postmodern fiction does not have an equivalent for Faulkner's "implacable and immemorial earth," nor does it for the depth of biological process represented by Lena Grove's pregnancy in *Light in August*. Consider the distance we have traveled from Lena Grove to Samantha Hughes, the main character of Bobbie Ann Mason's *In Country*, who says that "it used to be that getting pregnant when you weren't married ruined your life because of the disgrace; now it just ruined your life, and nobody cared enough for it to be a disgrace" (103). The mysteries of generation and anxieties about lineage so important to Faulkner find no place in DeLillo's *White Noise*, where in a family that combines children from several marriages the facts of paternity and knowledge of blood relation are given a glancing attention that reduces them to the level of trivia.[17]

As the metaphor of the deep surface suggests, the postmodern historical imagination is further distinguished by its paradoxical nature, which to an extent derives from its foregrounding of the paradox inherent in all historical explanation. DeLillo's fiction in particular reminds us that historical "depth" is two-faced. On the one side, the search for depth is a search for a metanarrative that legitimates and grounds our understanding of history. Whether history is seen as driven by conspiracy, class struggle, liberation of the individual spirit, or God's will, depth theories provide a principle of causality and thus an explanation for historical events. But on the other side, precisely because of its a priori nature as a ground for historical explanation, depth is also a source of mystery. As Hayden White has argued, the sense of rightness that we find in historical accounts ultimately derives from aesthetic and moral judgments, rather than from epistemological ones (*Metahistory* xii). Metanarrative is self-legitimating, the explanation that cannot be explained, narrative's prime mover. Historical explanation thus involves what Kenneth Burke has called an "antinomy of definition," in which a thing is understood in terms of what it is not (*Grammar of Motives* 21–58). In explaining the "paradox of substance," Burke writes that the word *substance* is commonly used to mean that which is intrinsic to or the essence of a thing, while etymologically *substance* refers to that which "stands under," supports, and is thus outside or extrinsic to that thing. So with historical explanation: a particular historical field must always be understood with reference to something outside itself—whether its context, its causal determining law, or its *telos*—and this appeal to something outside of the events to be explained must rest finally on the unknown. To "ex-plain" means to smooth out flat, to make something into a visible *surface*. But the surface laid bare by the explanations of depth, like crumpled paper smoothed, retains its invisible underside. "Ex-planation" produces "understanding," something which stands under history but which itself remains unknown. In DeLillo's fiction, the search for depth is revealed to be a search not so much for certainty as for the satisfactions of mystery.

All this would suggest that historical thinking, in any age, has its paradoxical aspect. But for historical thinking that engages mass cultural phenomena, such as we find in the fiction studied here, an important additional source of paradox lies within the concept of mass culture itself. The paradoxical quality of the concept of mass culture grows out of its attachment to cyclical theories of history, in which the progress of civilization necessarily entails its decline and fall. Patrick Brantlinger expresses this paradox most succinctly when he writes that "civilization leads to the death of civilization" (34–35). Since Juvenal placed the blame for the decay of the Republic on the fickle Roman populace, in love with *panem et circenses,* the concept of mass culture has developed within theories of social decay tied originally to the fall of Rome. In his study of nineteenth- and twentieth-century social thinkers, Brantlinger shows how theorists of mass culture usually operate within the mode of a "negative classicism" that associates mass culture with the fall, first from Republic to Empire, and finally into barbarism. The dual attitudes toward mass culture that such thinking entails are still found today: "As Rome was both the zenith and the burying ground of ancient civilization, so modern mass society with its mass culture is both zenith and nadir of modern progress, acme and end of the line for the 'dual revolutions' of industrialization and democratization. Or so negative classicists either fear or hope" (35). As Brantlinger's argument suggests, positive and negative valuations of mass culture, with their corresponding utopian and dystopian visions of the future, often lie so close to one another as to become inseparable. It is therefore not surprising that within works of fiction the historical valence of mass culture is often in fact an ambivalence.

In Pynchon's *Gravity's Rainbow,* for example, the technology and practice of film is associated with a history of exploitation and violence, while at the same time the text's allusions to film, popular music, comic books, and other mass-cultural artifacts are a continual source of playful, comic disruption that suggests a possible realm of freedom to be found in the popular. In Nicholson Baker's *The Mezzanine,* the products of mass corporate culture are brazenly celebrated as providing the only reliable pleasures remaining to a protagonist/narrator who finds himself enclosed within a seamless world of mass culture, yet at the same time the narrator's irony acknowledges the superficiality of such a celebration.

Donald Barthelme's *Snow White* bemoans the debased and anarchic nature of contemporary life under the pressures of mass culture, while it delights in the possibilities for verbal play that such anarchy provides. On one level this novel is about the marginality of "serious" literary fiction in a culture glutted with mass-cultural artifacts. The novel achieves much of its comic effect by capitalizing on the play of differences experienced in a culture where discourses are fragmented and scrambled without regard for hierarchies of cultural position or status. Paper towels, shower curtains, and talk about baby food rub up against fragments of philosophy, psychology, and literary criticism. As fragments of discourse, signifiers detached from their "high" cultural contexts, the names of Mozart, Shelley, Byron, Keats, Pushkin, Gogol, and Dostoevski appear alongside the names of Bloomingdale's, Volkswagen, the Yellow Pages, Old Gold cigarettes, and DDT. The reader's pleasure comes in part from seeing "high" cultural icons mixed shamelessly with the detritus of mass consumer culture. In an important sense, this novel, with its formal disruptions, fragmentation, and pastiche of cultural discourses, takes as its subject matter the way that the postmodern novel's bid for cultural comprehensiveness is doomed by its position within a culture too distracted for the sort of sustained attention that novel reading requires. But in its way, *Snow White* finds a form in which to represent that which it claims to be unrepresentable: the anarchic linguistic landscape of postmodern culture. The novel's contradictory attitude to its own operations is embodied in its ambivalent tone. One of the dwarfs complains that "analogies break down, regimes break down, but the way I feel remains. I feel abandoned" (137). On the other hand, the narrative doesn't stop "trying to break out of this bag that we are in" (179), takes continual delight in the resources of verbal play, and is nourished by "the ongoing circus of the mind in motion" (139). As much as the characters register their distress at the breakdown of traditional narrative structures and the fragmentation of the larger cultural systems in which such narratives are enmeshed, the novel as a whole is happy to romp through the ruins.

Dual attitudes toward mass culture are demonstrated most schematically in science fiction and fantasy writing. A novel such as Marge Piercy's *Woman on the Edge of Time* goes so far as to project two possible futures: an authoritarian dystopia in which all the most repressive features of contemporary technological mass culture are exaggerated, and a utopia in which the same technologies have been placed in the control of individuals and communities for personal and communal benefit, in effect eliminating "mass culture" by transforming the ways that the communications technologies are controlled and used. Donna Haraway has used the science-fiction concept of the cyborg—part human, part machine—as a way of projecting into the future our current condition as subjects within postmodern culture. To Haraway, such scenarios have positive and negative values: "From one perspective, a cyborg world is about the final imposition of a grid of control on the planet, about the final abstraction embodied in a Star Wars apocalypse waged in the name of defense, about the final appropriation of women's bodies in a masculinist orgy of war. From another perspective, a cyborg world might be about lived social and bodily realities in which people are not afraid of their joint kinship with animals and machines, not afraid of permanently partial identities and contradictory standpoints" (196). Within postmodern fiction the tension between the positive and negative values of mass culture typically results in a historical double vision in which mass culture is both the cutting edge of progress and the decline of civilization; it can be both the means by which the masses achieve democratic participation in culture and the means by which a power elite manipulates the masses into consumerist passion and political quietism; it both educates and indoctrinates, stimulates and enervates, pleases and bores. Mass culture is both problem and promise, and its insistent presence urges us to look backward to either a lost golden age or a time of drudgery and deprivation, forward to either paradise or disaster.[18]

Deep Surfaces

Each of the novels discussed in this study engages in some significant way the lived experience of mass culture. And not merely coincidentally, each text also exhibits some of the antifoundational features of postmodernist historical thought. Given the particular focus of this study on mass culture and history, the selective grouping of texts considered here cannot be said to represent the great diversity in American fiction writing today. Nonetheless, this grouping does demonstrate how a number of writers of considerably different styles and approaches can find in their engagements with mass culture the material for a similarly paradoxical attitude toward history and historical representation. Thomas Pynchon is a familiar figure in discussions of postmodernist fiction, and Don DeLillo is rapidly becoming one, but Bobbie Ann Mason is not usually considered as a postmodernist writer. Nicholson Baker, who is of a younger generation, has yet to receive substantial critical attention. E. L. Doctorow, the best-selling author discussed here, is often discussed in the context of postmodernism, and yet his fiction straddles in an interesting way the boundary between "serious" and "popular" that postmodernism is said to contest. Ishmael Reed's *Mumbo Jumbo,* though decisively postmodernist in its use of pastiche and its otherwise forthrightly avant-gardist posture, must also be read in relation to issues of African American identity and cultural tradition. In the deep surfaces that these texts construct out of their engagements with mass culture, we find a historical attitude that is not confined to a few select works of fiction but governs the postmodern historical imagination.

In attending to the lived experience of mass culture, one must sometimes attend to matters of seemingly trivial importance. How much does it matter that most of your zippers say "YKK" on them, or that the microchip in your personal computer is made by Intel? But a novel such as Baker's *The Mezzanine* demonstrates brilliantly that the seeming triviality of mass culture is essential to its function. It is the nature of large corporations to organize things both great and small and to introduce the results of their global machinations into our lives as incremental additions to pleasure and convenience, sometimes interesting, often beneath our notice, but seldom imparting any awareness of their connection to the large-scale organization of economic and social life that their production requires. Baker's fiction registers brilliantly the way that any attempt to represent the totality of experience within mass culture necessarily risks being overwhelmed by trivia, at the same time as it demonstrates that it is precisely in minute particulars that the power to organize material and cultural life can be best observed.

Fredric Jameson, who sees postmodernism as "the cultural logic of late capitalism" and ties his semiotic analyses of cultural forms to the mode of production in an economy organized on a global scale, argues that the postmodern "crisis of representation" arises precisely out of the impossibility of representing the structures of multinational capital that produce our omnipresent mass culture. This problem, implicit in Baker's fiction, is most powerfully elaborated by Don DeLillo, whose novels throughout the seventies and eighties show a profound engagement with the existential and epistemological problems raised by contemporary mass culture. In chapter 2, we see how in DeLillo's fiction the excesses of our contemporary image culture threaten the epistemological foundations of historical understanding, in part by fostering a televisual self-consciousness that threatens the Cartesian distinctions between subject and object. The central irony of Don DeLillo's fiction is that, although our media-saturated culture creates the impression that all of history and the self has been made into images and that "nothing escapes our scrutiny," the structures of power responsible for this image culture may remain invisible, unrepresentable, and mysterious.

From the belief that the line between image and reality is difficult to draw, it is just one short leap to the belief that there is no such line at all. At this point the world becomes all image, to be commodified and manipulated on those terms, and history like everything else becomes simply a collection of signs available for play. In a tone that accuses poststructuralism of acquiescence, if not complicity, in the disappearance of history, Fredric Jameson writes that "in faithful conformity to poststructuralist linguistic theory, the past as 'referent' finds itself gradually bracketed, and then effaced altogether, leaving us with nothing but texts" ("Postmodernism" 66). However, in chapter 3, a formal analysis shows how E. L. Doctorow's *Ragtime* and Ishmael Reed's *Mumbo Jumbo* do set out to represent particular periods of American history—do, that is, attempt to leave us with something more than mere "texts"—but do so in discontinuous "spectacular" forms that expose and call into question the conventions of narrative historiography. Borrowing the energies of spectacular performance from contemporary film and television, Reed and Doctorow self-consciously place their own representations of history within a particular history of representation. Through parataxis, pastiche, and other techniques that stress the unavoidable discontinuities in narrative, these texts comment upon their own unprecedented historical situation, in which the novel survives as a residual form in a culture dominated by electronic and visual media.

In the postmodernist texts discussed in these chapters, we see a narrative pattern emerge in which gestures toward "depth" of historical understanding are continually returned to the "surface" of postmodern image culture with its rejection of epistemological foundations and master narratives. This is a problematic result, but not a simplistic one, and one which bids us confront in a serious way the terms of our confinement to the realm of the image. The pattern is continued by Bobbie Ann Mason's *In Country*, discussed in chapter 4 as an example of "minimalist" fiction. Consciously constructed as a "low" postmodernism in response to the "high" postmodernism of such writers as Pynchon, Barth, Gass, Coover, and Barthelme, minimalist fiction is only one form of literary response to a widely shared skepticism about the ability of historical narrative to comprehend and organize the data of contemporary experience. Yet *In Country* contributes uniquely to our understanding of how this skepticism toward history is itself a product of its historical moment, when the aftermath of the Vietnam War and the social upheaval of the 1960s brought a loss of narrative coherence. As with other minimalist writers, such as Raymond Carver, Ann Beattie, and Frederick Barthelme, the sympathy that Mason shows toward mass culture allows her to register the characteristic feeling of the age of MTV and shopping malls, when life becomes "lifestyle" and when history and the self can seem to be mere projections on a screen. Rather than mourn, as Horkheimer and Adorno did, the surrender of history and authenticity to the "invading barbaric life" of mass culture, minimalist fiction maps the changing shape of the historical imagination under postmodern conditions of knowledge.

Thomas Pynchon's work most fully elaborates the challenges that image culture makes to concepts of self and history that have been with us since the Enlightenment. In *Gravity's Rainbow*, film stands in paradoxical relation to both history and the self: film is a figure for abstract instrumental reason and the principle of cause and effect; it is also a figure for the breakdown of the dualistic model of selfhood on which such reason and causality are based. Just as it destabilizes the self, Pynchon's narrative suspends us between alternative and competing imperatives for the shape of history, constructing a deep surface by refusing to establish a hierarchy among competing systems of historical explanation. In Pynchon's *Vineland*, we have entered a world where television seems to have swallowed history whole, where police play the theme music from "Jeopardy" on their sirens, and where children see their parents as characters in a sitcom. In this postmortem of the radical movements of the 1960s, Pynchon suggests that the real revolution may have been in the way history and the self have become mediated entirely by mass culture; oppressor and oppressed alike are so plugged into the Tube that any oppositional politics has become literally unthinkable. Nonetheless, Pynchon, like DeLillo, suggests that accepting such formulations too easily may blind us to the real forces of history that are out there, behind the scenes, running the show.

Toward the Postmodern Historical Imagination:
From Walker Percy's *The Moviegoer* to Nicholson
Baker's *The Mezzanine*

At certain points in both Walker Percy's *The Moviegoer* (1961) and Nicholson Baker's *The Mezzanine* (1988), the protagonists enter into a sort of enchantment in which the life of the zealous consumer becomes a marvelous self-sufficiency, an assurance that one is living on the cutting edge of progress, where one's physical, psychic, and aesthetic demands are met by methods ever more ingenious, efficient, and delightful. And yet this enchantment has its dark opposite, a disenchantment in which each character suspects that whatever is gained in self-sufficiency and pleasure is won at the terrible cost of his authenticity, the loss of connection to family and community, and the loss of any historical sense by which he is rooted in place and time. Patrick Brantlinger has suggested that the lived experience of mass culture typically prompts just this sort of duality. The very concept of mass culture, Brantlinger explains, assumes a cyclical theory of history beset by the paradox that "civilization leads to the death of civiliza-tion" (34–35). The darker view, which associates mass culture with civilization's fall into barbarism from the heights of some idealized classical past, is a histori-cal attitude that Brantlinger terms "negative classicism." Negative and positive views of mass culture are closely intertwined in both *The Moviegoer* and *The Mezzanine,* but in the earlier novel it is negative classicism that finally provides the governing historical attitude and ensures that the protagonist's enchantment with the moviegoer's life is only temporary. In *The Mezzanine,* however, negative classicism remains only as the residue of an irony that celebrates the pleasures of the consumer's life while acknowledging the superficiality of that celebration. *The Mezzanine* finds no alternative to the enchantment with the present and, in departing from the forms of historical thinking found in *The Moviegoer,* marks a shift to the postmodern historical imagination.

In Percy's novel, the recent history of the rise of mass culture becomes part of the older *mythoi* of the fall from grace and the loss of the values of the aris-tocratic, agrarian old South. In Baker's fiction, on the other hand, mass culture promises to replace history entirely; what history there is in the novel is that of the development and use of consumer goods. Whereas Percy's history of the suburbanization of the South attaches to a larger mythic (and specifically Christian) history, and thus establishes a depth of historical perspective that counters the perceived superficiality of the developing consumer culture, the history constructed by Baker's narrator is so extremely solipsistic, so limited to the secular, the personal, and the resolutely mundane, that any larger historical frame—whether the history of capitalistic production, the liberal *mythos* of "progress," or a spiritual tradition opposed to the materialism of consumer cul-ture—is gestured at only through the irony of its absence. In both novels the double historical vision prompted by mass culture persists: the mass cultural future is both celebrated as the way of progress and bemoaned for its oblitera-tion of a more "authentic" past. Yet in the earlier work, the rise of mass culture is assimilated into existing mythic structures and thus provides new content for traditional forms of historical imagination. In the later work, the absence of such structures is a given: the tragic "loss of absolutes" explored by modernism has become so familiar as to be hardly worth serious attention. Rather than mourn, the kind of postmodern historical imagination at work in Baker's fic-tion attempts to rid itself of modernism's nostalgia for master historical narra-tives. In place of gestures toward traditional historical depth that it finds too irrelevant and futile even to be regressive, Baker's fiction celebrates the pleas-ures of the mass cultural surface.

In his 1959 essay "Mass Society and Postmodern Fiction," Irving Howe described the emerging "postmodern" literature as a search for and validation of the margins, "those few pockets of elemental emotional life left in this country" that remained untrammeled by a homogenizing and atomizing mass society:

> By the mass society we mean a relatively comfortable, half-welfare and half-garrison society in which the population grows passive, indifferent, and atomized; in which traditional loyalties, ties, and associations become lax or dissolve entirely; in which coherent publics based on definite interests and opinions gradually fall apart; and in which man becomes a consumer, himself like the products, diversions, and values that he absorbs. (196)

The particular authors that Howe found to exemplify the new literature of the margins—Jack Kerouac, Nelson Algren, Norman Mailer, Saul Bellow—suggest that he was still thinking primarily about the margins of white male experience. It would take the political and social movements of the 1960s and 1970s to bring the margins that were suppressed in Howe's account to the forefront of literary expression. The boom in feminist fiction and in writing by African American women in the 1970s, for example, was to confirm, in ways that Howe could not have envisioned, the revitalizing effect of the marginal on American literature. The novels to be considered in what follows, however, are far from representing "marginal" experience. The protagonists of Walker Percy's *The Moviegoer* and Nicholson Baker's *The Mezzanine* are immersed in the mainstream of just the sort of mass society that Howe describes. Percy's novel is not postmodern, but Baker's novel is, a fact that says something important about the relationship that postmodernism has come to have to the mainstream. Far from Howe's margins, the experience registered in Baker's novel exemplifies a postmodernism that has relinquished marginality in favor of an ironic complicity with the dominant culture. Baker's irony thus expresses the paradoxical politics of postmodernism, which to Linda Hutcheon is always "doubly encoded as both complicity and critique" (*Politics* 168). While Baker's irony suggests a critique of the very culture he celebrates, by now we have come to recognize—in everything from television commercials to political rhetoric—that this sort of self-directed irony has become a routine strategy by which the dominant culture maintains its hegemony. Nonetheless, it is the elusiveness of Baker's irony, together with the richness and erudition of his prose, that makes his historical imagination something more than merely a superficial celebration of mass culture. *The Mezzanine,* finally, constructs a "deep surface" in which we may locate the full dimensions of both our pleasure and our unease with the way that mass culture shapes our historical consciousness.

The *Moviegoer* was published in 1961 and stands in the company of those novels and stories that document the malaise of the Eisenhower years, works that in various ways address the theme of spiritual poverty amidst material prosperity. It has a spiritual affinity with such works as Richard Yates's *Revolutionary Road* (1961); the first of Updike's Rabbit trilogy, *Rabbit Run* (1960); John Cheever's short stories throughout the fifties; and the fiction of J. D. Salinger. The 1962 paperback edition of *The Moviegoer* touts the novel as "a *Catcher in the Rye* for adults only." What has changed in the nearly thirty years that separate Percy from Baker is that mass culture has so completely engulfed society that the kind of critical position from which both Howe and Percy could write has been rendered nearly irrelevant. Neither Howe's leftist critique nor Walker Percy's conservative and Christian one can gain the same leverage in the world of *The Mezzanine*. The "microhistories" that Baker's narrator constructs are so seamlessly enclosed by the world of mass culture that "macrohistories"— whether Percy's decline of aristocratic virtue or Howe's class conflict—have been squeezed off the page. Whereas in *The Moviegoer* mass culture can still be seen as an alien presence rapidly colonizing the old South, in *The Mezzanine* the invasion is complete. Mass culture has become all culture, and we are the barbarians. By the late 1980s, *The Mezzanine* tells us, the kind of cultural geography by which the center could be reliably located in relation to the margins has been lost. If in *The Moviegoer* culture is suburbanized, in *The Mezzanine* it is Los Angelized.

What this means for the protagonist of the later novel is that both his ability and his desire to place himself within larger historical frameworks are diminished. The "uneven development" that Fredric Jameson sees as necessary to the modernist perception of rapid historical change persists in Percy's 1960 South, where suburban and urban industrial development can still be seen against a background of older agrarian forms of social and economic organization.[1] To Binx Bolling of *The Moviegoer*, history is visible in the landscape. In contrast, the framing action of *The Mezzanine* is set in the lobby of a corporate office building, and its protagonist occupies a self-enclosed totality in which the products of mass culture provide the ultimate horizon of any historical perspective.

What makes these differences between *The Moviegoer* and *The Mezzanine* most telling is how much the two novels have in common. Though separated by twenty-seven years, the protagonists of these novels are both young, college-educated white men making their first forays into independent living and the corporate world of work, and both pursue their projects of self-realization through an obsessive engagement with the products of mass culture. Both men find themselves in lucrative but uninspiring corporate jobs that they eventually leave, making their way to adult responsibilities, marriage, and more satisfying careers. Further, both novels stage a confrontation between the phenomena of mass culture and an essentially aristocratic sensibility, between low culture and high. Binx Bolling is the last scion of an old southern family with some aristocratic pretensions and has as his guardian an aunt who quotes Marcus Aurelius to him as a guide to his conduct.[2] The narrator of *The Mezzanine* displays an educated literary sensibility, a wit and erudition that sometimes rise to Nabokovian heights; he also happens to read Marcus Aurelius's *Meditations* on his lunch hour. Both novels tell of a coming of age, with the necessary descent from lofty ideals and acceptance of diminished possibility. Just as Binx Bolling must accept his ordinariness, so does the narrator of *The Mezzanine* come to say, "I was a man, but I was not nearly the magnitude of man I had hoped I might be" (54). Both protagonists achieve their coming of age in part through a negotiation between high culture and low, as they learn to forge an accommodation between their patrician and plebeian identities. The difference, finally, is that, despite being a devoted moviegoer, Binx Bolling at last finds the exit and is able to reenter the historical patterns of the world outside the theater. For the narrator of *The Mezzanine,* on the other hand, his decision to change jobs is only a decision to change seats; he sees neither the possibility nor the need of leaving the show.

The action of *The Moviegoer* is initiated when Binx Bolling rejects the ambitions traditionally held by young men of his position in favor of "living the most ordinary life imaginable, a life without the old longings; selling stocks and bonds and mutual funds; quitting work at five o'clock like everyone else; having a girl and perhaps one day settling down" (14). Selling stocks and bonds is to Bolling an absurdly easy way of making money, and one that avoids the trials of a life in search of knowledge or beauty: "Ten years ago I pursued beauty and gave no thought to money. I listened to the lovely tunes of Mahler and felt a sickness in my very soul. Now I pursue money and on the whole feel better" (180). At first he rejects the social complexities of his caste, turns away from the spectacle—painful to his guardian, the genteel Aunt Emily—of the dying out of the old Southern proprieties, decides to make money as painlessly as possible, and finally chooses to marry and care for his fragile cousin Kate Cutrer. At this point he makes his peace with the social world of his Aunt Emily, agrees to follow his father's path and pursue the career in medicine that his Aunt Emily wants for him—agrees, finally, to conform to the traditional proprieties of professional respectability and family duty. In return, he gets Aunt Emily to accept that "the Bolling family had gone to seed and that I was not one of her heroes but a very ordinary fellow" (217). It is not only a coming-of-age story, but also the mythic plot of a hero's journey and return, except that Binx Bolling receives a properly ironic twentieth-century version of the hero's rewards: a Penelope in need of psychiatric care, a clear sense of his own diminished powers, a realm not renewed so much as set back on the course of peaceful decline. Further, this hero tests himself not in the timeless dark forest or on the ancient winedark sea but in the newly sprung wilderness of mass culture.

Binx Bolling's foray into this mass society takes him out of the Quarter in New Orleans to a new suburb, where he rents a room on Elysian Fields, an optimistically named thoroughfare that "runs an undistinguished course from river to lake through shopping centers and blocks of duplexes and bungalows and raised cottages" (14). There he watches television, goes to a lot of movies, and revels in the feeling that he has cut himself loose to drift in mass culture. He becomes "a model tenant and a model citizen" and indulges in the pleasures of the zealous yet civic-minded consumer:

> I subscribe to *Consumer Reports* and as a consequence I own a first-class television set, an all but silent air conditioner and a very long lasting deodorant. My armpits never stink. I pay attention to all spot announcements on the radio about mental health, the seven signs of cancer, and safe driving—though, as I say, I usually prefer to ride the bus. Yesterday a favorite of mine, William Holden, delivered a radio announcement on litterbugs. "Let's face it," said Holden. "Nobody can do anything about it—but you and me." This is true. I have been careful ever since. (12)

The coolness in this voice, its complacent willingness to remain at the level of phenomena, is informed by an absurdist, existentialist fear of the void beneath that phenomenal surface.[3] The novel will finally resolve this tension, however, not in an existentialist act of violence or destruction that confirms the void, but by reestablishing a realm of depth, human connection, and emotional generosity.

Though the narrator of *The Mezzanine* is also absorbed by the phenomena of the surface, the existentialist fear of the void beneath has been replaced by the sunny confidence that there *is* no "beneath," that life at the surface is all there is, and is not so bad after all. The framing events of *The Mezzanine* are the beginning and end of a single trip up an escalator carrying the narrator, who is returning from his lunch hour, to the mezzanine level of the office building where he works. Despite the compressed narrative frame, *The Mezzanine* actually ranges over a much greater period of time than *The Moviegoer*, jumping

backward to the narrator's childhood, and forward to the time of narration itself, "several years after the escalator ride that is the vehicle for this memoir"
(37). By this time the narrator has, like Binx Bolling, married his true love and
come to terms with his ordinariness: "The feeling that you are stupider than
you were is what finally interests you in the really complex subjects of life: in
change, in experience, in the ways other people have adjusted to disappointment and narrowed ability. You realize you are no prodigy, your shoulders
relax, and you begin to look around you, seeing local color unrivaled by blue
glows of algebra and abstraction" (24). The "local color" that is of particular
interest to the narrator is "the mute folklore of behavioral inventions," the myriad ways that people adjust to the continual refashioning of their physical world
undertaken on their behalf by industry. The novel is a tissue of digressions in
which the narrator explores—often by way of lengthy footnotes—the "microhistories" of particular products, such as the cardboard milk container, the ice
cube tray, the stapler, the electric hand dryer, white bread, Jiffy Pop popcorn
("one of the outstanding instances of human ingenuity in my lifetime" [107]),
and the plastic straw. His obsessive pursuit of these histories is often both in-
ventive and lyrical:

> ¹Let me mention another fairly important development in the history of
> the straw. I recently noticed, and remembered dimly half noticing for sev-
> eral years before then, that the paper wrapper, which once had slipped so
> easily down the plastic straw and bunched itself into a compressed concer-
> tina which you could use to perform traditional bar and dorm tricks with,
> now does not slip at all. It hugs the straw's surface so closely that even
> though the straw itself is stiffer than the earlier paper straw, the plastic
> sometimes buckles under the force you end up using in trying to push the
> wrapper down the old habitual way. A whole evolved method for un-
> wrapping straws—one-handed, very like rapping a cigarette on a table to
> ensure that the tobacco was firmly settled into the tube—now no longer
> works, and we must pinch off the tip of the wrapper and tear our way two-
> handedly all the way down the seam as if we were opening a piece of junk
> mail. But I have faith that this mistake too will be corrected; and we may
> someday even be nostalgic about the period of several years when straws
> were difficult to unwrap. It is impossible to foresee the things that go wrong
> in these small innovations, and it takes time for them to be understood as
> evils and acted upon. Similarly, there are often unexpected plusses to some
> minor new development. What sugar-packet manufacturer could have
> known that people would take to flapping the packet back and forth to cen-

trifuge its contents to the bottom, so that they could handily tear off the top? The nakedness of a simple novelty in pre-portioned packaging has been surrounded and softened and made sense of by gesticulative adaptation (possibly inspired by the extinguishing oscillation of a match after the lighting of a cigarette); convenience has given rise to ballet; and the sound of those flapping sugar packets in the early morning, fluttering over from nearby booths, is not one I would willingly forgo, even though I take my coffee unsweetened. (94–95)

Both Binx Bolling and the narrator of *The Mezzanine* voice an ironic regard for the myth of technical and consumerist progress. But the irony serves a different purpose in each case. For Bolling, mass culture is a temporary escape from the history to which he must inevitably return, and thus can be treated ironically as a superficial realm that provides a false security from the realities of adult responsibility. In contrast, the anticipatory nostalgia with which the narrator of *The Mezzanine* looks forward to the solving of the straw-wrapper problem is the triumph of a corporate mass culture that substitutes innovation for change. Mass culture has itself *become* history, and if this voice treats the myth of progress ironically, it does so in a way that seems to leave no alternative except a regressive nostalgia for a lost childhood of glass milk-bottles and commercials for Prell shampoo. Whereas *The Moviegoer* opposes the superficiality of mass culture with the depth of both sacred and secular historical perspective, in *The Mezzanine* we have entered a world in which the conventional distinction between "surface" and "depth" no longer holds. Both terms are absorbed into the category of the "personal," and the desire for historical narrative manifests either in the cultivation of domestic childhood memories or in rapt attention to the minutiae of the consumer's life.

If there is a "macrohistory" that the narrator of *The Mezzanine* most frequently engages, however ironically, it is that of technical progress, as in this footnote on the development of perforated paper products:

> [1]Perforation! Shout it out! The deliberate punctuated weakening of paper and cardboard so that it will tear along an intended path, leaving a row of fine-haired white pills or tuftlets on each new edge! It is a staggering conception, showing an age-transforming feel for the unique properties of pulped wood fiber. Yet do we have national holidays to celebrate its development? Are festschrift volumes published honoring the dead greats in the field? People watch the news every night like robots, thinking they are learning about their lives, never paying attention to the far more immediate developments that arrive unreported. (74)

The histories that this narrator constructs do hold a distinct fascination. With a riveting veracity of detail, they perform a sort of perverse Foucauldian analysis, documenting the minutiae of material practices but without enabling any political critique. Of course, to talk about this writing only as a failure of historical imagination or a capitulation to consumerism is to miss the joke. It *is* funny, and on two levels. The writing performs that most fundamental comic function of validating our perceptions in unexpected ways: "fine-haired white pills or tuftlets" seems to get things exactly right, and we gain a pleasurable shock of recognition. But further, and more insidiously, the writing is funny because it makes fun of its own obsessiveness. The writing thus treats itself ironically in the way that television does: it allows us to feel superior to a situation without allowing us a way out of it. Just as many television commercials now gain our complicity by flaunting their own stupidity, allowing us the pleasure of condescension, so the narrator of *The Mezzanine* seeks our sympathy by announcing his moral poverty, begging our indulgence for "practicing philosophy on the scant raw materials of my life" (125). Thus the fundamental ambivalence that Brantlinger found inherent in the concept of mass culture is embedded in the structure of the irony itself. The narrator constructs his own history as the history of consumer goods while admitting the emptiness of the procedure: "I am not proud of the fact that major ingredients of my emotional history are available for purchase today at CVS" (115). In this self-deprecating irony we find the structure of a "deep surface" in which the superficiality of mass culture is criticized but not rejected, explored but finally not evaded.

The narrator is aware of the threat that nostalgia presents to history, knowing that in his own attempts at reconstructing the past he is "tempted away from history into all kinds of untrustworthy emotional details" (44). However, in seeking the end of "the rule of nostalgia" (47), he desires not an enlarged or more "authentic" historical grasp but rather the ability to live more entirely in the present moment, to do away with his attachment to a childhood that is his only remaining history outside of consumption. Complaining that we depend too much upon the narratives of childhood to authorize present perceptions, he asks: "Why should we need lots of nostalgia to license any pleasure taken in the discoveries that we carry over from childhood, when it is now so clearly an adult pleasure?" (39). Commenting on how 1950s designs of kitchen blenders are now antiquated enough to be considered decorative, he complains, "Why do these images have to age before we can be fond of them?" (78). The implication is not that our addiction to nostalgia is robbing us of a more authentic historical sense, but that it is limiting the pleasures we might take in our present commodity environment.

Like the narrator of *The Mezzanine,* Binx Bolling also worries about how mass culture has become the substance of his personal past:

> Other people, so I have read, treasure memorable moments in their lives: the time one climbed the Parthenon at sunrise, the summer night one met a lonely girl in Central Park and achieved with her a sweet and natural relationship, as they say in books. I too once met a girl in Central Park, but it is not much to remember. What I remember is the time John Wayne killed three men with a carbine as he was falling to the dusty street in *Stagecoach,* and the time the kitten found Orson Welles in the doorway in *The Third Man.* (12–13)

Bolling shows a moment's concern that, despite their obvious falseness, despite their substitution for the sort of direct experience that might once have been the substance of one's personal past, the movies have become his most significant source of experience. He compares movies not to experience itself, but to experiences he has read about "in books," suggesting that the movies operate at a Platonic third remove from the Real. Triumphing over print culture, movies are but shadows of the shadows found in books and so take us one rung further down the ontological ladder from Truth.

But Bolling's greatest fear does not center on the problem of constructing a meaningful personal past. Rather, his fear has to do with his status as a member of the mass movie *audience* and thus marks a concern with social relations not voiced in *The Mezzanine.* With the pleasures of the moviegoer's life comes the threat of losing one's individuality and sinking into the "everydayness" of the repetitive, massified life. "Everydayness is the enemy," Binx Bolling declares (135). Binx's enjoyment of the movies comes at the risk of disappearing into the anonymity of the mass audience, and he takes positive measures to combat this threat:

> Before I see a movie it is necessary for me to learn something about the theater or the people who operate it, to touch base before going inside. . . . If I did not talk to the theater owner or the ticket seller, I should be lost, cut loose metaphysically speaking. I should be seeing one copy of a film which might be shown anywhere and at any time. There is the danger of slipping clean out of space and time. It is possible to become a ghost and not know whether one is in downtown Loews in Denver or suburban Bijou in Jacksonville. (72)

Thus, for all his enjoyment of the movies ("I am quite happy at a movie, even a bad movie" [12]), Binx resists surrendering entirely to them. His experience in the theater must be framed by an external geography and social history. The same fear that attends his joining the movie audience also attaches to his arrival in the Chicago train station, where he risks becoming an anonymous stranger in the crowd:

> If only somebody could tell me who built the damn station, the circumstances of the building, details of the wrangling between city officials and the railroad, so that I would not fall victim to it, the station, the very first crack off the bat. Every place of arrival should have a booth set up and manned by an ordinary person whose task it is to greet strangers and give them a little trophy of local spacetime stuff—tell them of his difficulties in high school and put a pinch of soil in their pockets—in order to insure that the stranger shall not become an Anyone. (185)

Thus the threat of everydayness raised by the movies is only one part of the larger threat associated with growing urbanization and industrialization: "The everydayness is everywhere now, having begun in the cities and seeking out the remotest nooks and corners of the countryside, even the swamps" (135). In associating everydayness with urban culture, Walker Percy evokes one of the abiding themes of American literature: the threat of urbanization to the rural and frontier way of life. The continuity of feeling that Bolling experiences between the movies and the train station links the conventionally mythic symbol of American industrial expansion—the railroad—with the latest outpost of that expansion—the suburban movie house. Mass culture, as an agent of everydayness and urbanization, is thus placed within the traditional historical framework of the conquest of wildness and the constriction of frontier liberty. This general American theme is given its particular southern resonance by its association with the loss of the southern agrarian past. Binx Bolling demonstrates the way that, in Howe's words, "traditional loyalties, ties, and associations become lax or dissolve entirely" in the ease with which he disassociates himself from the land. In selling off his only inheritance from his father, the patch of land on which his father and uncles used to have a duck-hunting club, Binx is concerned only with getting the best possible price from the developer who wants to use it for a housing subdivision. In this episode we have a graphic example of how "uneven development" contributes to a sense of rapid historical change: Bolling can literally see a genteel, rural, and agrarian past being displaced by suburban development.

In *The Mezzanine* there is no question any longer of an agrarian patrimony; the effacement of "nature" is complete, and suburbanization has become limitless sprawl. The narrator of *The Mezzanine* has neither the desire to place his own behavior as a consumer within a broader system of social relations nor the desire to place the development of mass culture within a larger historical framework. In the following passage, part of a tour-de-force description of a CVS store, the narrator gestures at larger history only to dismiss it, finding in the shampoo aisle a parallel history with its own satisfactions:

> And here were the shampoos! Was there really any need to study the historical past of Chandragupta of Pataliputra, or Harsha of Kanauj, the rise of the Chola kings of Tanjore and the fall of the Pallava kings of Kanchi, who once built the Seven Pagodas of Mahabalipuram, or the final desolation and ruin of the great metropolis of Vijayanagar, when we had dynastic shifts, turbulence, and plenty of lather in the last twenty years of that great Hindu inheritance, shampoo? Yes, there was. Yet emotional analogies were not hard to find between the history of civilization on the one hand and the history within the CVS pharmacy on the other, when you caught sight of a once great shampoo like Alberto VO5 or Prell now in sorry vassalage on the bottom shelf of aisle 1B, overrun by later waves of Mongols, Muslims, and Chalukyas—Suave; Clairol Herbal Essence; Gee, Your Hair Smells Terrific; Silkience; Finesse; and bottle after bottle of the Akbaresque Flex. Prell's green is too simple a green for us now; the false French of its name seems kitschy, not chic, and where once it was enveloped in my TV-soaked mind by the immediacy and throatiness of womanly voice-overs, it is now late in its decline, lightly advertised, having descended year by year through the thick but hygroscopic emulsions of our esteem, like the large descending pearl that was used in one of its greatest early ads to prove how lusciously rich it was. (114)

Despite the narrator's assertion that there *is* a need to study the "historical past," this past is summoned only as the starting point for the "emotional analogies" by which the narrator locates himself in the history of shampoos. When *The Moviegoer* gestures toward a larger history, that history is validated as a frame for the narrative of Binx Bolling's odyssey through the wilds of mass culture. In *The Mezzanine* the values are reversed, and "real" history becomes oriental exotica of trivial interest compared to the history of consumption that bears the emotional weight of the personal past.

Baker's prose is often delightful; contemporary fiction could certainly use more phrases like "emulsions of our esteem." The lexical richness and metaphoric play are the means by which this narrative makes a *home* out of the materials of mass culture. The technical virtuosity with which this narrator practices philosophy on "the scant raw materials" of his life makes this text an ironic tour de force, celebrating in its own novelistic practice the same triumph of style over substance that it perceives in its mass cultural environment. And yet once again we must see that the irony cuts both ways; the celebration is not simply a tongue-in-cheek display that collapses back into the negative classicism we find in *The Moviegoer*. Binx Bolling's "everydayness" is not a concern for the narrator of *The Mezzanine,* precisely because he is genuinely at home in mass culture in a way that Binx Bolling is not. Whereas Bolling is threatened by the encroachments of "everydayness" on the countryside, the narrator of *The Mezzanine* is concerned only with changes within mass culture itself. Mass culture is what the countryside has become, and by constructing narratives of product development he gains the pleasure of mastering the landscape. His only concern is that the pace of innovation within mass culture will overwhelm his ability to construct new narratives:

> Theoretically, I suppose there is a point, too, at which the combined volume of all the miniature histories of miscellanea that have been collecting in parallel in my memory, covering a number of the different aisles of CVS and even some of the handiwork of civilization at large, will reach some critical point and leave me saturated, listless, unable to entertain a single new enthusiasm. (116)

The narrator does not fear losing a sense of history or identity so much as he fears losing the capacity for "enthusiasm." As the material on which his historical consciousness operates, consumer goods are valued not primarily as a basis for self-understanding but as a source of stimulation. *The Moviegoer*'s master narrative of the conquest of wildness by mass culture is replaced by an endlessly proliferating collection of little narratives of consumption. These "miniature histories" are collected "in parallel," suggesting that they are only paralogically related to one another within the narrator's historical consciousness, a condition that blocks their connection to a larger, unifying narrative structure.[4]

Of course the narrator of *The Mezzanine* is not alone in celebrating the enthusiasms of mass culture, which clearly enrich Binx Bolling's life as well. To Bolling, one of the positive values of the movies is their ability to confer a special sense of reality on what would otherwise be ordinary experience. Seeing the actor William Holden on a New Orleans street, Binx remarks that "an aura of heightened reality moves with him and all who fall within it feel it" (20). The movies' power to strengthen one's sense of reality also takes the form of what Bolling, defining special terms in the style of Kierkegaard, terms "certification," something that he and Kate experience while watching a movie that contains a scene showing the very neighborhood of the theater in which they sit. Seeing the neighborhood in the movie has certified the neighborhood's existence:

> Nowadays when a person lives somewhere, in a neighborhood, the place is not certified for him. More than likely he will live there sadly and the emp-

tiness which is inside him will expand until it evacuates the entire neighborhood. But if he sees a movie which shows his very neighborhood, it becomes possible for him to live, for a time at least, as a person who is Somewhere and not Anywhere. (61)

The movies thus offer a paradoxical rejuvenation, bringing to life the dead spaces of the urban environment that they themselves, in complicity with the industrialization and massification of the city, have helped kill. Bolling's "certification" also offers a precursory instance of what will become a postmodern commonplace: an experience is not "real" until it has been commodified as an "image," a paradox that threatens the classical separation between the real and the imaginary, and one that reproduces on a different level (to be explored in the next chapter) the collapse of the distinction between depth and surface.

Thus, despite the repetition that is the essence of both mass culture and of everydayness, the movies occasionally provide the kind of surprise that triumphs over everydayness and is for Binx Bolling the highest pleasure. Another form of this experience is termed a "rotation" in Binx's Kierkegaardian language: "A rotation I define as the experiencing of the new beyond the experiencing of the new" (134). When such a moment occurs at a drive-in movie that Binx attends with his secretary/girlfriend Sharon and his younger half-brother Lonnie, Binx experiences the pleasure that compensates for the risks of everydayness: "My heart sings like Octavian and there is great happiness between me and Lonnie and this noble girl and they both know it and have the sense to say nothing" (134).

Though the novel thus preserves the ambivalent attitude toward mass culture, its dominant mode is a negative classicism that associates mass culture with historical decline. For Aunt Emily to accept Binx Bolling's ordinariness she must accept a general familial decline that accords with her sense of the lateness of her cultural time in general. She expresses the feeling—common enough in postbellum southern literature—of living out the dying years of one's culture:

> The world I knew has come crashing down around my ears. The things we hold dear are reviled and spat upon. . . . It's an interesting age you will live in—though I can't say I'm sorry to miss it. But it should be quite a sight, the going under of the evening land. That's us all right. And I can tell you, my young friend, it is evening. It is very late. (53)

Aunt Emily's vision clearly conforms to the sort of negative classicism that Patrick Brantlinger describes; referring to the passing of Binx's father's generation, she declares that "the age of Catos is gone" (49). She quotes the emperor Marcus Aurelius Antoninus in an attempt to correct Binx's conduct and clearly sees a life of moviegoing as incompatible with the ideal of Roman virtue: "In this world goodness is destined to be defeated. But a man must go down fighting. That is the victory. To do anything less is to be less than a man" (53).

In Binx's eyes, of course, Aunt Emily is an anachronism, a slightly ridiculous figure whom he nonetheless loves and respects. Her insistence on the old proprieties seems incongruous beside Binx's own realization that he is

> living in fact in the very century of merde, the great shithouse of scientific humanism where needs are satisfied, everyone becomes an anyone, a warm and creative person, and prospers like a dung beetle, and one hundred percent of people are humanists and ninety-eight percent believe in God, and men are dead, dead, dead; and the malaise has settled like a fallout and what people really fear is not that the bomb will fall but that the bomb will not fall. (209)

Aunt Emily's eulogies for the old South are undercut in a way that they could not have been by Faulkner. The difference is that, while in Faulkner the ironic irrelevance of such speeches as Aunt Emily's is the stuff of tragedy, Percy empties their irrelevance of tragic force. This shift in tone is part of what marks Percy's novel as a transition from Faulkner's modernism to the postmodernist South of Bobbie Ann Mason. There, in a novel such as *In Country,* the old South is something seen only on television, and all attempts to reconnect with an agrarian past can only take the form of parody.[5]

But what matters most here is that, even though Emily's eulogy for the old South is rendered with a gentle irony, it is replaced with a narrative of the historic ravages of "scientific humanism" that is equally determined by negative classicism.[6] In the end Binx Bolling perseveres despite his knowledge of the death and merde around him, acting on the unspoken premise that flawed human nature is redeemed through selfless caring and charity. The novel concludes with a deathbed visit to his congenitally ill half-brother Lonnie and with evidence of his tender guardianship of his wife Kate. Mass culture is finally not a substitute for history, and Binx Bolling's identity as a moviegoer and consumer is not a substitute for the identity given him within the traditional structures of family and community. Rather than displace older forms of historical understanding, mass culture conforms to the existing *mythoi* of the fall from grace and the loss of the aristocratic, agrarian past. The movies are finally only a pleasant diversion during the twilight hours of the Empire, and mass culture only one element in a larger historical pattern of decline.

The presence of Marcus Aurelius in both novels, whether by deliberate allusion or simple coincidence, only confirms Patrick Brantlinger's argument that the concept of mass culture typically operates against the background of an idealized classical past.[7] But whereas Aunt Emily's invocation of Aurelius marks how far the contemporary world has fallen and how poorly his precepts apply to present-day conditions, the narrator of *The Mezzanine* persists in the hopeful project of acting on Aurelius's exhortation to philosophize, despite feeling that his life provides little in the way of philosophic material (125). *The Mezzanine* presents a postmodern historical imagination that, despite confessing the narrowness of its vision, refuses to validate utterly the narrative of negative classicism. While recognizing the distance between Roman virtue and consumerist zeal, *The Mezzanine* refuses to see that distance as a disabling one.

A charge commonly leveled against American fiction of the late 1970s and 1980s is that its concerns were limited to the domestic and personal spheres at the expense of an engagement with broader historical and political themes. As will be discussed in a later chapter, the most frequent recipients of such attacks are the "minimalist" writers, such as Raymond Carver, Bobbie Ann Mason, and Ann Beattie, whose characters—so the complaint goes—seem rarely to have jobs and spend a lot of time on the sofa watching TV.[8] Nicholson Baker is to be commended for taking us into the world of corporate work that, for all its importance to contemporary experience, is rarely treated of in fiction.[9] Don DeLillo's satire of the corporate world in *Players* seems superficial compared with Baker's minute observations of corporate bathroom behavior and elevator etiquette, the decorum of small talk with secretaries, and the social function of the interdepartmental memo, all the subcultural oddities of "the Hungarian 5/2 rhythm of the lived workweek" (92). But in a curious way, what Baker has done is merely transport the domestic and personal concerns of much recent fiction from the living room to the office. Despite promising to engage material beyond the domestic sphere, *The Mezzanine* ends by banishing the public sphere almost entirely. We never learn what his company *does*, though a brief reference to "a thirty-page cross-departmental requisition for a fleet of trucks" tells us that out there, somewhere, goods are being moved (61). The narrative ignores the central corporate function to focus on incidental personal details. Apologizing for this reversal of value, the narrator explains that in the time elapsed since he left the job it has become difficult to remember the actual problems that had kept him working late night after night:

> While the problems you were paid to solve collapse, the nod of the security guard, his sign-in book, the escalator ride, the things on your desk, the sight of colleague's offices, their faces seen from characteristic angles, the features of the corporate bathroom, all miraculously expand: and in this way what was central and what was incidental end up exactly reversed. (92)

Thus the narrative of production that would place the corporation in a network of material relations is banished, if not to Fredric Jameson's "political unconscious," then to some willfully constructed domain of the "uninteresting." *The Mezzanine* pushes the solipsism and domesticity of much contemporary fiction to the extremes of self-parody, producing a narrative that is by turns hypnotic in its obsession, maddening in its claustrophobic confinement to consumerist trivia, and hilarious in its acute voicings of normally unremarked mundane details.[10] The only overarching history in *The Mezzanine* is that of material progress, but the irony with which this narrative is invoked invalidates it as any ultimate ground for historical understanding, while at the same time rejecting the negative classicism that is its opposite. We are left with a deep surface, as the historical double vision created by mass culture refuses to resolve into a single narrative, and we are left only with history as the richly ironic search for the next enthusiasm.

On the basis of its title alone, *The Moviegoer* seems a likely candidate for the designation "postmodern." Indeed, the alterations in our concepts of self, of community, and of historical understanding prompted by a seemingly omnipresent image culture have become a common preoccupation of postmodernist writers, artists, and theorists. But *The Moviegoer* is a transitional text, treating postmodern themes in a late modernist mode. The difference between Percy and Baker is in part a matter of tone. Binx Bolling's coolness, his seeming easy acquiescence to change, his attempt to deny deep pathos in the face of the unmistakably pathetic, belongs more to postwar American existentialism than to postmodern schizophrenia or minimalist lack of affect, and in any case never quite crosses over into the unqualified celebration of the consumer's life that we find in *The Mezzanine*.[11] Knowingly ironic about this celebration, Baker seems to parody the postmodernism described by its most vitriolic opponents. Terry Eagleton's attack on postmodernism could serve, with certain modulations in diction, as dust-jacket copy for *The Mezzanine*: "it persuades us to recognize utopia not as some remote *telos* but, amazingly, as nothing less than the present itself, replete as it is in its own brute positivity and scarred through with not the slightest trace of lack" (61). Though Baker's self-parody anticipates precisely this sort of condemnation, it does not truly answer it. The ironies by which *The Mezzanine* undercuts its own procedures are not sanctioned by any depth of historical perspective that stands outside them as a norm, and the novel finally leaves us with no alternative to the narrator's celebrations.

Related to this shift in tone, but more important, is the fact that Bolling continues the effort, however problematic, to place the self in the sort of larger historical scheme that *The Mezzanine* can only mock. Binx Bolling eventually finds his way out of mass culture and back into the history of his family's and society's decline, a secular history that maps onto the sacred history of the soul's journey through a fallen world to salvation. The narrator of *The Mezzanine,* on the other hand, makes a home in the heart of the mass cultural machine, where consumption is the only activity around which the self and history can be constructed. *The Moviegoer* belongs to an earlier historical moment, a time when suburbanization and the advances of image culture could still be seen against a background of older social forms, when the materialism of consumer culture was still reliably opposed by a vital humanist and spiritual tradition, and when the cultural margins could still be located in relation to the mainstream. Whether these conditions have in fact been eliminated completely is debatable, yet *The Mezzanine,* and postmodernism generally, projects a world in which they have.[12] Inside *The Mezzanine,* we are inside a culture that has vanquished the marginal, and which therefore blocks any perception of historical change outside of the innovations of product development. Other postmodernist writers have responded to these same conditions either through the poststructuralist strategy of subverting historical representation itself, as in Ishmael Reed's *Mumbo Jumbo* or Thomas Pynchon's *Gravity's Rainbow,* or through the actualist strategy of constructing alternative histories, as in Marge Piercy's *Woman on the Edge of Time* or Angela Carter's *Nights at the Circus.* Baker's approach, a third way, is to quit fighting and declare victory. However tempted we might be to wish for a more politically satisfying result, one that engages possible futures based on renewed scrutiny of the past, Baker's fiction provides a compelling and unnervingly delightful vision of a postmodern condition in which celebrating the present seems the only option left.

Don DeLillo's Invisible Histories

Stephen Spender once wrote that "there seems to be a transparent quality about American life, as though everything has been put under the microscope and talked about over the loudspeakers" (52). Especially at a time when our deepest secrets, all our desires and fears, anxieties and hopes are continually appropriated by market researchers, journalists, and talk-show hosts for the slick productions of film, television, and advertising, it can seem that we are continually on display. Carried further, the experience of self-exposure leads to the self-conscious feeling that we have actually become our images: when we see ourselves as though seen on TV, the old distinctions between inside and outside, self and society no longer hold, and the self merges with its image environment. This is an idea that has spanned the length of Don DeLillo's career. David Bell, the protagonist of DeLillo's first novel, *Americana* (1971), is a young television executive haunted by the feeling that he and his colleagues "existed only on video-tape. . . . We seemed to be no more than electronic signals and we moved through time and space with the stutter and shadowed insanity of a TV-commercial" (23–24). In DeLillo's ninth novel, *Libra* (1988), Lee Harvey Oswald finds his moment of greatest self-realization in the instant of being shot by Jack Ruby, but this self-awareness takes the form of a man watching himself on tele-vision: "He could see himself shot as the camera caught it. Through the pain he watched TV" (439). DeLillo's protagonists are restless seekers of self, and their search typically involves both an engagement with and a repulsion from a cul-ture glutted with images, information, and jargon. In this culture of the image, the self is both exposed and concealed, both constructed and dispersed, both made real and shown to be nothing but shadows. The sense of televisual expo-sure DeLillo's characters suffer develops into a self-consciousness that is not the development of a sustainable interiority but rather an emptying of the self into the domain of image-production. With the fear that image culture has abolished the borders between inside and outside, self and world, comes the fear that, if turned inside out, the televisual self would be revealed to have no inside at all.

Michel Foucault observed that the discourse of continuous history and the discourse of the unified human subject are two sides of the same system of thought. The idea of continuous history depends on the idea of a unified and continuous human consciousness that can serve as the subject of that history (*Archaeology* 12). It follows that any alteration in the discourse of the self will si-multaneously entail an alteration in the discourse of history, and vice versa. It is also true that, at least since Emerson, the impulse to conflate constructions of self with constructions of history has been a peculiarly American one. For Emerson, all of history was contained in the individual, and "if the whole of history is in one man, it is all to be explained from individual experience" (221). The question then arises, what are the consequences for historical understand-ing of the sort of televisual self-consciousness found in DeLillo's characters? In DeLillo's fiction, just as the self is both served up for display and made to disap-pear into its own images, so history is made both visible and mysterious. The sense that the self is being constructed by information and image-producing systems whose structure lies "just outside the range of human apprehension" is redoubled in a sense of history as both visible and inscrutable.

The major emblem for this view of history in DeLillo's work is the assassina-tion of President Kennedy. His first novel, *Americana,* ends with the protago-nist driving a rented car along the route of the presidential motorcade through Dallas, keeping his hand on the horn all the way through Dealey Plaza (377). References to the Kennedy assassination and to assassinations in general run throughout the novels, creating in hindsight the sense that *Libra,* DeLillo's finest novel to date, is the book he had spent a career preparing to write. In an interview, DeLillo remarked, "Since the assassination, we've entered a world of randomness and ambiguity—a sense that history is being manipulated. I don't think my books could have been written in the world that existed before" (Roberts 5). In *Libra,* DeLillo's narrator describes the stretch of film showing the assassination of President Kennedy as "the seven seconds that broke the back of the American century." He refers here not to the president's death itself, but to the way that this film seemed to make history *visible* in an unprecedented and problematic way. It becomes a central irony of DeLillo's fiction that at the same time that the operations of history and the self *appear* to have been made visible and obvious, continually served up for our scrutiny on the evening news, the true structures of power behind the images seem to have become ever more irrational and mysterious.

In DeLillo's novels, the excesses of our televisual information age force the search for a separate, secret order in which history and the self can be located. DeLillo's characters repeatedly stumble into a world of conspiracy, political intrigue, and terrorism that lurks beneath the surface of ordinary lives. "This is the age of conspiracy," says a character in *Running Dog* (1978). "This is the age of connections, links, secret relationships" (111). A fascination with secrecy and conspiracy runs through every DeLillo novel from *Great Jones Street* (1973) forward, taking center stage in *Libra* (1988), where DeLillo imaginatively reconstructs the intersection of the life of Lee Harvey Oswald with the plot to assassinate the president, and providing the denouement of *Mao II* (1991), in which the reclusive writer Bill Gray attempts to contact a secret terrorist organization in Beirut. As in the fiction of Thomas Pynchon, the sense that the boundaries of the self are dissolving is accompanied by the fear that other, larger structures may be in control. A steady current of paranoia runs through DeLillo's work, and his characters often sense that "nameless energies" and "deeper levels" may be determining the course of events. As a form of historical explanation, conspiracy is not only a paranoid imposition of order in response to disordered contemporary conditions but an attempt to fashion a self by creating a realm of secret "deep" knowledge apart from an image culture that continually exposes the self and refuses the satisfactions of depth.

Finally, however, conspiracy is no refuge. In novels such as *Players* (1977) and *Libra,* for example, the effort to recover depth and order through the conspiratorial act turns back on itself, returning the self to the externalized condition of an image on a screen and rendering historical process more mysterious than ever. For both Lyle in *Players* and Lee Oswald in *Libra,* the involvement in conspiracy becomes a symptom of the *loss* of self, as their identities are invaded by someone else's plans for history, plans that themselves remain beyond apprehension. As one of the CIA plotters in *Libra* sees it, "nothing can be finally known that involves human motive and need. There is always another level, another secret, a way in which the heart breeds a deception so mysterious and complex it can only be taken for a deeper kind of truth" (260). Jack Gladney of *White Noise* (1985) finds that the deepest regions of the self—even his own death—have become the operand of information and image-producing technologies, and his attempt to impose order on his life through a secret murder plot becomes nothing but a bungled effort to impose on his life the form of a literary cliché.

In the deep surfaces that DeLillo's fiction constructs, the search for depth only substitutes one confusion for another, as deep mystery and terror replace the disorder of the visible surface. This is not to say that DeLillo's fiction is pure mystification. More than any other American novelist working today, he is a connoisseur of cultural surfaces, with a keen eye for life within the new consumer environments of the supermarket and the shopping mall, and for the ways that such key postwar technologies as the television and the computer have transformed our ways of thinking and working. At the same time, however, that he provides acute observations of the workings of television networks, intelligence organizations, corporations, government agencies, and the academic world, he reminds us of the extent to which all these institutions may be in thrall to chance, contingency, and structures of power beyond our apprehension. As a "deep surface" Don DeLillo's postmodern historical imagination confounds the distinctions between surface and depth, while exploring the conditions under which history and the self can be known in an era of televisual exposure.

Losing the Real: A Dialectic of Vision

Before taking up DeLillo's fiction in greater detail, it will be helpful to explore the sources of concern among novelists and cultural critics over the possibility that mass cultural images have robbed us of any genuine understanding of history and the self. The terms in which the problem is stated are themselves the product of an epistemology of vision, inherited from the Western philosophical tradition, that makes vision the primary analogue for knowledge and thus makes the image a metonym for all forms of information and communication. With the unprecedented power of today's mass media, the pressure of this metonymic substitution is too great for the image to bear. The much touted "crisis of representation" said to characterize the postmodern condition is the result of making traditional epistemological demands of images at a time when the nature of the image has been transformed by the technologies of the mass media and the corporate structures of late capitalism.

In their seminal essay on the "Culture Industry," Theodor Adorno and Max Horkheimer complained that "real life is becoming indistinguishable from the movies" (126). The concern that we have lost the distinction between reality and the images produced within mass culture has become a commonplace among postmodern theorists and culture critics. Just as poststructuralism draws from the experience of intertextuality that there is no getting "outside" of language, postmodernist cultural theory draws from the experience of mass culture that there is no getting "outside" of images. In place of whatever we might have once considered "authentic" experience, mass culture presents what Jean Baudrillard (after Plato) calls "simulacra," reproductions for which originals never existed. William Gass observes, for example, that there is no "real" Mickey Mouse, just as there is no "real" Marilyn Monroe: "where their image is, they are—that's it" (67). This effect is raised to a higher power by a performer such as Madonna, who knowingly acts upon the premise that she is nothing but her various masks (including her impersonation of Monroe) and in her shifting personae offers herself up for consumption as a series of images with no essential connection to a unifying self. A nonvisual example of the postmodern simulacrum would be popular music "recordings," which are in fact no longer recordings of original performances but amalgamations of electronic signals produced by machines with input from human performers and engineers who may never have been in the same room together.[1] Like the images of Madonna, such music becomes pure surface, referring neither to some originating event nor to any coherent self as its willing agent. As Jean Baudrillard puts it, with customary mordant wit: "Everything is destined to reappear as simulation. . . . You wonder whether the world itself isn't just here to serve as advertising copy in some other world" (*America* 32).

For the present study, the ontology of media stars, whether Mickey or Madonna, is not in itself of great concern. But in postmodern fiction the loss of the distinction between image and reality within mass culture serves as a paradigm for a general shift in the conditions of knowledge. Pynchon's *Gravity's Rainbow*, Doctorow's *Ragtime*, and Reed's *Mumbo Jumbo*, for example, in their own ways present the history of image-producing technologies—particularly photography and movies—as the history of an epistemology. In their representations of particular times and places—Europe during World War II, New York in the 1900s, the Harlem Renaissance—each novel calls attention not only to the processes by which history gets constructed but to the particular effects that mass-cultural forms of representation have had on those processes. DeLillo's *Libra* reminds us that the experience of watching the Kennedy and Oswald killings on television unavoidably controls our historical understanding of these events, just as it governs DeLillo's narrative reconstruction of them. Frank Lentricchia, for one, describes the shift from the fiction of Dreiser and Dos Passos to that of Don DeLillo in these terms: "The social environment of the typical naturalist character is displaced in DeLillo by the charismatic environment of the image, a new phase in American literature and culture" ("Don DeLillo" 10). Though Lentricchia doesn't use the term, DeLillo's fiction can be seen as a new "realism" in that images have come, paradoxically, to form the real and determining cultural and social context of his characters' lives. Under such conditions, the binary opposition between the real and the imaginary breaks down. As Lentricchia argues, making a typically postmodern claim, the realm of the image has become both real and inescapable: "The environment of the image *is* the landscape—it is what 'landscape' has become, and it can't be turned off with the flick of a wrist. For this environment-as-electronic-medium radically constitutes contemporary consciousness and therefore (such as it is) contemporary community—it guarantees that we are a people of, by, and for the image" ("Don DeLillo" 7). In such an environment of the image, as in Guy DeBord's "Society of the Spectacle" and Jean Baudrillard's seamless world of "simulacra," the "real world" has disappeared, and any attempts to effect its return are themselves outpaced by illusion.

Though mass culture considered broadly encompasses a range of image-producing practices—photography, film, computer simulations—it is television that, for DeLillo, as for other writers and critics, provides the paradigmatic form of the image within postmodern culture. Brian McHale writes that "where the movies had arguably functioned in the modernist period as cultural dominant, modernism's preferred model or metaphor for itself, TV has come to function as postmodern culture's privileged model or metaphor. TV, it might be argued, is the medium in which postmodern culture prefers to represent itself *to* itself" (*Constructing Postmodernism* 125). Jean Baudrillard writes that television is "the ultimate and perfect object for this new era" ("Ecstasy" 127). Despite the apocalyptic tenor of much of Baudrillard's writings on postmodern culture, many of his basic insights on the effects of the mass media are widely shared. As television programmers sell our attention to advertisers, we are removed from the scene of history in two ways: first, we are removed from a relationship to our immediate surroundings by our focus on the screen, increasing our physical and social isolation; second, we begin to view television images not as re-presentations of events that have taken place elsewhere (and which can at least in principle be experienced directly or in forms other than the tele-visual) but as first-order phenomena, as events themselves. The referent of the images becomes unnecessary, redundant, and finally lost to consciousness. The first of these effects—the loss of contact with our immediate surroundings—is described by Baudrillard in his essay on "The Ecstasy of Communication":

> It is well known how the simple presence of the television changes the rest of the habitat into a kind of archaic envelope, a vestige of human relations whose very survival remains perplexing. As soon as this scene is no longer haunted by its actors and their fantasies, as soon as behavior is crystallized on certain screens and operational terminals, what's left appears only as a large useless body, deserted and condemned. The real itself appears as a large useless body. (129)

To anyone who knows what happens to conversation when a television is turned on, this assessment seems all too convincing. To Baudrillard, images are "murderers of the real," and Western technological, postindustrial culture has progressed to the point where images have replaced reality entirely. This second and most drastic effect—the loss of the reality to which television refers—Bau-drillard describes in a much noted passage from *Simulacra and Simulations:*

> These would be the successive phases of the image:
> 1 It is the reflection of a basic reality.
> 2 It masks and perverts a basic reality.
> 3 It masks the *absence* of a basic reality.
> 4 It bears no relation to any reality whatever: it is its own pure simula-crum. (*Selected Writings* 170)

For Baudrillard, simulation displaces the reality principle by displacing the old binary opposition between the real and the imaginary. The simulacrum, as a reproduction for which no original ever existed, is the *only* reality, one re-quiring a new label: the hyperreal. With the loss of the reality principle comes the loss of any realm outside of the systems of signs in which simulacra are produced. Thus the postmodernist critique of image culture aligns itself with Saussurian linguistics in its claim that meaning—and thus historical under-standing—must necessarily be produced on a "surface" constructed by the dif-ferential play of signifiers without recourse to the depth and authority of any transcendental signified.

The excesses of contemporary image culture, and their threats to conven-tional distinctions between the real and the imaginary, would not be perceived as such a problem were not a metaphorics of vision central to the Western philosophical tradition. When René Descartes made clarity and distinctness the criteria for certainty, and thus founded knowledge on the model of vision, he preserved the traditional theological resonance of the dialectic between light and dark that has been with us since the original *fiat lux*. The Book of Genesis establishes vision as fundamental to being, and with the words "God divided the light from the darkness" we understand that light has no existence apart from its dialectical relation to darkness. The perception of truth, for Descartes, came by way of a "natural light" provided by God, and it was only the certainty that God was not a deceiver that assured him that any thing of which he had a clear and distinct conception must be true (136).[2] True to the nature of the dialectic, however, the rationalist elevation of clarity and distinctness was never more than a holding action against the inroads that obscurity and confusion must inevitably make. Those who would celebrate postmodernism as an unprecedented triumph over Cartesianism (Death to the *cogito!* Down with *claritas!*) would do well to remind themselves that from the beginning the doctrines of clarity and the unitary subject were threatened, anxious attempts to rescue knowledge and selfhood from dispersal and confusion.[3]

In 1757 Edmund Burke wrote that "a clear idea is another name for a little idea." Thus in the midst of the English Enlightenment he announced a rebellion against Cartesian *claritas* and the Lockean theory of language so important to Enlightenment thought. In a radically antimimetic and anti-Lockean treatment of poetic language, Burke argued that words characteristically function by arousing the passions rather than by exciting their corresponding images or ideas in the mind (163). In hindsight, Burke's attack on clarity and his elevation of the power of confusion in his treatment of the sublime are often viewed as an opening toward romanticism; however, it is more faithful to Burke's actual historical position to see his attack on the Lockean and Cartesian traditions as growing out of a humanism that looks backward toward a prescientific rhetorical and ethical tradition.[4] But the fact that there is a certain affinity, both of conception and affect, between Burke's backward-looking humanism and the later romanticism only points up the fact that clarity and distinctness have always been in dialectical contention with obscurity and confusion. We should expect to see certain similarities among attacks on clarity despite the otherwise quite different discursive and historical contexts in which they appear. As recent studies of the relationship between the postmodern and the romantic sublime have suggested, we can read both romanticism and postmodernism as dialectical turns of the spiral away from the values of clarity and distinctness toward the values of dispersal and confusion.[5]

This view is corroborated by Walter Ong, who has written that our too heavy reliance on vision as a symbol of intellect, our too easy equation of knowing with seeing, leads inevitably to an "oscillation into chaos" (125). The use of vision as the primary analogue for knowledge has served a specific purpose within the Western philosophical tradition. As the most abstract of the senses, sight was most readily associated with the distance and objectivity required for the development of abstract, scientific thought (Ong 121–44). The danger in making vision the primary sense is that sight can remove us from the world; the movement from sight to hearing, to smell, taste, and finally to touch is a movement back toward the world, until we are more securely anchored in our surroundings. "Sight gives precision, but lacks intimacy," Ong writes. "Touch is intimate, but lacks clear definition" (135). Our knowledge of persons—and thus our very morality, as Ong would have it—is as notoriously *in*distinct as our sense of touch, so by founding knowledge on the analogue of sight we distort our epistemology and create an obsession with certainty that can never be satisfied in the life world we inhabit.

In the American context, the primacy of vision was given an emphatic development by the Calvinism of the Puritan settlers, with their need to produce visible signs of godliness. As Sacvan Bercovitch has explained, the Puritan concept of "calling" involves demonstrating one's inward state through a social vocation by which the *visibilia* of the saint are displayed in oneself (7). We might see, in this early construction of the American self, something of our own need for self-display, our compulsion to make our most inner selves manifest, if not through a social vocation, then through our psychic investment in consumer goods: with my fitted shirts, my German automobile, my hardwood floors and interesting shrubbery, my taste in exotic brands of mustard, I proclaim the richness and rightness of my inner being. The problem is that the meanings generated by these external signs are unstable: our desire to know is sometimes defeated by our compulsion to see. The instability in the Puritan concept of *visibilia* is brilliantly explored in Nathaniel Hawthorne's *The Scarlet Letter,* in which the letter on Hester Prynne's breast comes to mock the desire to couple visibility with knowledge. Given the fiery and rebellious adornments of Hester's needle, worn over a breast containing unrepentant, radical thoughts, yet the mark of a woman whose outward bearing is one of saintly humility and charity, the scarlet letter finally eludes all efforts to control its signification, as Hester both performs and parodies the punishment set out for her by the community. Rather than provide a stable mark of a spiritual condition, the scarlet letter in its visual clarity and distinctness mocks the moral obscurity and confusion that is both Hester's and Boston's. *The Scarlet Letter* warns against trying to represent the confusions and complexities of the moral world with the deceptive clarity of visual signs.

What must be grasped, finally, about the dialectic of vision under postmodern conditions is that the current swing away from the values of clarity and distinctness is occasioned not by a de-emphasis of the visual but by an *excess* of visibility.[6] The irony is that as vision, traditionally a metaphor for knowledge, becomes more nearly the literal condition of knowledge in the televisual age, visual clarity and distinctness are demoted in value. This is a dialectical result in that the epistemology of vision is undone by its own success. Recall that, for Descartes, a perception is "distinct" if we can separate it from all other perceptions, a difficult condition to meet in the age of split screens, multiple exposures, jump cuts, and subliminals. The paradigmatic form here is perhaps MTV, where Samantha Hughes, the main character of Bobbie Ann Mason's *In Country,* finds "everything flying, shifting, changing in the blink of an eye" (230). A further and even more common challenge to Cartesian distinctness is found in those environments where one is subject to multiple, heterogeneous flows of information. Talking on the phone while driving a car is a small feat next to that of the teenager who simultaneously listens to the radio, watches television with the sound turned off, talks to a friend on the phone, and solves homework problems in a notebook. The very fact that one is tempted to redefine the terms *listening, watching, talking,* and *solving* in this context suggests how poorly this sort of multitrack consciousness is accounted for by an epistemology founded on the model of distinct, unified vision. In the next chapter we will see how such challenges to distinctness are registered in narrative as "spectacular form," which uses formal discontinuity and the combination of heterogeneous discourses to frustrate the conventional expectations of linear, unified historical narrative.

To Descartes a perception is "clear" if we are sure that we are really having it; this condition is not easily met in a world where the distinction between image and reality is continually abrogated. Cartesian *claritas* depends on the separation between subject and object, but Don DeLillo's characters typically suffer from a form of televisual exposure that makes them feel as though their most carefully hidden secrets, their most desperate drives, even their own deaths, have been taken from them and displayed on the screen. In his short story "Videotape," a man watches the television broadcast of a home video that happened to capture the random shooting of a man driving a car on the highway. Despite its tedium the video fascinates by seeming an anticipation or projection of the man's own consciousness: "It is the jostled part of your mind, the film that runs through your hotel brain under all the thoughts that you know you're thinking" (15). *Libra* has Oswald, just before the assassination, watch a film on TV in which Frank Sinatra plays a man trying to assassinate the president with a high-powered rifle, and then a second film in which John Garfield plays a man trying to assassinate a Cuban dictator. Oswald, deep into the plot to kill the president, "felt he was in the middle of his own movie," that "they were run-ning a message through the night into his skin" (370). Incorporated into the plots of several of DeLillo's novels is a situation in which, as Walter Ong writes, "the 'media' are more significantly within the mind than outside it" (46). In-deed, DeLillo's fiction suggests that the interface between mass culture and consciousness has become so problematic that it sometimes makes little sense to speak of our having an "inside" at all.

In one sense DeBord's "society of the spectacle" or Lentricchia's "charismatic environment of the image" simply extend a tradition that makes vision the pri-mary metaphor for both epistemology and ontology: to know is to see, to be is to be seen. But what is different is that, whereas clarity was once routinely set against obscurity, light against darkness, contemporary mass culture now creates the impression that we live in a world of total illumination. As the nov-elist Robert Stone writes, "The world of popular culture casts no shadows." The cameras are standing by, says a character in DeLillo's *White Noise.* "Nothing ter-rible escapes their scrutiny"(66). The environment of the image can seem to be one of surface only, flooded with an illumination both terrible and wonderful. The culture of the surface is one in which, according to Lawrence Grossberg, today's youth in particular feel well at home: "The surface becomes the site at which reality is collected, the space within which power and pleasure are pro-duced. The surface becomes nothing but a collection of quotations from youth's own collective historical debris, a mobile game of trivia. The narrative is less important than the images" (140). This conjunction of several uses of the "surface" metaphor is made possible precisely by the customary use of vision as an equivalent for knowledge. *Surface* here refers at the same time to a visible surface illuminated by the glare of TV lights, to the surface of the video screen itself, to the "surface" of linguistic signifiers detached from their signifieds, and to the "surface" of the intertext, to which Grossberg alludes with his echo of Barthes's definition of the text as a "fabric of quotations resulting from a thou-sand sources of culture" ("Death of the Author" 1132).

But the challenge to the historical imagination by the conditions of the sur-face does not belong to youth only, as Grossberg seems to suggest. The problem is general, and bids us all to confront the terms of Fredric Jameson's sobering pronouncement that contemporary mass culture "is characterized by a histori-cal amnesia—a repression both of past and of imaginable future—far more in-tense than in any other social formation in human history" (Interview 74). To Jameson, the postmodern historical novel registers our confinement to the realm of the image by replacing a more "genuine" apprehension of history with nostalgia, making us "aware of a new and original historical situation in which we are condemned to seek History by way of our own pop images and simulacra of that history, which itself remains forever out of reach" ("Postmodernism" 71).

Life in the Filmed Century

The idea that the consumption of images can lead to error and blindness both epistemological and moral is at least as old as Plato's cave. Yet the idea that images can substitute for and finally replace a prior reality acquires particular force in a time when the technologies of the mass media make the reproduction and distribution of images a ubiquitous fact of our lives. When the narrator of Maxine Hong Kingston's *The Woman Warrior* (1976) asks "What is Chinese tradition and what is the movies?" she expresses a typically postmodern concern with the confusion between the realm of image and what is projected or desired as a realm of "authentic" experience. When Horkheimer and Adorno complained that "real life is becoming indistinguishable from the movies," they were, first of all, remarking on the development of the technology itself. The producer of the sound film had an unprecedented ability to reproduce reality: "The more intensely and flawlessly his techniques duplicate empirical objects, the easier it is today for the illusion to prevail that the outside world is the straightforward continuation of that presented on the screen" (126). Horkheimer and Adorno fear a seamless technical perfection that will eliminate the distance between image and reality, a distance that maintains and is maintained by the ironic and critical consciousness of the viewer.

But their complaint has to do with more than the technology in itself. Horkheimer and Adorno point to the *form* of the popular film, its pacing and sensory complexity, as denying the audience the opportunity for the kind of reflective thought required to distinguish between image and reality. Sound films, they write, "are so designed that quickness, powers of observation, and experience are undeniably needed to apprehend them at all; yet sustained thought is out of the question if the spectator is not to miss the relentless rush of facts" (127). The result is that the moviegoer's powers of imagination are stunted. In a highly suggestive attack on the power of the mass media to alter consciousness, Horkheimer and Adorno go so far as to suggest that Kant's categories—those fundamental concepts which are the a priori basis of perception and cognition—have been replaced by categories supplied by the culture industry: "Kant's formalism still expected a contribution from the individual, who was thought to relate the varied experiences of the senses to fundamental concepts; but industry robs the individual of his function. Its prime service to the customer is to do his schematizing for him" (124). Kant's categories were, of course, by definition beyond the reach of any such manipulation, yet Horkheimer and Adorno treat Kant's system on the level of political allegory in order to serve their polemic: the function that was once reserved to the individual—that of fitting empirical conditions into preexisting categories of experience—has been usurped by the apparatus of the culture industry. The modes of perception fostered by the mass media have altered us so deeply that it is *as if* our a priori categories of perception had been changed.

The idea that we have become a people whose perceptions are organized by the forms of mass culture is a recurring theme in Don DeLillo's fiction. In *The Names* (1982), the filmmaker Frank Volterra explores the nature of representation in a world seemingly conquered by the image:

> "Film is more than the twentieth-century art. It's another part of the twentieth-century mind. It's the world seen from inside. We've come to a certain point in the history of film. If a thing can be filmed, film is implied in the thing itself. This is where we are. The twentieth century is *on film*. It's the filmed century. You have to ask yourself if there's anything about us more important than the fact that we're constantly on film, constantly watching ourselves. The whole world is on film, all the time. Spy satellites, microscopic scanners, pictures of the uterus, embryos, sex, war, assassinations, everything." (200)

To say that film is "the world seen from inside" is to claim that our subjectivity has evolved to conform to the modes of experience offered by film. Volterra thus echoes the claim made by Horkheimer and Adorno that film has altered the fundamental categories of perception. Our perceptual and cognitive apparatus has been so shaped by film that, in order for a thing to be an object of perception, film must "be implied in the thing itself." Becoming a thing "as seen on film" is necessary to its being seen at all.

Like Foucault's description of Bentham's panoptic prisons, Volterra's vision grasps how panopticism helps shape a particular self-conscious subjectivity. In the twentieth-century panopticism that Volterra describes, as in the eighteenth-century panopticon, the fact of universal observation is less important than its potential. Just as the prisoner in his cell acts on the assumption that he is always being watched, even though he knows that this cannot in fact be the case, so with the idea that everything *could* be on film one begins to see and behave as though everything *were* on film.[7] Thus the potential for universal observation becomes the fact of universal self-observation, and film becomes, as Frank Lentricchia puts it, "the culturally inevitable form of our self-consciousness" ("Don

DeLillo" 21). As our experience is shaped by the idiom of film and television, and we see our own lives in flashback, instant replay, slow-motion, and close-ups, it becomes difficult if not impossible to draw the line between our own ideas and those provided for us by the media culture. One could say that the boundaries of the self become blurred, only that in saying it one senses that such terminology has already become obsolete.[8]

The problem is further complicated by the sense that our grasp of a coherent agency behind mass media images has been weakened. To say that the media culture "provides" us with images is to pass over the difficult question of the intentionality and causality behind these images. At a time when corporations seem effortlessly to transform oppositional practices into new products (as when, for example, McDonald's becomes the nation's foremost champion of recycled paper) and when both politicians and corporations base an increasing share of decisions on up-to-the-minute opinion polls and focus groups, it is no longer so easy to say who is acting upon whom.[9] Horkheimer and Adorno's theory of the culture industry as "mass deception," which grew out of the spectacle of the Nazi propaganda machine as well as that of American mass culture in the 1940s, relied on a hierarchical model in which the masses were manipulated from above by political leaders in collusion with the captains of industrial capitalism. But "mass culture" is no longer the culture of the industrial working classes only, as the term was first used in the nineteenth century. In the age of television, mass culture has in an important sense become all culture, a development concomitant with the increased difficulty of locating oneself in regard to a distinct class structure and of perceiving clearly the ways in which both private and public institutions operate on one's life. The adequacy of the centralized, hierarchical model of mass culture is further weakened by the advent of cable and satellite television, which multiplies the sources of programming and divides the receiving audience into ever smaller and more specialized fractions. More recently, the rise of the Internet marks yet another and even more striking phase of this dispersal of agency and accountability. Horkheimer and Adorno's model assumed a cultural geography in which the center of power could be reliably located in relation to the margins, and one knew who the bad guys were. In contrast, much of postmodernist thought, and the fiction of Don DeLillo in particular, presents a vision of a culture with no one clearly in charge. DeLillo's fiction, with its gestures toward unknowable "deeper levels" of causality beneath surface appearances, accompanies a postmodernism notoriously unable to theorize agency in the face of its deconstruction of the idea of the individual subject and its elevation of the concept of "discourse" as the object of historical and political analysis.[10] Having dethroned the sovereign individual as the agent of history, postmodernist cultural theory has been at a loss for a replacement that can be held to account. For intellectuals on the political left, the lack of a concept of historical agency has presented difficulties for any theoretically coherent oppositional politics, while in DeLillo's fiction, it creates an opening for the paranoid suspicion that behind the apparent lack of agency lies an invisible structure of power. Not only are the boundaries of the self blurred, but, more insidiously, we are unsure of who or what is doing the blurring. On the one hand, when it appears that media images, corporate-produced jargon, and computer simulations have come to constitute fundamental elements of the psyche, it becomes legitimate to question what, if anything, can be meant by the term "individual." On the other hand, when the institutions we might point to as the cause of this condition are themselves seen to be riddled with contingency, accident, and lack of coherent intention, we are left with a poor sense of just what the "individual" might be up against. DeLillo has updated a central concern of the American literary tradition: the problems of the relations between the individual and society, inside and outside, self and world. In DeLillo's disturbing vision of life in the culture of the image, such distinctions may no longer be possible.

White Noise: *Inside the Aura*

Early in DeLillo's eighth novel, *White Noise*, the college professor Jack Gladney accompanies his colleague Murray Siskind, an expert in popular culture, on a visit to "the most photographed barn in America." Driving through the countryside, Gladney and Siskind pass several signs announcing their approach to the barn. Murray explains that "once you've seen signs about the barn, it becomes impossible to see the barn" (12). The barn, the object in itself, has been replaced by its images. Even the act of photographing the barn—the act by which the tourist possesses the object and makes it his or her own—is significant not as an individual act but only as part of a collective activity by which the barn itself is effaced by the image: "We're not here to capture an image," Siskind explains, "we're here to maintain one. Every photograph reinforces the aura. Can you feel it, Jack? An accumulation of nameless energies" (12). The process by which the barn disappears into its images also includes Siskind and Gladney themselves: "We can't get outside the aura. We're part of the aura. We're here, we're now" (13).[11]

But Gladney is not entirely comfortable with being "part of the aura." Throughout the novel, Gladney attempts to keep some ironic, critical, and aesthetic distance between himself and his mass cultural environment. However, his effort to preserve some degree of autonomy and authenticity, to organize a self around something other than consumption of the products of mass culture, is continually compromised. Gladney's experience registers the typical postmodern predicament in which there is no getting outside of culture, no escape from the systems of signs and images in which we are enmeshed. In perhaps the ultimate test of this postmodern hypothesis, the novel asks whether death itself, presumably beyond the reach of simulation, has been compromised by technology. If death represents the last authentic preserve of the self, the final reality that images are not supposed to penetrate, then Gladney's experience of death's inauthenticity represents the final triumph of the imaginary over the real.

Gladney's effort to get outside the aura of image culture is part of a recurring pattern in DeLillo's novels. In *Players* and *Libra,* to be discussed in greater detail later, the protagonists attempt to exit the surface of mass culture by entering into the secret world of conspiracy. In *Americana,* the young television executive David Bell lurches out of his fast-track career path in a quest for self-discovery, but in a sense Bell's cross-country auto trip—in which he self-consciously repeats the formula of the American road novel—only takes him more deeply into the culture that he seeks to escape. Fleeing the realm of corporate-produced images, he journeys into another realm of images: those he produces himself while shooting a fragmented, expressionistic film of his own life. In *Great Jones Street* (1973), rock star Bucky Wunderlick decides suddenly to leave his band in mid-tour and hole up in a tiny New York apartment, where he hides from the media and his frenzied admirers. In withdrawing from the world of rock 'n' roll stardom, Wunderlick seeks escape from language itself, seeking "withdrawal to that unimprinted level where all sound is silken and nothing erodes in the mad weather of language" (265). However, as is the case with David Bell, Wunderlick's attempt to escape his culture is unsuccessful: he finds that being "outside" is not much different from being "inside"; the media machine continues to crank out varying accounts of his whereabouts, and he gains no greater control over his life than he had when fully immersed in his role as pop-culture icon. Wunderlick, like David Bell, Lyle, Lee Oswald, Gary Harkness of *Endzone* (1972), Billy Twillig of *Ratner's Star* (1976), and Jack Gladney, ends up escaping *into* the culture rather than out of it. In seeking self-discovery and/or self-annihilation, DeLillo's characters attempt to escape their ordinary routine only to find that it can be impossible to tell whether one is "outside" one's culture or at the very heart of it. Indeed, the terms *inside* and *outside* no longer seem to apply to a world fully conquered and absorbed by the culture of the image, where (as we saw in comparing *The Moviegoer* to *The*

Mezzanine) one has lost the sort of cultural geography by which the center could be reliably distinguished from the margins. The contemporary American rebel no longer has Huckleberry Finn's option of "lighting out for the territories"; the frontier has been closed not by conquest of arms or industry but by the camera's eye.

In response to Murray Siskind's effusions over the most photographed barn in America, Gladney makes the typically wry observation that Siskind "seemed immensely pleased by this." Siskind can be placed among those sunny postmodernists who have stopped worrying and learned to love the culture of the image. A celebrant of the mass-cultural surface, Siskind comes into his own in the supermarket, where he finds in the glut of information there an exhilaration bordering on mystical experience:

> Everything is concealed in symbolism, hidden by veils of mystery and layers of cultural material. But it is psychic data, absolutely. The large doors slide open, they close unbidden. Energy waves, incident radiation. All the letters and numbers are here, all the colors of the spectrum, all the voices and sounds, all the code words and ceremonial phrases. It is just a question of deciphering, rearranging, peeling off the layers of unspeakability. Not that we would want to, not that any useful purpose would be served. This is not Tibet. Even Tibet is not Tibet anymore. (38)

In the degree to which he accepts the swarm of signs at the mass cultural surface, Siskind surpasses even the narrator of *The Mezzanine.* He gestures toward the depth of "layers of unspeakability" that may lie beneath that surface but waves off the attempt to reach them as not useful and presumably no fun. Siskind stands as the representative of an emergent form of consciousness that gladly accepts the white noise of "all the colors of the spectrum" and finds the disappearance of the real not a loss but a liberation.

Gladney is not so sanguine. Bombarded by information and images that continually threaten to disintegrate into the meaningless jumble of signals indicated by the novel's title, Jack Gladney worries about how television's "narcotic undertow and eerie diseased brain-sucking power" affects not only himself but his children (16). Gladney is one in a series of troubled family men to appear in DeLillo's fiction, beginning with James Axton of *The Names,* and continuing through Lee Oswald of *Libra.* As Jack Gladney and his wife Babette struggle to raise a collection of children from their previous marriages, they must face the unprecedented challenges posed by their children's exposure to torrents of information and imagery. Watching his children sleeping, Gladney sees in their faces "a quality of trust so absolute and pure that [he] did not want to think it might be misplaced" (154). In a moment both poignant and chilling, he bends over his sleeping daughter, full of a "desperate piety" as he strains to catch the words forming on the child's lips, "clearly audible words, familiar and elusive at the same time, words that seemed to have a ritual meaning, part of a verbal spell or ecstatic chant." Listening closely, Gladney realizes that the words are "Toyota Celica." Though they form only the name of an automobile, Gladney wonders why he finds the words "beautiful and mysterious, gold-shot with looming wonder. . . . Supranational names, computer-generated, more or less universally pronounceable. Part of every child's brain noise, the substatic regions too deep to probe" (155). In this moment we sense that the deepest regions of the psyche have been invaded by the brand-name babble of multinational corporations. But for Gladney, the moment is uplifting: "Whatever its source, the utterance struck me with the impact of splendid transcendence." Neither Gladney nor DeLillo can leave such a moment untouched by irony, however, and what follows is a one-sentence paragraph: "I depend on my children for that." The ironic deflation of this line signals Gladney's characteristic suspicion not only of any moment of transcendence, but of his own ability as a parent to respond adequately to the unprecedented conditions in which his children are growing up.

He feels guilty, for example, at the enjoyment he and his children get out of watching coverage of disasters on the TV news. Gladney, who is founder and chairman of the Department of Hitler Studies at a small midwestern college, is assured by his colleagues who teach popular culture that his feelings are normal:

> "Because we're suffering from brain fade. We need an occasional catastrophe to break up the incessant bombardment of information. . . . The flow is constant. Words, pictures, numbers, facts, graphics, statistics, specks, waves, particles, motes. Only a catastrophe gets our attention. We want them, we need them, we depend on them. As long as they happen somewhere else. This is where California comes in. Mud slides, brush fires, coastal erosion, earthquakes, mass killings, et cetera. We can relax and enjoy these disasters because in our hearts we feel that California deserves whatever it gets. Californians invented the concept of life-style. This alone warrants their doom."

The speaker is Alfonse (Fast Food) Stompanato, one of the "smart, thuggish, movie-mad, trivia-crazed" New York emigrés who make up the department officially known as American Environments. He goes on to lament the fact that the potential for total panoptic surveillance has not yet been realized:

"Japan is pretty good for disaster footage," Alfonse said. "India remains largely untapped. They have tremendous potential with their famines, monsoons, religious strife, train wrecks, boat sinkings, et cetera. But their disasters tend to go unrecorded. Three lines in the newspaper. No film footage. No satellite hookup. This is why California is so important. We not only enjoy seeing them punished for their relaxed life-style and progressive social ideas but we know we're not missing anything. The cameras are right there. They're standing by. Nothing terrible escapes their scrutiny." (66)

When Gladney continues to express his guilt over enjoying such spectacles, Alfonse offers a further defense: "For most people there are only two places in the world. Where they live and their TV set. If a thing happens on television, we have every right to find it fascinating, whatever it is" (66). With the distinction between "where they live and their TV set," the separation between the private and public sphere is complete, as television performs an ontological division of the world in two. As the images on the TV screen lose their connection to the real, their significance becomes a function only of the sensory stimulation they provide. As Murray Siskind attests, "in the psychic sense a forest fire on TV is on a lower plane than the ten-second spot for Automatic Dishwasher All" (67).

But the further irony is that the distinction between "where they live and their TV set"—the distinction that gives Alfonse both moral sanction and a sense of place—cannot be maintained. Whereas such a model would preserve an authenticity associated with the privacy of the home and the integrity of one's own body, *White Noise* goes on to show that these, too, have been invaded by the image. The discussion of TV disaster footage sets up the irony of the second section of the novel, in which Jack Gladney must evacuate his family from the threat of the poisonous vapor leaked from a nearby train tanker car. Conditioned by television to believe that such events happen "somewhere else," Gladney at first tries to reassure his skeptical son, arguing that such fates are reserved to the "poor and the uneducated" and "the people who live in mobile homes. . . . I'm a college professor. Did you ever see a college professor rowing a boat down his own street in one of those TV floods?" (114).

Faced with a catastrophe that has finally happened where he lives rather than on the TV screen, Gladney discovers that the difference between the two is not absolute. He and his family listen on the radio as the cloud of vapor is described first as a "feathery plume," then as a "black billowing cloud," before being given its official designation as an "airborne toxic event," a term spoken by Gladney's adolescent son "in a clipped and foreboding manner, syllable by syllable, as if he sensed the threat in state-created terminology" (117). The shifts in language from concrete metaphor to literal description to abstract, official jargon map the progress of the state bureaucratic apparatus in exerting "control" over the situation, transforming the danger from one that can be apprehended directly by the senses into an absent "event" that can be managed by state agencies on the citizens' behalf. By managing the language surrounding the event, the bureaucracy does its best to turn the disaster into pure information, something that can be broadcast on the airwaves and received with a comfortable indifference by a passive audience.

But rather than remain in the distanced realm of images on a screen or words from a radio, information invades the private realm of the body: Gladney's daughters dutifully exhibit whatever symptoms of toxic exposure the radio announces they should have, starting with sweaty palms, working up to nausea and a sense of déjà vu. As the radio informs them of increasingly harrowing possible health effects, including "convulsions, coma, miscarriage," Jack worries about his daughters' susceptibility to suggestion, and wonders at the limits of the media's power over the body: "Could a nine-year-old girl suffer a miscarriage due to the power of suggestion? Would she have to be pregnant first?" (126).

Thus two sets of conventional expectations about the relation of mass media images to the real world are violated. On one side, the toxic spill at first seems a comeuppance to those who feel that the referent for the television image has disappeared; it reminds us that the real world, with real chemicals and real illnesses, still exists. But rather than unequivocally assert the existence of a material reality beyond the realm of the image, the "airborne toxic event" is quickly absorbed by the image-making apparatus of the media and forced to conform to the bureaucratic imperatives of the official and quasi-official agencies that respond to the catastrophe. On the other side, we see that "information" itself can be a material cause of "real" events. What has happened is not that the referent for mass-media images has disappeared but that the binary opposition between the real and imaginary has itself broken down.

Jack finds that his son's pleasure in observing the toxic cloud through binoculars and listening to radio reports is not qualitatively different from that of watching distant disasters on television. In fact, Jack learns with some concern that the disaster's real proximity has only intensified his son's pleasure; Heinrich speaks about the day's events "enthusiastically, with a sense of appreciation for the vivid and the unexpected," and finds the whole disaster "brilliantly stimulating" (123). Further, Gladney discovers that, to the people in charge of managing the evacuation, the difference between a real emergency and a simulated one is no more than an inconvenience to be overcome. In the evacuation center to which he, along with hundreds of others, has brought his family, Gladney learns that the "SIMUVAC" insignia worn by evacuation officials stands for "simulated evacuation." The team handling the evacuation is using the real evacuation as a means of testing their simulation models, in a bid for government funding. Jack asks one of them how it's going:

> "The insertion curve isn't as smooth as we would like. There's a probability excess. Plus which we don't have our victims laid out where we'd want them if this was an actual simulation. In other words we're forced to take our victims as we find them. We didn't get a jump on the computer traffic. Suddenly it just spilled out, three-dimensionally, all over the landscape. You have to make allowances for the fact that everything we see tonight is real. There's a lot of polishing we still have to do. But that's what this exercise is all about" (139).

When the veracity of the "real" event is tested against the standard of the simulation model, we have moved into Jean Baudrillard's realm of the "hyperreal," the world of simulacra.

There remains one event that Jack Gladney would like to think lies beyond the reach of simulation: his own death. Death is, in fact, the principal theme of *White Noise,* and the novel in various ways posits death as the limit test of the mediating power of mass culture. Not only do computers and the electronic media have the power to alter death, but chemistry, as a corporate enterprise to alter the basic structure of matter by developing synthetic compounds, has produced new forms of death. The "airborne toxic event" produced by the spill of Nyodene-D is only one such episode in the novel. Gladney and his son are spectators at the scene of a large building fire, a mythic experience that is spoiled by the "sharp and bitter stink" of burning synthetics, "overpowering the odor of smoke and charred stone . . . it was as though we'd been forced to recognize the existence of a second kind of death. One was real, the other synthetic. The odor drove us away but beneath it and far worse was the sense that death came two ways, sometimes at once, and how death entered your mouth and nose, how death smelled, could somehow make a difference to your soul" (240). Early in the novel, one of Gladney's children has her school evacuated because "kids were getting headaches and eye irritations, tasting metal in their mouths. A teacher rolled on the floor and spoke foreign languages." Investigators in Mylex suits speculate that the source of the problem may be any one of an alarmingly long list of toxic and synthetic materials in the building, "or perhaps something deeper, finer-grained, more closely woven into the basic fabric

of things" (35). As in *Ratner's Star,* in which a scientist remarks that "no definition of science is complete without a reference to terror" (36), scientific understanding is only a thin cover for "something deeper," for the mystery that
underlies whatever system of symbols we develop as a defense against terror.

Mass culture's ability to transgress the ontological boundary between image
and reality becomes an ability to transgress the ultimate ontological boundary
between life and death. Even death, Gladney finds, is subject to the techniques of
the simulators. When he questions the SIMUVAC official about the effects of his
exposure to Nyodene-D during a two-and-a-half-minute period he spent outside of his car, he finds that the very concept of death has been altered by its insertion into a system of computerized, statistical knowledge. To the seemingly
simple question, "Am I going to die?" he receives the unsatisfactory answer: "Not
as such" (140). The official taps into various computer records of Jack Gladney's
personal and medical history, adds the new information about the toxic exposure, and reports gravely that Gladney is "generating big numbers":

> "This doesn't mean that anything is going to happen to you as such, at
> least not today or tomorrow. It just means you are the sum total of your
> data. No man escapes that."
> "And this massive so-called tally is not a simulation despite that arm-
> band you're wearing. It is real."
> "It is real," he said. (141)

But just what it means to say that a data tally is "real" is not clear. Jack Gladney
is disturbed not only by the news that his exposure is potentially fatal but by
the form in which the knowledge comes to him: "You are said to be dying and
yet are separate from the dying, can ponder it at your leisure, literally see on the
X-ray photograph or the computer screen the horrible alien logic of it all. It is
when death is rendered graphically, is televised, so to speak, that you sense an
eerie separation between your condition and yourself. A network of symbols
has been introduced, an entire awesome technology wrested from the gods. It
makes you feel like a stranger in your own dying" (142). Here the techniques of
computer simulation—another way of making images—separate Gladney
from that most private and essential part of himself, his own mortality. With
his own death somehow taken from him and placed in a "network of symbols,"
Gladney perceives directly and with visceral unease that death, in Paul DeMan's
provocative phrase, has become "another name for a linguistic predicament."

The idea that death itself is embedded in symbolic systems helps explain the
final action of the novel, in which Jack Gladney hunts down and attempts to
kill a man who he learns has had sex with his wife. The husband's jealous

rage, his stalking of the man with a gun, seems oddly formulaic in a novel that until this point has been consistently innovative and surprising. But Jack's murderous hunt ends up as neither the thriller novel's bid for cheap closure nor the existentialist assertion of authenticity through violence. Instead, it is the deliberate enactment of a literary cliché. Swayed by Murray Siskind's argument that "to plot is to affirm life, to seek shape and control" (292), Jack attempts murder not out of "authentic" jealousy but rather out of a self-conscious desire to impose the order of a literary formula on conditions in which his own death has been taken from him, dispersed into the "white noise" of computer-generated statistical data. This section of the novel treats ironically what Frank Kermode has shown to be our need for a sense of an ending when our own endings have become uncertain. Gladney's motives are similar to those of an earlier DeLillo protagonist, David Bell, who toward the end of *Americana* admits that his cross-country trip has been "merely a literary venture, an attempt to find pattern and motive, to make of something wild a squeamish thesis on the essence of the nation's soul" (349). However, for David Bell, as for Jack Gladney, whatever remains "merely literary" is no match for life's contingency and uncertainty. Having already surrendered any bid for authenticity to his own self-consciousness in enacting a stereotypical "male rage," Gladney compromises his effort further by bungling the job. After shooting the man twice, and being shot himself in the wrist, he ends by saving his victim's life, driving him to a hospital run by nuns, who upbraid him for presuming that they still believe in God and heaven: "Do you think we are stupid?" (319). Under the relentless pressure of DeLillo's irony, by which all human action can seem the repackaged productions of television and pulp novels, Gladney's attempt at self-definition by leaving the bounds of his ordinary life unravels into farce. When he first considers murder, Gladney finds that simply carrying a handgun "created a second reality for me to inhabit . . . a reality I could control, secretly dominate" (297). But in the end the realm of secret order that Jack seeks to establish through his murder plot merely empties back into the world of ordinary cliché, returning him to his normal routine, in which "there was nothing to do but wait for the next sunset, when the sky would ring like bronze" (321).

White Noise stages a confrontation between the forces of mass culture and death itself. Death asserts a final boundary, and if *this* life has been conquered by the image, if mass culture has eliminated the public sphere and rendered the private sphere inauthentic, then death is the only possible remaining preserve of the real. Death stands as the limit test of the powers of mediation, the ultimate realm of "depth" into which the image may not go. But as we have seen, *White Noise* puts death's inviolability into question. Early in the novel Murray

Siskind compares the supermarket experience to the Tibetan ritual preparation for death: "Here we don't die, we shop. But the difference is less marked than you think" (38). In the supermarket we find an intense concentration of information flows, the intersection of innumerable cultural codes—"all the letters and numbers are here, all the colors of the spectrum"—but the problem of deciphering these codes remains, especially when the systems by which they are deployed remain beyond our control. The novel's ending returns us to the supermarket, where shoppers are confused by a sudden rearrangement of the shelves:

> There is a sense of wandering now, an aimless and haunted mood, sweet-tempered people taken to the edge. They scrutinize the small print on packages, wary of a second level of betrayal. The men scan for stamped dates, the women for ingredients. Many have trouble making out the words. Smeared print, ghost images. In the altered shelves, the ambient roar, in the plain and heartless fact of their decline, they try to work their way through confusion. (326)

In this image of information degenerating into the disorder of white noise, we see how DeLillo's cultural criticism typically operates on the levels of both analysis and mystification. His analysis of the experience of chaos on the phenomenal level summons the suspicion of order on some "higher" or "deeper" level of control. In the world that this novel creates, it is presumed that the rationale for the corporate directive to rearrange the supermarket shelves remains beyond the bounds of knowledge, just as it is presumed that despite the apparent confusion there remains some hidden level on which an order is maintained: "But in the end it doesn't matter what they see or think they see. The terminals are equipped with holographic scanners, which decode the binary secret of every item, infallibly. This is the language of waves and radiation, or how the dead speak to the living" (326). Shopping has become our ritual preparation for death, with the information flows and simulating practices of our consumer environments containing hidden messages to ease our passage to the next world. But if mass culture transgresses even this final boundary, if the dead speak to us in laser beams and in the sound of expressway traffic like "dead souls babbling at the edge of a dream" (4), there remains the problem of understanding what the dead have to say. For in the end DeLillo suggests that, even if mass culture does resituate or even abolish the boundaries between image and reality, private and public, living and dead, this remains a process whose workings are beyond control and whose results are "just outside the range of human apprehension" (36). DeLillo insists on mystery's power to reassert itself: "The

American mystery deepens" (60). For all its ability to colonize the real and alter the fundamental conditions of knowledge, mass culture may leave the *pragmatics* of knowledge unchanged.

Conspiracy: The Backstage of History

Defending the difficulty of his work in a 1979 interview, DeLillo explicitly positioned his fiction in relation to mass-cultural conditions in which too much is known and exposed, saying that he writes "out of the sense of drowning in information and in the mass awareness of things. Everybody seems to know everything. Subjects surface and are totally exhausted in a matter of days or weeks, totally played out by the publishing industry and the broadcast industry. Nothing is too arcane to escape the treatment, the process. Making things difficult for the reader is less an attack on the reader than it is on the age and its facile knowledge-market. The writer is driven by his conviction that some truths aren't arrived at so easily, that life is still full of mystery" (Interview 87). In DeLillo's fiction the persistence of mystery is expressed repeatedly by the idea that there are forces at work in history behind what is visible and obvious. But conspiracy theories are not simply the result of a desire for mystery; they are also a search for a degree of order and precision lacking in ordinary life. As a form of historical explanation, conspiracy theories have a paradoxical effect: they provide an orderly explanation for events while at the same time promoting a mystified sense of historical causality as always occurring in orders beyond the visible. For DeLillo's protagonists, conspiracy is an escape from life at the surface, where televisual exposure breeds confusion and indifference, to a realm of depth in which history and the self can be constructed around a secret order. Entering into the realm of conspiracy, DeLillo's characters feel the thrill of gaining access to history's backstage. The final irony, however, is that nowhere is one safe from televisual exposure and its resulting self-consciousness. In the culture of the image, one can never be sure if one is truly behind the scenes or just another part of the show.

One aspect of the "facile knowledge-market" in which "everybody knows everything" has been described by media theorist Joshua Meyrowitz as the loss of "backstage" areas of social behavior, those parts of our lives once hidden from general view but now subject to televisual exposure. In *No Sense of Place,* Meyrowitz employs Erving Goffman's distinction between "onstage" and "backstage" regions of social space; as social "performers"—whether as parents, teachers, lovers, or professionals—we all need to have "backstage" areas in which to prepare for our performances "onstage." The two areas are distinguished by different patterns of access to social information. It is important that clear distinctions be maintained between the two informational worlds: much behavior that would be appropriate in a teacher's lounge, for example, would be strictly inappropriate in front of one's class. Likewise, men's and women's "locker room" conversations are a form of backstage preparation for one's encounters with the opposite sex, and a politician's "backstage" behaviors may be quite different from his performance in front of a camera. Much of the shock created by the tapes of President Nixon's conversations in the Oval Office resulted from the fact that normally "backstage" behavior was brought "onstage"—with devastating results both for Nixon and for the institution of the presidency. That it no longer seems possible to have "great" political leaders in this country has much to do with how the electronic media have painfully demonstrated the truth of the old saying that "no man is a hero to his valet."

Television in particular is characterized by its "front region bias," its tendency to expose backstage areas once kept hidden. The primary cause for the exposure of backstage areas, according to Meyrowitz, is not the *content* of television programming but the social conditions of its reception. Given the nature of broadcast technology and the commercial imperatives behind it, the electronic media tend to merge audiences that are more strictly segregated in print culture. In merging informational worlds previously kept separate, television breaks down barriers between once distinct social situations and fosters new kinds of social behavior. As one example, consider the different effects that print and television have on children's access to social information. The nature of reading itself, as a complex skill that must be acquired in stages over years of effort, separates readers according to age and reading experience. Children's literature becomes a sort of "informational ghetto" in which children's access to social information can be carefully controlled (239). In contrast, television comes with very few prerequisites; one does not "learn" to watch television by advancing through a graded series of increasingly difficult programs. On the contrary, children readily adapt to watching "adult" programming and often show a preference for it. The result is that adult "backstage" areas are increasingly exposed to children, and children become more knowing about adult behavior and the adult world. The controversy over television's deleterious effects, Meyrowitz argues, is not in response to the content of the programming per se but to the fact that television communicates everything to everybody and fails to segregate its audience (87).

Television thus contributes to the changes taking place in the social definitions of "childhood" and "adulthood." Today's children tend to dress, speak, and think much more like adults, and vice versa. In shopping malls across

America—those structures designed to house and sell the products advertised on television—fathers and sons stroll side by side licking identical ice-cream cones, wearing identical Mickey Mouse T-shirts, on their way to play the same video games at the arcade. DeLillo captures the changing social construction of the distinction between child and adult in the character of Heinrich in *White Noise*. In his mastery of the technical jargon and consumerist lingo of his time, Heinrich is far ahead of his parents (he also has a receding hairline). Heinrich's fluency in the mass-mediated codes further erodes his father's already threatened sense of his own competence as a parent, reducing him to a childlike fear of death and a crushing sense of his inability to provide shelter and security for his family in the face of newly created dangers and anxieties "not provided for by instinct" (116).

But Heinrich also understands that the kind of knowledge provided by the mass media is superficial and that his own fluency with jargon masks a profound ignorance about how things really work. Spending the night in a shelter to which they and much of their town have been evacuated following the toxic chemical spill, Heinrich challenges his father on the usefulness of their knowledge:

"It's like we've been flung back in time," he said. "Here we are in the Stone Age, knowing all these great things after centuries of progress but what can we do to make life easier for the Stone Agers? Can we make a refrigerator? Can we even explain how it works? What is electricity? What is light? We experience these things every day of our lives but what good does it do if we find ourselves hurled back in time and we can't even tell people the basic principles much less actually make something that would improve conditions. Name one thing you could make. Could you make a simple wooden match that you could strike on a rock to make a flame? . . . Here it is practically the twenty-first century and you've read hundreds of books and magazines and seen a hundred TV shows about science and medicine. Could you tell those people one little crucial thing that might save a million and a half lives? . . . What good is knowledge if it just floats in the air? It goes from computer to computer. It changes and grows every second of the day. But nobody actually knows anything." (147–49)

Heinrich's attack on the "facile knowledge-market" of mass culture makes DeLillo's point that the demystifying nature of mass culture can in fact only blind us to the mysteries that remain. The visibility of a TV culture that relentlessly exposes our "backstage" areas and creates the feeling that all specialized knowledge has become general is in fact only creating the *illusion* that "everybody knows everything."

One result of the feeling that everybody knows everything is that people become increasingly dissociated from what they see. In fact, the audience's disengagement from the televisual image is a necessary condition for its mass distribution. We would be driven mad if we took television too seriously. In contrast with print, television has what Meyrowitz calls a relatively weak "association" factor. People identify with and take responsibility more for what they read than for what they watch on television. This can be grasped by comparing the relative weight of "I am a reader of X" with "I am a watcher of X" as statements of self-definition (89). "Ironically," Meyrowitz observes, "the ability of viewers to dissociate themselves from the content of television allows for the most widespread sharing of similar information in the history of civilization" (89–90). Television demystifies by exposing what was once hidden, thus robbing the hidden of its power: "with television, the very notion of 'taboo' is lost" (92). Like Meyrowitz, DeLillo links the informational excesses of the media to a social and cultural environment in which "half-heartedness and indifference is very much to the point" (Interview 83).

Television's encouragement of passivity and moral disengagement has, of course, long been the focus of television's critics. We have already seen how DeLillo provides a satirized defense of the medium through Alfonse in *White Noise,* who claims that "if a thing happens on television, we have every right to find it fascinating, whatever it is" (66). What is more disturbing is the possibility that the lack of commitment viewers feel toward television spills over into all areas of life, a condition that is registered vividly in DeLillo's *Players.* For Lyle, television and the movies are, in fact, more stimulating than the real world. Even as he gets involved with a secret group of terrorists planning to bomb the New York Stock Exchange, he finds it difficult "to feel wholly engaged. It was happening around him somehow. He was slipping right through. A play. It was a little like that. He found himself bored, often, at the theater (although never at the movies), even when he knew, could see and hear, that the play was exceptional, deserving of total attention. This kind of torpor was generated by three-dimensional bodies, real space as opposed to the manipulated depth of film" (100). To Lyle's televisual consciousness, the difference between theater and real life is less marked than the difference between both of these and film. The crucial distinction is not between art and life but between the three-dimensionality of live bodies and the "manipulated depth" of the two-dimensional screen. Lyle is one of the "players" of the novel's title because he displays both the self-consciousness of the actor and the moral disengagement of the adult who treats life as a child's game.

Lyle is a Wall Street stockbroker who is bored with his life and with his wife, Pammy, who works for the "Grief Management Council." Lyle watches a lot of television, changing channels every few seconds, not in search of engaging content, but rather because "he simply enjoyed jerking the dial into fresh image-burns" (16). But Lyle's indifferent life at the televisual surface only stimulates his longing for mystery and depth. A member of the New York Stock Exchange, Lyle finds in the stock market an exhilarating sense of secrecy, and describes the Wall Street district of Manhattan as an enclave of the invisible: "The district grew repeatedly inward, more secret, an occult theology of money, extending ever deeper into its own veined marble. . . . At the inmost crypt might be heard the amplitude pulse of history, a system and rite to outshadow the evidence of men's senses" (132). It is not mystery only but system that Lyle craves, seeing in the operations of the trading floor the possibility of a history in which one could find one's identity: "In the electronic clatter it was possible to feel you were part of a breathtakingly intricate quest for order and elucidation, for identity among the constituents of a system" (28). The quest for a secret order in which history and the self might be located takes Lyle ever further from everyday routine into a world in which violence, sex, and death become the ultimate means of breaking through the superficiality of the televised life.

Lyle's quest for self-identity through a violent conspiracy repeats a pattern established throughout DeLillo's work. In *Great Jones Street*, Bucky Wunderlick abandons his life as a rock star and gets caught up in a competition between various shadowy underworld and countercultural groups for possession of a package of a mysterious new drug. In *Running Dog*, the journalist Moll Robbins's investigation of a story leads to her affair with Glen Selvy, who turns out to be a spy for a nebulous spin-off organization of the CIA and who ends by dying a pointless and brutal death in the desert. In *The Names*, James Axton's search for an occult meaning in the seemingly random murders of a shadowy terrorist group takes him progressively further from his corporate career as a "risk analyst" and into the violent world of the terrorists. In *White Noise*, the quest for a secret order leads Jack Gladney to attempt the murder of Willie Mink, seeking in the "secret precision" of the murder plot an affirmation of his own life (291). Pammy, Lyle's wife in *Players*, seeks escape from her own boredom through a secret sexual affair with a troubled gay man who ends up taking his own life. Lee Oswald of *Libra*, like Lyle of *Players*, is lured into conspiracy by the promise that in the secretly planned, dramatic act of violence one can merge oneself with history. And Bill Gray, the reclusive author in *Mao II*, decides to quit working on his masterpiece-in-progress and leave his seclusion to make a doomed solo journey to contact a group of terrorists in Beirut who are holding a prominent writer hostage. If conspiracies are hatched to establish a kind of order and control not available in ordinary life, to give their members a sense of shaping history and the self, then in the botched, senseless, or accidental violence with which each of these quests ends we see the betrayal of conspiracy's purpose.

In his fascination with conspiracies whose motivations are either unclear or based in primal urges that defy analysis, DeLillo could be accused of making the sources of power in our society needlessly obscure, thus blurring whatever political insight his books might contain. John Kucich links these repeated gestures toward violence to a failure of political imagination, to DeLillo's "inability to reason out an alternative politics" to the negative postmodernist one that denies the possibility of meaningful opposition to all-embracing systems of power (341). Kucich desires what DeLillo's novels despair of attaining: a politics based in reason, and strategies of opposition rooted in "coherent intellectual agendas" (338). Neither the world of the surface, in which the epistemology of vision is defeated by televisual excess, nor the realms of mystery and depth in which DeLillo's characters seek refuge, provide the conditions in which this kind of reason and coherence can operate. DeLillo refuses to provide a hopeful vision of the resources of the individual in the struggle against a corrupt and often terrifying society, nor does his work express much hope for successful collective action. Leaving aside the question of what it would mean for *any* work of fiction to have a "coherent intellectual agenda," it does seem fair to say that, in his attraction to mystery, DeLillo forgoes the articulation of an oppositional politics in favor of enumerating the odds against its success.

DeLillo's characters fail to establish a secret order beneath the surface of ordinary lives because of the postmodern predicament: there is no getting outside of culture, no escape from the systems of signs and images within which history and the self are constructed and over which we seem to have little control. Conspiracy is no safe haven and is always subject to the sort of televisual exposure in which the secret self that one has attempted to construct is exposed and flattened to an image on a screen. In *Players,* Lyle explains to the terrorist leader that his deepening involvement with the conspiracy is motivated by "the secret dream of the white collar. To place a call from a public booth in the middle of the night. Calling some government bureau, some official department, right, of the government. 'I have information about so-and-so.' Or, even better, to be visited, to have them come to you. . . . Imagine how sexy that can be for the true-blue businessman or professor. What an incredible nighttime thrill. The appeal of mazes and intricate techniques. The suggestion of a double life" (100). The problem is that the terrorist conspiracy to bomb the New York Stock Exchange takes on the inscrutability of the government it opposes. Kinnear, the apparent leader of the terrorist ring, sees the U.S. government as a "haze of conspiracies and multiple interpretations" and works on the assumption that "behind every stark fact we encounter layers of ambiguity" (104). Rather than perform the sort of demystifying analysis necessary to organized radical politics, Kinnear takes ambiguity as the working condition of knowledge, thus dooming his conspiracy to ever greater obscurity and incoherence. After his initial meeting with Kinnear, Lyle becomes progressively removed from close contact with the conspirators and is given telephoned instructions, the purpose of which is ever more in doubt. At the end of the novel, he has left his job and gone to Canada, where he waits in a motel room for a phone call we feel certain will never come. In the novel's closing sentences, the narrative pulls away from Lyle, who is "barely recognizable as male. Shedding capabilities and traits by the second, he can still be described (but quickly) as well-formed, sentient and fair. We know nothing else about him" (212).

Thus in the novel's last section, titled "The Motel," Lyle is returned to the condition in which he is first introduced. The novel's opening section is titled "The Movie," and begins with someone saying "Motels. I like motels. I wish I owned a chain, worldwide. I'd like to go from one to another to another. There's something self-realizing about that" (3). In the 1979 interview, DeLillo explained that in this section "all the main characters, seven of them, are introduced in an abstract way. They don't have names. Their connections to each other are not clear in all cases. They're on an airplane, watching a movie, but all the other seats are empty. They're isolated, above the story, waiting to be named" (82). The movie they are watching shows terrorists attacking and killing a group of golfers. The novel's ending is thus a symmetrical inversion of the beginning. At both beginning and end, Lyle is anonymous, stripped of "capabilities and traits." In the beginning, Lyle is the spectator of the images of violent death on the screen, whereas at the end, Lyle is the would-be agent of such violence himself, transformed both by his own ineffectiveness and by the narrative distance of the closing sentences into a screen image, pure light and surface. Rather than being a place of self-realization, the motel room at the end of the novel seems to Lyle

the *idea* of something, still waiting to be expressed fully in concrete form. Isn't there more, he wants to ask. What's behind it all? It must be the traveler, the motorist, the sojourner himself who provides the edible flesh of this concept. Inwardness spiraling ever deeper. Rationality, analysis, self-realization. He spends a moment imagining that this vast system of nearly identical rooms, worldwide, has been established so that people will have somewhere to be *afraid* on a regular basis. The parings of our various searches. Somewhere to take our fear. (209–10)

Lyle is finally denied any self-realization through conspiracy, and the strange woman who has been sent to share his motel bed mocks the "edible flesh" of the communion mystery. Lyle's search for depth, his desire to locate self and history in a secret order beneath the world's televisual surface, ends up only emptying him of content, making him into one more character displayed on the screen.

Libra: *The Truth at the Edge of Human Affairs*

All of the operations of the contemporary culture of the image—the overwhelming of the epistemology of vision through an excess of visibility, the confounding of the distinction between the imaginary and the real, the development of televisual self-consciousness, the exposure of backstage areas, the lure of nostalgia—can be observed in the way that in the last three decades we have learned to make a spectacle out of the mortality of our presidents. When President Grover Cleveland disappeared for five days in 1893 for an operation to remove his entire upper left jaw and part of his palate, for sixty days no outsider learned what had occurred, and the main details of the operation remained secret for twenty-five years (Meyrowitz 285). Even as late as the 1950s, President Eisenhower could linger near death in a hospital while press releases fabricated an image of an active, vital president. But the Zapruder film showing the assassination of President Kennedy marks a decisive end to a time when we might be spared the most graphic evidence that politicians are mortal. In the mid-1960s, President Johnson would show his surgical scar to the cameras as if to his most intimate friends, and by the late 1970s, we were treated to daily news updates on the condition of President Carter's hemorrhoids.

The 1981 assassination attempt on President Reagan was not only highly visible but involved such a dizzying interpenetration of art and life as to make it a paradigm for the postmodern breakdown of the distinction between image and reality. The most fantastic of our contemporary novelists would not have dared imagine a scene in which a cowboy actor-turned-president is gunned down by a real bad guy named John Hinckley, who is staging his own version of the movie *Taxi Driver* in order to impress the real Jodie Foster, who acted in the movie. The whole event is captured on videotape and then broadcast within four minutes after the first shot is fired, making Hinckley a real celebrity and Reagan a real hospital patient whose handlers continue to script one-liners for him as he goes under the surgeon's knife: "Who's minding the store?" Indeed. (It turned out to be Secretary of State Alexander Haig, whose sprint to the press briefing room and breathless, mistaken claim of his succession to the presidency was necessitated, so he felt, by the very fact that the video of the shooting had already been sent out on the airwaves.) Finally, in the late 1980s, as the Nickelodeon cable television channel exploited our nostalgia for 1960s sitcoms, we marked the twenty-fifth anniversary of John Kennedy's assassination with the grisly ritual of watching endless slow-motion reruns of those seven seconds of grainy film shot in Dallas. Not only have the mass media enhanced our ability to make politics into entertainment, but out of the wounded and diseased bodies of our presidents the media have made a spectacle of our national morbidity.

Perhaps this last sentence gives these developments too great a narrative coherence. What is maddening about the trend toward increased visibility in American life is that in insisting that everything be made visible, we end up seeing far more than we can know or understand. Visibility is no guarantee of intelligibility, and our love of the spectacular is often at odds with our need to understand ourselves and our history. This idea is central to Don DeLillo's *Libra,* which constructs the life of Lee Harvey Oswald, attempting to get behind those seven seconds of the Zapruder film and their sequel, in which Jack Ruby shoots Oswald before a live television audience.[12] The Lee Harvey Oswald that we know literally comes into being with the televisual image. In the act of shooting President Kennedy, and in being shot by Jack Ruby on television, Oswald stepped out of the state of nonbeing in which he lacked "capabilities and traits" and became part of our collective history. *Libra* takes on the question of the extent to which the "layers of ambiguity" behind the stark facts of those deaths will ever yield to our understanding, and to what extent satisfactory historical understanding can ever be achieved under televisual conditions. A key problem is that the media spectacle surrounding these deaths is itself history; the images themselves *are* the events, and to speak of these killings separately from our experience of watching them on television is in a way, paradoxically, to deny their essential reality. Of all of DeLillo's novels to date, *Libra* most sharply focuses the problems for historical understanding posed by our search for historical depth beneath the televisual surface.

The novel's central epistemological problem is focalized through the character of Nicholas Branch, a retired senior analyst of the CIA, who has spent fifteen years, starting in 1973, analyzing an ever-growing accumulation of data in order to write "the secret history" of the assassination of President Kennedy:

Six point nine seconds of heat and light. Let's call a meeting to analyze the blur. Let's devote our lives to understanding this moment, separating the elements of each crowded second. We will build theories that gleam like jade idols, intriguing systems of assumption, four-faced, graceful. We will follow the bullet trajectories backwards to the lives that occupy the shadows, actual men who moan in their dreams. Elm Street. A woman wonders why she is sitting on the grass, bloodspray all around. Tenth Street. A witness leaves her shoes on the hood of a bleeding policeman's car. A strangeness, Branch feels, that is almost holy. There is much here that is holy, an aberration in the heartland of the real. Let's regain our grip on things. (15)

This passage recapitulates the basic impulse to move from image to reality, from surface to depth, that motivates the historical imagination under postmodern conditions. We begin with the tantalizing precision of the "six point nine seconds" of the Zapruder film, analyzable frame by frame, yet whose blurs frustrate the desire to translate seeing into knowing. Branch's problem is not a lack of data but its excess, from the dreams of witnesses the night after the assassination to microphotographs of Oswald's pubic hair to Jack Ruby's mother's dental chart: "photo enhancements, floor plans, home movies, biographies, bibliographies, letters, rumors, mirages, dreams . . . an incredible haul of human utterance. It lies so flat on the page, hangs so still in the lazy air, lost to syntax and other arrangement, that it resembles a kind of mind-spatter, a poetry of lives muddied and dripping in language" (181). From the teasing visibility of the Zapruder film we make our way through myriad disconnected facts toward the depths of "a strangeness that is almost holy." As an "aberration in the heartland of the real," the assassination is cut off from the flow of historical causality, losing its discursive quality to become an object, a mute jade idol, enigmatic and sacred.

Our understanding of the assassination, like the novel itself, is to become a work of art. Nicholas Branch is a surrogate for the author of *Libra,* which we can take to be a version of the "secret history" that Branch might write if he were ever to put an end to the "branching" of possibilities, overcome the inertia of "the paper hills that surround him" (378), and write with the artist's license to select and create. DeLillo concludes the novel with an "Author's Note," in which he writes that "because this book makes no claim to literal truth, because it is only itself, apart and complete, readers may find refuge here—a way of thinking about the assassination without being constrained by half-facts or overwhelmed by possibilities, by the tide of speculation that widens with the years" (458).

DeLillo's claim to have constructed a system of order "apart and complete," somehow purged of the extraneous, echoes an image from the start of the novel. As a young boy Lee Oswald skipped school to spend entire days riding the subways of Manhattan, which to him "held more compelling things than the famous city above. There was nothing important out there, in the broad afternoon, that he could not find in purer form in these tunnels beneath the streets" (4). The subway tunnels provide an image for the kind of space the novel constructs, secret and dark yet illuminated by flashes of light ("A tenth of a second was all it took to see a thing complete" [3]), a realm of depth beneath the teeming city, mysterious yet contained and ordered. The subway purifies one's movement through the city; once a line is chosen, one is compelled to ride it on rails.

The desire for a realm that is both mysterious and governed by a perceptible order, that provides a map of human experience while remaining outside of it, "apart and complete," is evident again in the astrology of the novel's title: "Astrology is the language of the night sky, of starry aspect and position, the truth at the edge of human affairs" (175). While the positive Libran has balanced the scales and achieved self-mastery, Oswald is the "negative Libran who is, let's say, somewhat unsteady and impulsive. Easily, easily, easily influenced. Poised to make the dangerous leap" (315). To the conspirators who seek to draw Oswald into the assassination plot, it is just a question of tipping Oswald's scales in their direction. David Ferrie, the conspirator who "handles" Oswald, tries to persuade him that he is wired into history on some deep level beyond conscious control: "There's a pattern in things. Something in us has an effect on independent events. The conscious mind gives one side only. We're deeper than that" (330). Ferrie is the most committed to a mystified sense of history and is given to precious mystic utterance: "Truth isn't what we know or feel. It's the thing that waits just beyond" (333). He is also subject to the covert operator's routine paranoia, believing that history "is the sum total of all the things they aren't telling us" (321). But Ferrie's is just the most extreme case of a mystified sense of history that is widely shared by the characters in this novel. For Marina, Oswald's wife, as for Ferrie and the other CIA agents involved in the conspiracy, the desire for a coherent history points beyond the boundaries of the sensible: "Destiny is larger than facts or events. It is something to believe in outside the ordinary borders of the senses, with God so distant from our lives" (204). Astrology provides a governing metaphor for a sense of history that is both deterministic and inscrutable. Astrology is also kitsch, and it is typical of DeLillo's irony throughout his work that this sort of historical depth is both indulged in and exposed as a hoax, made both mystical and ridiculous.

Conspiracy theories of history, like astrology, like the novel itself, provide a system of order "apart and complete" by which one can understand the course of events. The impulse to order manifested in *Libra*'s theory of the conspiracy to kill the president is shared on the diegetic level by the characters themselves, for whom the urge to conspire is the urge to consort with the gods, to be part of history's backstage. To Win Everett, the disaffected CIA agent who hatches the assassination plot, "secrets are an exalted state, almost a dream state. They're a way of arresting motion, stopping the world so we can see ourselves in it" (26). Conspiracy is a form of control that leads to a self-realization not attainable in the ordinary world. Laurence Parmenter, one of Everett's coconspirators, sees the quasi-official corporate network established by the CIA "as a better-working version of the larger world, where things have an almost dreamy sense of connection to each other. Here the plan was tighter. These were men who believed history was in their care" (127). The secret realm of conspiracy is a refuge from the visibility of the "larger world," which Everett finds "eerie and real" (16).

But conspiracy shows the two faces of historical depth: a "tighter" order, but also a "dreamy" and thus mystified sense of connection, suggesting that the search for order must end in mystification rather than clarity. Though the conspirators want to believe that "history was in their care," they also suspect that they are "all linked in a vast and rhythmic coincidence, a daisy chain of rumor, suspicion and secret wish" (57). It is the job of intelligence agencies, of course, to make visible and intelligible that which would otherwise remain hidden, and thus to overcome the sense that history is determined by mere "coincidence." To Parmenter, intelligence and espionage are forms of psychoanalysis: "It's the job of an intelligence service to resolve a nation's obsessions" (258). But as a form of understanding in depth, psychoanalysis through espionage explains in a way that preserves mystery. Despite the belief in the power of intelligence agencies to make things known and visible, despite the fantasy of panopticism represented by the U-2 spy planes, which "like ancient monks" collect "all the secret knowledge of the world" (77), Parmenter remains committed to mystery. Like Kinnear, the terrorist ringleader in *Players,* Parmenter takes ambiguity as the fundamental condition of knowledge: "He believed that nothing can be finally known that involves human motive and need. There is always another level, another secret, a way in which the heart breeds a deception so mysterious and complex it can only be taken for a deeper kind of truth" (260). Thus the metaphorics of depth involve this duality: when contrasted with knowledge of surface appearances only, "depth" signals a knowledge grounded in some greater authority; and yet, if there is always "another level," knowledge in depth becomes bottomless and without foundation. Far from clarifying historical causality, the insistence on depth leads to the mystifications of a David Ferrie, for whom the line connecting Lee Harvey Oswald to the conspiracy to kill the president "comes out of dreams, visions, intuitions, prayers, out of the deepest levels of the self. It's not generated by cause and effect like the other two lines. It's a line that cuts across causality, cuts across time. It has no history that we can recognize or understand" (339).[13]

The pervasive sense of mystified history is ironic in a novel as meticulously researched, as committed to the accumulation of veracious detail as *Libra*. The sequence of events that DeLillo imaginatively reconstructs is this: Win Everett, a veteran CIA plotter of the Bay of Pigs invasion, who felt betrayed by Kennedy, wants to stage "an electrifying event" that will focus public attention on the Cuban threat. What he plans is a failed attempt on the president's life, a "spectacular miss," that will appear to be the work of Cuban agents and will force the government into a more militant anti-Castro stance. Everett plans to "create" a lone gunman out of forged documents and clues, to "script a person out of ordinary pocket litter" (28). Events quickly get out of Everett's control; first, the execution of the plan is placed in the hands of T. J. Mackey, an even more bitter Bay of Pigs veteran who doesn't tell his shooters that their shots are supposed to miss; second, the fictitious gunman appears in the person of Lee H. Oswald. Having set things in motion, Everett loses contact with Mackey and fears that the plot will get out of control, following the dictates of its own narrative logic: "There is a tendency of plots to move toward death. . . . He had a foreboding that the plot would move to a limit, develop a logical end" (221). Everett's foreboding echoes that of Jack Gladney in *White Noise*, who likewise comes to be convinced that "all plots tend to move deathward" (26). Everett and Gladney are similar: both are fundamentally weak characters, good family men, pathetically dependent on their wives and inordinately fearful for their own and their wives' continued good health. Whereas Everett is the weak man whose fantasies are overtaken by events, Mackey is the strong man, highly skilled in "the fundamentals of deadly force," able to move history according to his own design.

Thus the novel presents us with a range of distinctly unattractive models for historical understanding. First there is the historian Branch, overwhelmed by data and paralyzed by possibilities. Then we have the ineffectual fantasist Win Everett, whose plans escape his control. Laurence Parmenter has a somewhat firmer grip on events but remains finally in the thrall of mystery and complacency. David Ferrie is a hypochondriac whose paranoia manifests in a thoroughly mystified sense of history. And finally there is T. J. Mackey, the one character capable of shaping events to his will, but whose command of history can be exercised only in violence.

In contrast to these characters, each limited and distorted by a single obsession, Lee Harvey Oswald seems expansive, even endearing. Oswald is also gripped by obsession, but by one that is less focused and makes him an American Everyman: he is obsessed with self-creation. It is as though Oswald, in an effort to realize the "secret life" within him, the "world within the world," is consciously struggling to replace our televised images of him with a compelling interiority. It is his failure to do so that makes for the novel's poignancy and provides the most chilling vision of the effort to construct both self and history in a way that escapes televisual exposure and provides the satisfactions of depth.

Forever the outsider and loner, spending most of an impoverished childhood living alone with his widowed mother, Oswald continually struggles to construct a secret self that will somehow merge with the currents of history. Oswald finds in books of Marxist theory "the secret of who you are" and is able to see himself as "the product of a sweeping history" (41). The fact that they are "forbidden and hard to read" only increases the books' value, providing him a refuge from the taunts of his schoolmates: "Nobody knew what he knew. The whirl of time, the true life inside him. This was his leverage, his only control" (46). Oswald seeks a self with depth and interiority, not only through the secret study of Marxist theory, but eventually by learning the Russian language: "hearing his own flat voice take on texture and dimension, he could almost believe he was being remade on the spot, given an opening to some larger and deeper version of himself" (113). But Oswald's hopeful assertion of interiority, his repeated observation that "there is a world within the world" (13, 47, 277), becomes only a further source of isolation unless he is somehow able to connect his self-understanding with larger historical forces: "The only end to isolation was to reach the point where he was no longer separated from the true struggles that went on around him. The name we give this point is history" (248). Oswald places his hopes in the Cuban revolution, and travels to Mexico City where he tries unsuccessfully to get a Cuban entry visa: "He wants to sense a structure that includes him, a definition clear enough to specify where he belongs. But the system floats right through him, through everything, even the revolution. He is a zero in the system" (357). With his consuming self-consciousness, Oswald has gotten the Emersonian project the wrong way around: rather than project the self outward, and so shape history out of the individual's experience, Oswald is a sort of camera obscura, desperately trying to shape a self around the introjected images of history appearing on the screen of his mind.

Oswald never achieves the depth of self-conception required to support a steady purpose. His appropriation of Marxist economic theory only makes him a creature of jargon, a speaker of clichés who never really gets beyond his mother's oceanic sense of herself as the victim of vague injustices. (Oswald joins the growing list of historical figures whom DeLillo has cast as mama's boys, the other two being Hitler and Elvis, so labeled in a memorable scene in *White Noise*.) Oswald's desire to put his secret self in the service of some larger secret, to merge himself with history, only makes him an easy target for those who would use him for their own political purposes. Agent Bateman of the FBI, one of many agents, both Soviet and American, who have tried to "develop" Oswald over the years, tells Oswald: "You're an interesting fellow. Every agency from here to the Himalayas has something in the files on Oswald, Lee" (311). Oswald has become a creature of agency files, handed on from one intelligence service and security organization to another, none of which ever solves the riddle of who he is. Neither does Oswald. The confusion of his inner life leads Oswald, the pro-Castro activist, to end up shooting the president as part of an anti-Castro conspiracy.

Alone in his cell after his arrest, Oswald thinks that he has found a new vocation in trying to clarify his own vision of events:

> It was beginning to occur to him that he'd found his life's work. After the crime comes the reconstruction. He will have motives to analyze, the whole rich question of truth and guilt. Time to reflect, time to turn this thing in his mind. Here is a crime that clearly yields material for deep interpretation. He will be able to bend the light of that heightened moment, shadows fixed on the lawn, the limousine shimmering and still. Time to grow in self-knowledge, to explore the meaning of what he's done. He will vary the act a hundred ways, speed it up and slow it down, shift emphasis, find shadings, see his whole life change. (434)

Oswald's search for depth follows the same pattern as Branch's. The event is perceived in visual, filmic terms as a compilation of light and shadow that can be replayed at various speeds; as such, it provides the material for "deep interpretation." Branch does not share Oswald's hope for some final, deep understanding, however. To Branch, the Zapruder film is "a major emblem of uncertainty and chaos. There is the powerful moment of death, the surrounding blurs, patches and shadows" (441). Unlike those outsiders who "assume a conspiracy is the perfect working of a scheme," that "a conspiracy is everything that ordinary life is not," Branch concludes that "the conspiracy against the President was a rambling affair that succeeded in the short term due mainly to chance. Deft men and fools, ambivalence and fixed will and what the weather was like" (440–41). The ultimate irony of the novel is that, just as Oswald's search for self-identity fails, so the promise of depth held out by a conspiracy theory of history is finally unfulfilled. Conspiracy proves to be as riddled with accident and contingency as ordinary life and provides no final refuge from the discontinuity and spectacularity of life on the televisual surface.

Conspiracy is certainly no refuge for Oswald. A restless, confused seeker whose life has been one long self-misunderstanding, Oswald would never have achieved the kind of self-knowledge he yearns for, even had his life not been cut short. What self-awareness he does attain, in the moments after being shot, is that of a man watching himself on television: "He could see himself shot as the camera caught it. Through the pain he watched TV. . . . Through the pain, through the losing of sensation except where it hurt, Lee watched himself react to the augering heat of the bullet" (439). This televisual self-consciousness links Oswald to the people who really do watch the event on television. One of these is Laurence Parmenter's wife, Beryl, who, despite her revulsion, watches repeated showings of Oswald's murder on television:

> There was something in Oswald's face, a glance at the camera before he was shot, that put him here in the audience, among the rest of us, sleepless in our homes—a glance, a way of telling us that he knows who we are and how we feel, that he has brought our perceptions and interpretations into his sense of the crime. Something in the look, some sly intelligence, exceedingly brief but far-reaching, a connection all but bleached away by glare, tells us that he is outside the moment, watching with the rest of us. (447)

Oswald does have the sensation of watching his own death "in a darkish room, someone's TV den" (440), but finally the claim of understanding and connection between Oswald and his audience must be read ironically. Beryl Parmenter's feeling of connection is little more than a desperate and hopeful defense against despair. Even to the extent that Oswald is somehow connected in thought and feeling with his television audience, he only joins the community of the ignorant, stunned by their inability to make a coherent narrative out of what they witness on the screen: "The camera doesn't catch all of it. There seem to be missing frames, lost levels of information. Brief and simple as the shooting is, it is too much to take in, too mingled in jumped-up energies" (446). Having reconstructed Oswald's life and led us through the maze of conspiracy, *Libra* ends by returning us to our living rooms, watching on television. This is a characteristic gesture of DeLillo's "realism," for it suggests that these images and our experience as television watchers are the primary ground of our experience of this history, the starting point and perhaps the limit of any "deeper" narrative structures we might erect to explain events. DeLillo's elaborate and chillingly plausible construction of the events leading to the deaths of Kennedy and Oswald creates a history based on accident, coincidence, and thwarted intentions as much as on intelligible, willed conspiracy. It is a history that does not correspond, somehow, to the apparent simplicity and brute physicality of the events we have witnessed on the screen.

Libra leaves us with fundamental questions concerning the historical imagination under postmodern conditions. First, DeLillo reminds us that visibility does not translate reliably into intelligibility, that seeing should not be mistaken for knowing. The sense that "everybody knows everything" in our mass-mediated environment can be a dangerous delusion, masking a larger ignorance about how history is being shaped. The sense that televisual culture breaks down the distinction between image and reality can blind us to the real power behind the scenes. Though DeLillo's fiction, along with that of Pynchon, Mason, and Reed, shows us that the nature of the relation between image and reality is being renegotiated under the pressure of the mass-cultural image, it also shows us that the distinction remains no less important for being elusive. History is not being effaced by spectacle, nor has the realm of the image somehow eliminated the real. What has happened is that mass-culture has transformed our means of access to history, so that depth can no longer assume its old forms and privileges. Living as we are in "the filmed century," in a televisual America, our past takes on a teasing visibility that both stimulates and frustrates our desire for connection and coherence. *Libra* suggests that a key historical development is the way that we have come, as Oswald has in his last moments, to watch ourselves in the act of being watched by others. Whatever historical narratives we do construct must bear the burden of our own spectacular self-consciousness.

The Spectacular Fictions of Ishmael Reed and E. L. Doctorow

Recent film theory has defined spectacle as a kind of visual excess that threatens narrative coherence. To Laura Mulvey, spectacle occurs when causal or narrative logic gives way to unrestrained scopophilia. To Claudine Eizykman, spectacle is the moment when the kung-fu movie becomes pure kinetic display, when we forget who is fighting whom or why, this liberation from narrative coherence providing the spectator with a moment of *jouissance*. To Dana Polan, spectacle is the ending of the 1950 movie *Summer Stock*, in which the song-and-dance numbers of Judy Garland and Gene Kelly overwhelm the movie's narrative of pioneer conquest and replace it with "a new dream of America as endless performance" (180).[1] The spectacular nature of film has particular bearing here because, in the 1970s and 1980s, postmodern fiction found new ways of using and registering film, television, and the other mass-cultural forms that have become such a dominant presence in contemporary consciousness and culture. Indeed, despite the experimental and formally challenging nature of much fiction in recent years, fiction writers, like all postmodern artists, have had difficulty achieving the oppositional character of earlier avant-gardes in part because the techniques of spectacular disruption of narrative have become the standard forms of commercial film, television programming, and advertising.[2] The hypothesis underlying this chapter is that postmodern culture in general can be characterized by the curious cohabitation of spectacle and narrative, a cohabitation whose very pervasiveness in both "serious" art and popular forms can be read as a sign of the broad shift to postmodern conditions of knowledge. By studying how spectacular performance occurs within postmodern fiction, we can observe how this larger epistemological shift is registered on the level of novelistic form.

Generally speaking, to the extent that an artistic performance—whether textual, filmic, theatrical, or musical—disrupts the continuity and closure of its narratives, it can be said to be "spectacular" in form. The spectacular work need not be entirely nonnarrative, however. For example, consider the tradition of performance art in the twentieth century, which can be characterized by its indifference, if not outright hostility, toward narrative. From the provocations of the futurists and dadaists to the experiments of the surrealists and the formal explorations of Bauhaus, through to the "happenings" and conceptual works of the 1960s and the multimedia performances of the 1970s and 1980s, performance art has rarely concerned itself with narrative (even more rarely with plot in the Aristotelian sense) and has been far more likely to take an aggressively antinarrative stance.[3] Yet works of performance art do often contain narrative elements—from relatively conventional plots to autobiographical narratives to the most indeterminate fragments—and after all it is perhaps impossible for any performance entirely to defeat the audience's desire to impose narrative form upon it as a way of constructing meaning. Indeed, the persistence of narrative even within virulently antinarrative productions suggests that, just as narrative is continually threatened by spectacular disruption, so spectacle always summons narrative as a dialectical possibility. The concept of spectacle flexibly applies to an entire range of artistic practices, from the most antinarrative of performance works to that form which historically is most committed to narrative: the novel.

Spectacular fictions can be said to "perform" in two different senses of the word. The first, as has already been suggested, is a consequence of the fact that the contemporary novel survives as a residual form in a mass-cultural environment dominated by television, film, radio, and advertising in all its formats.

One of the ways in which contemporary fiction has responded to this historical development is by absorbing, on the level of narrative form, some of the kinetic, discontinuous, visual, and spatial approaches to form that we find in the productions of mass culture. As the novel has become immersed in and partially constituted by the society of the spectacle, it has itself come increasingly to draw on the energies of spectacular performance. The second sense in which postmodern fiction can be said to "perform" draws on the linguistic notion of the "performative" developed by J. L. Austin to identify utterances that do not merely have a constative or denotative function, but which themselves are the performing of an action (e.g., "I pronounce you husband and wife" or "I bet you five dollars"). As postmodern fiction stages its attacks on the traditions of realism and mimesis, it can be said to move from an emphasis on the constative and denotative function of texts to their "performative" function. Whereas realistic fiction—historical fiction especially—traditionally relies on the denotative, referential function of the text as the primary source of its authority, postmodern "performing" fictions substitute for the diminished authority of the referent an authority founded on the text's own energetic activity. The common thread uniting the two senses of "performing" is mass culture itself, which to an unprecedented extent has saturated contemporary society and the contemporary psyche with images and has thus imperiled the distinctions between image and reality, self and world, inside and outside that have grounded claims to knowledge in the Western rational and empirical traditions. Mass culture is one of the primary means by which the postmodern conditions of knowledge are established as a condition of everyday life. In borrowing the energies of spectacular performance from mass culture, postmodern fiction not only foregrounds its own performativity as its primary authority, but does so in part to adjust to an epistemological shift that mass culture has itself helped to bring about.

In the last chapter we saw how the excesses of our contemporary image culture threaten the epistemological foundations of historical understanding, in part by fostering a televisual self-consciousness that threatens the Cartesian distinctions between subject and object. This chapter will show how the epistemological challenges presented by image culture are manifested on the level of narrative form. Ishmael Reed's *Mumbo Jumbo* (1972) and E. L. Doctorow's *Ragtime* (1975) set out to represent particular periods of American history, but do so in spectacular forms that expose and call into question the conventions of historical narrative. Before examining how spectacular form operates within these texts, it will be helpful first to examine briefly how the contest between spectacle and narrative is being played out in mass culture. By observing certain formal affinities between postmodern fiction and television, for example, we can see that Reed's and Doctorow's challenges to historiographic convention are part of a larger cultural condition in which the rise to dominance of electronic culture has been accompanied by a renewed skepticism toward narrative authority. If the depth and authority of historical narratives have traditionally lain both in their formal poetics (as Hayden White argues) and/or in the depth of the master narratives of history that stand behind them (as Jean-François Lyotard argues), then spectacle returns us to a "surface" by denying formal poetic closure and disrupting master narratives. The contest between narrative and spectacle within postmodern culture is a contest between depth and surface in which there is no winner. Instead, the historical imagination survives in the paradoxical shape of the deep surface.

Spectacle and Narrative

While acknowledging the marked presence of spectacle in contemporary culture, one must at the same time recognize that narrative is alive and well. Narrative is, of course, an indispensable form of knowledge, and, as Hayden White has compellingly argued, narrative underwrites any historiographic enterprise.[4] Though postmodernism may mark the end of a faith in the *grands récits*, those master narratives of history that Lyotard argues have become untenable under postmodern conditions of knowledge, the *petits récits* of history are flourishing. According to Lyotard, the postmodern condition is one in which discourses of knowledge are no longer legitimated by appeal to a master narrative, on the one hand, or by appeal to the criteria of truth or justice on the other, but rather are legitimated through their own performativity.[5] This condition by no means marks an end to the importance of narrative. On the contrary, Lyotard argues, "the *petit récit* remains the quintessential form of imaginative invention" (60).

What we find in postmodernism, then, is not a triumph of spectacle over narrative but peculiar ways in which the two cohabit in cultural space such that the authority of narrative is continually undercut by the disruptions of spectacle. For example, from one perspective it would seem that popular film and television are still firmly committed to traditional narrative. Indeed, television programming, along with popular genre fiction, remains perhaps the last bastion of the kind of realism we associate with the nineteenth-century novel. But analyzing individual television programs for their narrative content—still the standard method of most media criticism—misses something essential to the actual experience of watching television. Not only is each program interrupted at intervals with advertisements wildly incongruous with the program content, but the viewers themselves increase the discontinuity and spectacularity of the experience by switching between channels. This experience is described and satirized in a passage from Don DeLillo's *Players:*

> Lyle passed time watching television. Sitting in near darkness about eighteen inches from the screen, he turned the channel selector every half minute or so, sometimes much more frequently. He wasn't looking for something that might sustain his interest. Hardly that. He simply enjoyed jerking the dial into fresh image-burns. He explored content to a point. The tactile-visual delight of switching channels took precedence, however, transforming even random moments of content into pleasing territorial abstractions. (16)[6]

Contrary to Charles Newman's assertion, it is not "story at all costs" that the television viewer seeks (130) but distraction by any means. Narrative discontinuity is indispensable to how the technology is put to use by both the television producer and the viewer. A few years ago while watching a "nature" show about the protection and conservation of African elephants, I happened to turn the channel to a hunting program in which men were blasting elephants with high-powered rifles. Far from an aberration, the pleasures of this sort of irony are the *essence* of good television for those who routinely subvert the programmer's commercial imperatives of selling viewers' attention to advertisers.

Television's response to this subversion by the viewer has been the anticipatory strategy of incorporating discontinuity and a self-directed irony into the very form of its own programming. Commercials in particular increasingly employ techniques of rapid-cutting montage that seem intended to simulate and outpace the viewer's ability to switch channels by remote control. We have become accustomed to television shows that parody their own conventions (David Letterman as a parody of Johnny Carson, *The Simpsons* as a parody of an entire history of family sitcoms) and to commercials that mock their own stupidity (Joe Isuzu selling cars, retired athletes arguing whether Lite Beer is "less filling" or "tastes great"). These self-mocking strategies preposition the viewer as cynical commentator while preempting more serious criticism; the viewer is allowed the pleasures of ironic superiority so long as the tube stays on.

John Fiske has argued that television's ability to respond to the viewers' desire for interaction and discontinuity distinguishes it from both cinema spectating and novel reading, and leaves its narratives more open to negotiation: "The segmented, fractured nature of television, its producerly texts, and its active audiences, come together to oppose any forces of closure within its narrative structures" (147). What must be emphasized, however, is that television is at its most effective when it satisfies the viewer's desires for interactive and even sub-versive viewing while still moving the product. It may be true, as Fiske claims, that in the 1980s the polysemy of the MTV-created Madonna allowed her to be both an empowering image for young girls and a sex object for readers of *Play-boy* (125–26), but only so long as she continued to sell records to both groups. What we see in television is that spectacle does not always overwhelm narrative so much as open it up to multiple readings, allowing viewers to inscribe them-selves in a number of different subject positions. Fiske correctly points out that television's success depends on a functional polysemy by which it can appeal to a heterogeneous audience consisting of subgroups with very different interests and investments in the television text (148). But as is typically the case in the study of mass-cultural forms, this analysis points simultaneously toward both utopian and dystopian possibilities: in television, the disruption of narrative by spectacle becomes both a source of viewers' pleasure and a means of producers' control; it summons an ironic, critical consciousness in the viewer at the same time that it more effectively moves the goods.

Much of what has been said about television can also be said of postmodern fiction, in which the cohabitation of spectacle and narrative is registered as an appetite for narrative discontinuity, pastiche, and a suspensive irony toward novelistic conventions that creates functional instabilities of meaning. With its disruptions of linear narrative causality and exposure of the conventions of both reading and writing, postmodern fiction calls attention to the contingency inherent in the process by which both writers and readers construct texts and thus demands a high level of reader participation in constructing the text's meanings. The self-conscious text summons the self-conscious reader, as in the first sentence of a novel by Italo Calvino: "You are about to begin reading Italo Calvino's new novel, *If on a winter's night a traveler.* Relax. Concentrate." Of course, poststructuralist theory has in various ways argued that texts have al-ways been contested spaces constructed to some extent by the reader's interven-tion in the confluence of competing and at times contradictory discourses that inform both the work itself and the particular reading situation. But postmod-ern fiction is unique in the extent to which it has taken on the task of represent-ing this insight through narrative form itself, using spectacular disruption of the text to figure the disruptions and contingencies of the reading and writing processes.

In finding the means of registering their metafictional concerns, many of the more experimentally minded contemporary writers have drawn on tele-vision and film as sources of new formal and technical possibilities. Film has, of course, long been an influence on the novel, as cinematic form has influenced writers' conception of scene, point of view, pacing, and transition. Don DeLillo has described film as "the not-so-hidden influence on a lot of modern writing" and said that, despite the importance to him of such writers as Joyce, Faulkner, and Nabokov, "probably the movies of Jean-Luc Godard had a more immediate effect on my early work than anything I'd ever read" (Interview 84). The troubled distinction between reality and the images of film and television has been an important thematic concern throughout DeLillo's work and has provided a structural principal for the plots of several of his novels, including *Americana, Running Dog, White Noise,* and *Libra.* As we will see in a later chapter, Thomas Pynchon's *Gravity's Rainbow* plays seriously with the ability of the filmmaker Gerhardt von Göll to insert his film images into reality, and throughout the novel film serves as one way that Pynchon challenges the Enlightenment "fictions" of causality and the human subject. On the formal level, Pynchon's frequent use of the ellipsis and dash, his jump-cuts between scenes, and his parody of the movie voice-over technique construct a syntax of discontinuity that reinforces what the novel does on the thematic and metaphoric levels to destabilize the boundary between film image and reality.

Despite film's long history of influence on the novel, it is also clear that television, with its more rapid pace, more frequent breaks of narrative frame, and continual shifting between "fictional" and "factual" discourses, has proved to be particularly stimulating to postmodern writers. Robert Coover has remarked that "video has now discovered new, really wild techniques for putting, you might say, sentences together or conjoining paragraphs or juxtaposing imagery. I find it a pleasure to work inside all of those possibilities" (245). Ishmael Reed has commented that "I've watched television all my life, and I think my way of editing, the speed I bring to my books, the way the plot moves, is based upon some of the television shows and cartoons I've seen" (Interview 131). E. L. Doctorow has told critics that *The Book of Daniel* was structured like the television show *Laugh-In,* explaining: "Beginning with *Daniel,* I gave up trying to write with the concern for transition characteristic of the nineteenth-century novel. . . . Obviously, the rhythms of perception in me, as in most people who read today, have been transformed immensely by films and television." The reader, says Doctorow, will have little difficulty following the discontinuous narratives of his novels because "anyone who's ever watched a news broadcast on television knows all about discontinuity" (Interview 40, 41).

All this is not meant to suggest that the formal affinities between television, film, and postmodern fiction should be understood simply as a matter of "influence." For one thing, although the mass-cultural spectacles of television and film are the dominant cultural forms of our day, it could be argued that any influence between image and print culture is to some degree reciprocal. To the assertion that the rise of film entails the novel's decline, Don DeLillo has responded that "movies and novels are too closely related to work according to shifting proportions. If the novel dies, movies will die with it" (Interview 85). The larger issue is not how to conceptualize a direct causal relationship between recent mass-cultural forms and novelistic ones but rather to understand how these linked developments in *both* mass culture and fiction can be seen as part of a shift to conditions of knowledge and conventions of representation that may meaningfully be termed postmodern. It is in the terms of this larger inquiry that, further, we can distinguish postmodern spectacle from similar formal innovations within modernism, within other twentieth-century avant-gardes, and within earlier periods of the novel's history.

Spectacular Fictions: Reed vs. Sterne

We can go some way toward grasping the historical particularity of spectacular form in postmodern fiction by comparing an earlier "spectacular" work, *Tristram Shandy* (1759–67), with a postmodern novel such as Ishmael Reed's *Mumbo Jumbo* (1972). The plot of *Mumbo Jumbo* parodies the detective novel genre: here the "detective" is PaPa LaBas, a master adept at voodoo, on the trail of the Knights Templar and the Wallflower Order, ancient and secret white European sects that are locked in a thousands-of-years-old struggle with the forces of Jes Grew, the source of African religious practices. The immediate object of competition is control of the ancient Egyptian Book of Thoth, which is thought to serve as the founding text for Jes Grew. Last in the hands of a member of the Knights Templar, the text had been divided into fourteen pieces and distributed among an equal number of African Americans, who are then manipulated into sending the pieces to one another in an ongoing circle. The conflict arises when one of the fourteen, Abdul Sufi Hamid, attempts to reassemble the scattered pieces into the complete book in the hope of turning its power to his own political purposes; Hamid is hunted down by the forces of the Knights Templar and the Wallflower Order, who are desperate to stop the book's coming into being. Though the immediate setting for the novel is the Harlem Renaissance of the 1920s, the plot opens up on the entire history of both Western and Egyptian/African civilizations. *Mumbo Jumbo* thus carries forward the larger project of Reed's career: the conceptualization and promotion of Neo-Hoodoo, Reed's term for a developing global culture based on a pluralistic, multicultural sense of history. In contrast to the intolerance of Christianity and the oppressive selectivity of Eurocentric versions of history, PaPa LaBas offers the inclusiveness of the vodun aesthetic: "pantheistic, becoming, 1 which bountifully permits 1000s of spirits, as many as the imagination can hold" (35).

But to suggest that any simple plot summary adequately tells what *Mumbo Jumbo* is "about" is to make the sort of claim for the primacy of traditional narrative convention that the novel explicitly rejects. The "plot" serves only as the matrix for Reed's use of the practice of pastiche, in which the text becomes a collation of elements drawn from disparate historical and textual sources. Reed's title plays upon the Eurocentric view of black language and religions as just the sort of nonsensical jumble that the pastiche text plays at being. Henry Louis Gates Jr. has noted that the text of *Mumbo Jumbo* is framed by cinematic devices, beginning with the false start of the novel's prologue that functions as a film title sequence, and ending with the text's last words: "freeze frame" (Gates 305). But beyond questions of the influence of film and television on Reed's formal approach, there is the larger issue of how the text's use of pastiche points away from the typographically constituted novel toward a world in which the circulation of heterogeneous forms of representation has become essential to the mass cultural economy. Gates provides a catalogue of Reed's textual sources that in its own plenitude suggests how the energies of the sublime are released in the encounter with Reed's text:

> dictionary definitions, epigraphs, epigrams, anagrams, photo-duplicated type from other texts, newspaper clips and headlines, signs (such as those that hang from doors), invitations to parties, telegrams, "Situation Reports" . . . yin-yang symbols, quotations from other texts, poems, cartoons, drawings of mythic beasts, handbills, photographs, book-jacket copy, charts and graphs, playing cards, a representation of a Greek vase, and a four-page handwritten letter, among even other items. Just as our word "satire" derives from *satura*, "hash," so Reed's form of satire is a version of "gumbo," a parody of form itself. (301)

It is instructive to compare the terms on which *Tristram Shandy,* often invoked as the "postmodern" novel of its time, makes its own "parody of form." Though *Tristram Shandy* is a highly disruptive and digressive text, Sterne's use of pastiche—his inclusion of marbled pages, blank pages, one page completely black, and rows of asterisks—plays on the typographic and bound nature of the book, just as the digressions and suspensions of the narrative play on the emerging conventions of what was not yet routinely called "the novel." In playing within and against the bookness of the book, *Tristram Shandy* encloses itself within the world of the book, a world typographically constituted and bound between covers. By contrast, the pastiche of *Mumbo Jumbo* continually points *away* from the book, making us see the typographically constituted book as a contingent form amidst a heterogeneous collection of forms of representation that circulate through mass culture. What makes *Tristram Shandy* so dizzying is precisely that it restricts its play to the domain of the book, undercutting novelistic conventions while providing no escape from them; the reader remains bound within the conventions of novelistic discourse even as those conventions are exposed and rendered inadequate to the reader's expectations. *Tristram Shandy* redirects the reader's pleasure toward a level of play that supersedes the self-enclosed mid-century Richardson versus Fielding debate over the nature of "the novel"; nonetheless, the space that it clears for itself as its field of play remains bound within the very conventions that it seeks to destabilize. *Tristram Shandy* is a monument to the emergence of a dominant print culture precisely because print culture is so exclusively the object of its attack. In its historical attitude, *Tristram Shandy* points both backward to an earlier rhetorical tradition that the book is rapidly transforming and forward to an era in which the book, and the novel in particular, will consolidate its cultural power. By contrast, the pastiche of *Mumbo Jumbo* acknowledges a condition in which the book is in some sense already obsolete. *Mumbo Jumbo* points backward to the history of the book's dissolution (a history figured in the literal dismemberment and scattering of the ancient Book of Thoth) and points toward a future in which the typographic no longer dominates the many forms of representation that are deployed in the mass cultural field.

The contrast between Shandean play and postmodern pastiche can be seen as well in the texts' different approaches to the conventions of illustration. Hogarth's illustrations of *Tristram Shandy*, commissioned by Sterne once the book proved successful, are conventional in that they assist the reader's visualization of the narrative and thus redirect the reader's attention back *into* the narrative. Reed's text, on the other hand, "signifies" on the convention of illustration by including materials that not only are disparate in form and historical origin but are often only obliquely and mysteriously related to the text in which they are situated. The visual materials in *Mumbo Jumbo* typically provide an ironic counterpoint to the narrative, rather than an "illustration" of it, and often send the reader off on tangents leading away from the main narrative line. The main narrative is set in the 1920s, yet the text includes material ranging from the Renaissance forward to the time of the text's composition in the late 1960s and early 1970s. A photograph that shows Ishmael Reed himself is just one example of how the text calls attention to its ontological status by disrupting illusion and pointing outside the book to its own production (184). During PaPa LaBas's revisionary retelling of the myth of Osiris and Set, a long passage that is both a digression from and the "climax" of the action, the text is interrupted by a chart of "U.S. Bombing Tonnage in Three Wars" (163). The chart, which compares the tonnage of bombs dropped by U.S. forces in World War II, the Korean War, and the Indochina War, would seem to comment upon the violent and life-denying character of the Western European effort to suppress the cult of Osiris, and also to point outside the text to the social and political contexts of the text's production. At an earlier point in the novel, we find a photograph, apparently contemporary, of a woman kneeling beside a young girl on what appears to be a well-lit stage with a black backdrop (61). Both are dressed in bulky lamé evening dresses, the woman wearing a U.S. flag as a cape, the girl holding a small U.S. flag in her upraised hand. Together they peer off out of the frame of the photo with stagy intensity, as if at a ship on the horizon. The photo can be read as a commentary on the vacuity of a U.S. patriotism that must continually be staged with the help of glitter and props (the girl's beauty-contest-winner tiara) and must be articulated as a defense of (white) women and children. But as with all of Reed's "illustrations," this one invites interpretation without authorial direction, involving the reader in an open-ended process of sifting meaning through the text's multiple ironies. Reed's charts and photographs suggest the conventions of illustration while violating them, just as his quirky footnotes and "Partial Bibliography" suggest the scholarly apparatus of an academic approach to history writing that his narrative technique mocks.[7]

One of the reasons that Hogarth's engravings for *Tristram Shandy* seem to fit Sterne's satiric style so perfectly is that Sterne was working within satiric conventions that had themselves already been influenced considerably by Hogarth's work. But the illustrations for *Tristram Shandy* are also in accord with the dominant epistemological conventions of the period in a fundamental sense. The last chapter discussed how when René Descartes made clarity and distinctness the criteria for certainty he founded knowledge on the model of vision. The mid-eighteenth-century conventions of illustration would thus seem to find ready sanction in Enlightenment epistemologies of vision, especially if we understand that *illustration* not only means to illuminate and make clear but carries with it also the spiritual sense of "enlightenment." This etymology restores the theological resonance of Descartes's reliance on a "natural light" that enables the clear and distinct perception of ideas. Hogarth's illustrations of *Tristram Shandy* direct the reader's vision *into* the text and thus participate in the emerging mid-eighteenth-century convention by which the reader's response to the novel is mediated largely through the visual imagination.[8] Reed's visual elements, on the other hand, deflect the reader's vision *away* from the text, working against the reader's inclination to create clear and unified mental images of the narrated "scene." Reed's pastiche thus refuses the metaphysical basis of the epistemology of vision by denying the existence of any transcendental "image" that can legitimate the text's truth-claims. Without the unifying process of vision, the reader is denied the satisfactions of a selfhood that finds its "enlightenment" in the focusing power of the "illustration."

The text's denial of the unifying act of vision is part of Reed's attack on the unified or naturalistic black subject. As Henry Louis Gates has shown, Reed's pastiche disperses the unified black subject that Richard Wright's naturalism assumed, putting in its place a decentered, heterogeneous subject that refuses representation in established forms. But Reed's signifying practice in regard to the conventions of illustration also points up the performative function of spectacular form. In disrupting the continuity and closure of its narratives, the spectacular pastiche text invites the reader to construct narratives that lie outside or alongside the ones that the text explicitly develops. As a performative text, *Mumbo Jumbo* is concerned neither with the unitary "truth" of its narrative nor with the construction of the unified reading subject necessary to achieve such truth. The text's success is measured by its performativity rather than by its truth, by its ability to stimulate the construction of other narratives rather than by its ability to achieve closure for its own.

Accordingly, none of the narratives in *Mumbo Jumbo* are allowed closure, including the historical narrative that PaPa LaBas constructs as an Africanist life-enhancing alternative to the deathward-tending Eurocentric history promoted by the Knights Templar and the Wallflower Order. Any attempt to found the narrative of the black subject on the ancient Book of Thoth must eventually fail: in a final twist on the novel's detective plot, the book itself is never recovered and is thus revealed to be an object of desire that functions only through absence. The book is banished and closure is refused, a condition that returns us from depth to surface at the same time that it assures continued narrative performance. In *Mumbo Jumbo* the liberation of the black subject from the confining forms and assumptions of naturalist fiction is simultaneously a break away from the typographically constructed domain of the book. Whereas Sterne's performative disruptions point toward the conventions of print culture, Reed's break from the book points toward an image culture in which narratives are valued not for their truth but for their power to enable further performance.

Performing Ragtime

E. L. Doctorow's *Ragtime* provides a quite different and less obvious example of the presence of spectacle in narrative form, for whereas Reed's pastiche provides immediate visual evidence of its challenges to narrative conventions,

Doctorow practices his subversions from squarely within the popular novelistic tradition. While Reed's performance is more self-consciously avant-garde in character, Doctorow's is a tightrope act that has managed to attract readers committed to popular forms of realism as well as those interested in postmodern experimentation. Indeed, despite its parodic and self-reflexive play with narrative conventions, *Ragtime* was an immediate popular success, selling 232,340 hardcover copies in its first year, making the *Publishers Weekly* annual best-seller list, and setting a new record for the sale of paperback rights to Bantam for $1,850,000 (Maryles). *Ragtime* was a critical success as well, winning the National Book Critics Circle Award. And yet to Charles Newman, the novel's attempt to be both experimental and conventional results in the poor compromise of a "historical realism patinaed with the 'special effects' of Modernism— journalistic portraiture updated by ironical caveat, cinematic fragmentation, and didactic narration, whose market code word is the 'accessible serious,' and whose primary effect is a kind of double nostalgia both for absorbed Modernist innovation *and* 19th-century narration" (93). Whether the novel's technique is a poor compromise or a skillful blending of approaches, what is clear is that *Ragtime* manages to be quite a different novel to different readers. Just as television programming depends on polysemy and self-directed irony to appeal to a heterogeneous audience with quite different experiences and interests, so *Ragtime* manages its ironies in such a way that readers can approach it as "serious" historical fiction and/or a parody of the historical novel, as leftist political critique and/or pop entertainment. *Ragtime* satisfies the reader's expectations for affective engagement, plot, and narrative closure, but does so with a knowing wink and a showman's hustle, suggesting that all we can reasonably ask for our nickel is not truth but performance.

The spectacularity of form in *Ragtime* is the result of a number of techniques by which Doctorow constructs a syntax of narrative discontinuity. Beginning at the level of sentence structure, we find that the heavy use of short declarative sentences and the avoidance of subordinating conjunctions establishes right away the primacy of sequence over consequence. The pronounced paratactic quality of the text's transitions gives the impression that history is constructed on the principle of coincidence and free association rather than cause and effect. The novel's long first paragraph (640 words) ranges over a collection of widely disparate historical events, social phenomena, and characters both historical and fictional, often moving swiftly through a series of short statements: "Women were stouter then. They visited the fleet carrying white parasols. Everyone wore white in summer. Tennis racquets were hefty and the racquet faces elliptical. There was a lot of sexual fainting. There were no Negroes. There were no immigrants" (4). One can, of course, connect the dots here: from women's bodies to women's fashion ("the fleet" an ominously inassimilable element, presaging the World War that brings the ragtime era—and the novel—to its end); from the "whiteness" of the general fashion to that of tennis apparel, a sport whose physical exertions provide the link to "sexual fainting." The taboo subject of sexual pleasure summons related repressions: "Negroes," whose supposedly unrepressed sexuality is the stuff of popular myth and whose very existence threatens the "whiteness" of prevailing fashion; and finally "immigrants," whose presence provides another threat to fantasies of racial and ethnic purity. The business of making these connections is left largely to the reader, however. The narrative pursues its associative, combinatorial logic without an authoritative narrative voice to provide transitions or a scale of relative value of the various names, events, and phenomena introduced. We are given no indication, for example, that the nouns "Negroes" and "immigrants" index what will become two of the novel's major plot lines: the stories of Coalhouse Walker and Tateh.

This long first paragraph begins and ends with dates and thus invokes the discourse of veracious, nonfictive history. Yet if it is the fundamental act of history writing to link events in some causal nexus, using narrative to establish meaningful connections between events, *Ragtime* right away signals a curious disregard of the conventions of historiographic narrative. Anthony Dawson has likened this technique to that of cinematic montage and has rightly observed that such discontinuities in narrative syntax are one way in which the text calls attention to the artifice involved in its constructions of history, involving us "in an interplay between a sense of the authenticity of its past images and an awareness of how that sense is induced" (211). *Ragtime* continually reminds us of the two senses of the word *history:* the supposedly objective "past" that is independent of representation, and the writing by which that "past" is represented. In requiring the reader to leap across the gaps left by the lack of narrative transitions, the text calls attention to the writing of history as an act of performance. Despite its invocation of veracious historical discourse and its commitment to representing a particular historical past, *Ragtime* mesmerizes us with performativity of the text itself.[9]

As Barbara Foley has shown, *Ragtime* departs both from the conventions of nineteenth-century historical fiction, in which historical events serve as the background to fictional plots involving fictional characters, and from the naturalist conventions of Dos Passos, where historical events provide the plot into which the lives of the fictional characters are fitted. In *Ragtime,* the distinction between fictional foreground and historical background is blurred when the paths of historical and fictional characters intersect. Father, Mother, Grandfather, Little Boy, and Mother's Younger Brother are given only generic names, signaling their fictive status amidst a collection of historical names that includes Stanford White, Harry K. Thaw, Evelyn Nesbit, Emma Goldman, Winslow Homer, and Teddy Roosevelt. Though the first paragraph keeps the historical characters separate from the fictional ones, suggesting that perhaps the lives of the "foregrounded" fictional characters are being set against the historical "background" in which the "real" characters operate, the novel's second paragraph begins by linking names from the two categories: "Mother's Younger Brother was in love with Evelyn Nesbit" (6). In combining proper nouns from the real and fictional realms, the text sets into motion one of the novel's plot sequences. Moreover, the plot strands that are generated by this sort of cross-pollination are given not historical shapes but patently fictional ones: the story of Coalhouse Walker, borrowed from Heinrich von Kleist's 1808 novella, *Michael Kohlhaus,* follows a tragic trajectory, while the story of Tateh's rise and marriage to Mother follows a comic one.[10]

The adherence to fictional convention is seen as well in other devices by which the text handles transitions. One is the use of a voice that resembles the voice-over in a documentary film: "This was the time in our history when Winslow Homer was doing his painting" (4). This voice returns periodically throughout the novel (20, 30, 103, 177, 230) and is part of what Doctorow has described as his attempt "to create something not as intimate as fiction nor as remote as history, but a voice that was mock-historical—pedantic" (Saltzman 90). The voice calls attention to its own artificiality even as it directs our attention to historically verifiable "facts." Other transitional techniques play on the stock methods of popular fiction and film, such as Doctorow's "back at the ranch" crosscutting between different plot strands. After getting Peary to the north pole at the end of chapter 10, the narrator begins the next chapter with "Back home a momentous change was coming over the United States" (93). And after following Evelyn Nesbit to the end of chapter 11, the narrator begins the next chapter with "And what of Tateh and his little girl?" (101). A related page-turner device involves ending one chapter with an intriguing tangent that turns out to be the main element opening the succeeding chapter. While the discussion of Freud at the end of chapter 5 seems to digress from the focus on Houdini, a flip of the page reveals Freud to be the main subject of the start of chapter 6. In his knowing play with popular conventions, Doctorow attempts to have it both ways, exploiting the techniques of the fast-paced popular novel while pointing to their artificiality, giving us the pleasure of a "good read" while reminding us that such transitions are always essentially rhetorical means of managing the text's discontinuities.

The text's pop transitions can be viewed as performative utterances in the linguistic sense developed by J. L. Austin, for whom the name *performative* "indicates that the issuing of the utterance is the performing of an action" rather than simply the making of a statement (6). When the narrative asks rhetorically "And what of Tateh and his little girl?" it is also implicitly making the performative utterance: "I will now make a transition to the story of Tateh and his little girl." Such transitional language is performative in that its very utterance performs the transition. If the primary mode of utterance in historical discourse is constative—statements of fact—then Doctorow's showy use of the performative mode can be seen as a deliberate challenge to the conventional truth-claims of the historical text. This is because the primary criterion for evaluating a performative utterance is not its truth or falsehood but its efficiency in performing an intended action. It is not necessary—nor does it often make sense—to ask at such transitional moments whether the transitional utterance is "true," but only how well it performs.[11] With these performative transitions, Doctorow reminds us that as a work of historical imagination his text is a willful arrangement of narrative elements in a spatial order. It should be noted, moreover, that the paratactic transitions described earlier—the lack of subordinating conjunctions or other connecting language between clauses and sentences—indicate by the *absence* of explicit transition the same willful act of spatial arrangement. That is, *Ragtime*'s transitions are characterized either by a *lack* of transitional material—parataxis—or by an *excess* of transitional material, as in the hypotactic use of pop page-turning devices. By turns absent and over-obvious, these transitions call attention to the discontinuities that unavoidably result when historical events are spatialized in narrative.

That the transitions in *Ragtime* present historical narrative as a collection of elements ranged in a spatial order goes some way toward explaining the repeated figure of the collector and the collection in Doctorow's work. The Little Boy in *Ragtime* is a collector of castoffs. The boy cannot value objects unless they have been discarded by others, because "in his mind the meaning of something was perceived through its neglect" (131). The boy is fascinated with trash because in its cast-off state the discarded object bears the traces of time itself. The boy's recovery of the neglected object figures the novel's recovery of this country's neglected prewar radical past, yet does so in a way that emphasizes the volatility of any such recovery. Though the collection of discarded objects might suggest a desire for permanence and continuity, the boy is equally fascinated with ephemera, with change, with the discontinuous transformation of one thing into another. Hence his interest in the tales from Ovid's *Metamorphoses* told him by his Grandfather: "Grandfather's stories proposed to him that the forms of life were volatile and that everything in the world could as easily be something else" (132–33).

In Doctorow's *Billy Bathgate* (1989), the figure of the collector appears in the character of Arnold Garbage, a boy who lives in the basement of an orphans' home. Garbage wanders the streets with a shopping cart collecting junk, his obsessive purpose being "to love what was broken, torn, peeling. To love what didn't work. To love what was twisted and cracked and missing its parts. To love what smelled and what nobody else would scrape away the filth of to identify. To love what was indistinct in shape and indecipherable in purpose and indeterminate in function. To love it and hold on to it" (32). While this passage suggests that Arnold's junk has been stripped of both use value and exchange value to become an aestheticized collection, we learn that this is not entirely the case: Arnold willingly sells Billy the gun (found "in a wet marsh off Pelham Bay") with which Billy launches his life into the criminal trades. Thus the recovery of lost objects can retain an instrumental purpose. Despite his own ambitions, Billy cannot help but respect Arnold Garbage, whose life was one of "such mysterious single-minded and insane purpose that it seemed natural, and logical, and you wondered why you didn't live that way yourself" (32). And this, perhaps, is the point: while Billy's life of adventure follows the arrow of time and assumes a patently fictional shape, Arnold Garbage provides a model of an alternative mode of existence outside history in the stasis of the collection.

The objects of a collection have a dual relation to history. While the castoff object, for both the Little Boy of *Ragtime* and Arnold Garbage of *Billy Bathgate*, is marked by its posteriority and thus is valued as a token of time itself, it takes on an ahistorical value in its role as one element of a collection. Susan Stewart has articulated this insight in distinguishing between the souvenir and the collection. Whereas the souvenir (the miniature Eiffel Tower) summons the past and has as its referent the personal narrative of its acquisition ("My Trip to Paris"), the item in a collection (stamps or coins) tends to refer only to other items in the collection. At its extreme, the collection becomes a hermetically sealed set, concerned only with its own seriality and referring to nothing outside of itself (Stewart 132–69).

Thus the cast-off object finds its referents through two quite different kinds of operations. As an individual souvenir, the object refers diachronically to a narrative of the past; as a member of a collection, the object refers synchronically to the other objects in the collection. Both modes of reference are clearly at work in the case of the time capsule, a form of collection that Doctorow makes prominent in his 1985 novel, *World's Fair*. The novel ends with an act of collection in which the narrator/protagonist Edgar and his friend Arnold bury tokens of their lives and their historical period in a cardboard tube. Among the objects the two boys bury are a Tom Mix decoder ring, an M. Hohner Marine Band harmonica, a torn silk stocking, and "two Tootsy Toy lead rocket ships, from which all the paint had been worn, to show I had foreseen the future" (287–88). The boys' private time capsule is inspired by the public, official one installed at the 1939 World's Fair "to show people in the year 6939 what we had accomplished and what about our lives we thought meaningful." As the narrator reports, this collection includes, among other things, "the Lord's Prayer in three hundred languages, and a dictionary and photographs of factories and assembly lines, and assorted comic strips and *Gone with the Wind*, by Margaret Mitchell, which I had not yet read; and finally newsreels of President Roosevelt giving a speech, and scenes of the United States Navy on maneuvers and the Japanese bombing of Canton in the war with China, and a fashion show in Miami, Florida" (283–84). In this list, history becomes a heterogeneous collection of exhibits granted equivalent value by the coordinating conjunction "and." Their connection is that of spatial contiguity only; any more significant principle of association—causal, contextual, structural, teleological, or otherwise—is up to the reader to provide. As a means of access to the historical past, the time capsule collection tempts us to puzzle out the combinatorial logic of the collection itself, catching us in the maze of its own internal relations rather than referring us outward to the "real" historical events and conditions that these objects might otherwise signify.

As concluding gestures, the twin time capsules of *World's Fair* are particularly appropriate to a novel that, in its anecdotal and episodic structure, is itself a kind of time capsule. The novel is openly nostalgic, keenly and seriously engaged with its narrator's childhood perceptions of a particular place and time, yet does not impose upon the collection of episodes any of the conventional fictional shapes we see in *Billy Bathgate* and *Ragtime*, whether *bildungsroman*, comic rags-to-riches, or tragic fall. What is interesting is that, on the level of its sentences, *World's Fair* shows a complex syntax, a willingness to subordinate and qualify that is notably lacking in *Ragtime*. Thus sentence-level syntax is at odds with narrative-level syntax in both novels, yet with the relation reversed: in *Ragtime* parataxis at the sentence level serves the construction of conventional, tightly interwoven plots, whereas in *World's Fair* hypotaxis at the sentence level serves an essentially disconnected, loosely structured text. By any measure E. L. Doctorow must be considered one of our most persistent and successful practitioners of the historical novel. And yet, whether in the figure of Arnold Garbage, in the time capsule collections of *World's Fair*, or in the paratactic and performative transitions of *Ragtime*, Doctorow repeatedly suggests that the writing of history is a willful, contingent act of collection that depends for its plausibility on the performative efficiency of its transitions rather than on any appeal to historical "truth."[12]

Thus *Ragtime*'s transitional techniques not only make this one text "spectacular" but also foreground the spectacularity inherent in all narrative representations of history. But once again, as was the case in distinguishing Sterne's spectacular form from that of Reed, the text's formal devices must be seen within a particular historical context. The spectacularity of *Ragtime* is not a matter of syntax only. Doctorow also suggests a link between the problems of historical representation and the emergence of new "spectacular" technologies of representation: photography and film.

Ragtime is both a reproduction of history and a history of reproduction. The most prominent figure in this regard is Tateh, the Jewish socialist immigrant who transforms the traditional art of the handcrafted silhouette into the new technology of the movies. His intricately executed scissors-and-paper silhouettes eventually find their way into "private collections," their aura of originality allowing them to become commodities prized by collectors fetishizing the handcrafted past, while his flip-books and eventually his movie scripts are reproduced to reach a mass audience of lower social status. While transforming the technique of handcraft into the technology of mass production, Tateh transforms himself from socialist worker to capitalist entrepreneur, along the way remaking himself in the image of the exiled aristocrat, the Baron Ashkenazy.

In detailing Tateh's involvement with both the inventors and investors necessary to the start-up of the movie industry, *Ragtime* places the history of this new technology of reproduction within the history of a particular organization and deployment of capital. In so doing, the novel points forward to the development of an economy in which the production of material goods will become inseparable from the production of images. Houdini, the novel's central figure of spectacular performance, serves to focus two central questions simultaneously: that of the distinction between illusion and reality, and that of the distinction between "serious" art and popular entertainment. Lamenting that he is "a trickster, an illusionist, a mere magician" whose appeal is primarily to the lower classes, Houdini recognizes the unbridgeable gulf between himself and the likes of Henry Ford, J. P. Morgan, and Harry K. Thaw, who had "a kind of act that used the real world for its stage" (112). Despite the narrator's assertion that today "the audience for escapes is even larger," Houdini's presence in the novel suggests that the difference between popular entertainments then and now is not merely quantitative. Rather, the figure of Houdini prompts a nostalgic desire for a period when reality and illusion could be more clearly distinguished—or, to put it differently, when illusion could be safely bracketed as "entertainment," distinct from the mechanism of material production. In a postmodern environment, where mass-produced images are neither simply entertainment nor mere "reflections" of economic and cultural conditions but rather are a primary mechanism of the consumer economy, the distinction between the world of illusion and the world of real material production is not so easily made. While in *Ragtime* Houdini can feel himself clearly apart from the "real" actors of the world, in the culture of television we find increasingly that entertainment and industrial capitalism act on the same stage.

The character of Houdini is just one example of Doctorow's abiding interest, throughout his work, in traditional forms of spectacle and the carnivalesque: one thinks of the passage describing the Bathgate Avenue market that concludes *Billy Bathgate*. The 1939 World's Fair at the end of *World's Fair* and Disneyland at the end of *The Book of Daniel* represent the modernist and postmodernist transformations, respectively, of the traditional carnival. *Ragtime* concludes with Harry K. Thaw marching in the Armistice Day parade. The novel finds room not only for the mass spectacles of a political picnic excursion up the Hudson River, the Lawrence textile mill strike, and the mayhem of an Emma Goldman rally, but also for the Barnum and Bailey circus freaks hired to entertain the party guests of Mrs. Stuyvesant Fish, and for a baseball game that in Father's eyes becomes a freak show as well as an occasion for class loathing. Thus one of the sources of nostalgia in *Ragtime* is the way that it sets the emerging technologies of mass culture against the more traditional spectacles that they will rapidly come to dominate.

The appearance of Henry Ford's Model T at his assembly plant in Highland Park, Michigan, serves as one instance of mass reproduction in an era in which, suddenly, "the value of the duplicable event was everywhere perceived" (153). Mother's Younger Brother keeps a newspaper drawing of Evelyn Nesbit in his bedroom, while Houdini places photographs of his deceased mother around the house to simulate her presence. The value of duplicability is perceived quite clearly by the early entrepreneurs of the movie industry, who see in Evelyn Nesbit their first sex goddess and are eager to transform the engravings done of her by newspaper illustrators into photographic images projected on the screen (95). Not merely the instrument of desire and nostalgia, the photographic medium is also shown to shape events more directly. Desiring good pictures, the newspapers "agitated for several editions" to have Coalhouse Walker's destroyed Model T raised from Firehouse Pond (273). Seeing the resultant photos in the newspapers, the Coalhouse Walker gang is further emboldened: "This tangible proof of the force of Coalhouse's will made them all feel holy" (284).

The potential of photography as a historical force in its own right is suggested early in the novel with the brief appearance of Jacob Riis, whose photographs of the housing conditions of Manhattan's poor were intended to promote social change (20). Both Riis and the novelist Theodore Dreiser, described even more briefly in the following chapter, function in the novel as implicit presences, as important early practitioners of the kind of documentary realism of the lower classes that *Ragtime* both practices and parodies. This linking of the novelist and the photographer, Doctorow's naturalist forebears, would seem to suggest Doctorow's own consciousness of his relation to the image culture of his time. If Dreiser's literary realism was the naturalist analogue to Riis's photographic realism, then in Doctorow's spectacular text we see the postmodernist analogue to the spectacularity of postmodern image culture.

It is, of course, always the case in writing history that the historical situation of the text's production to some degree dictates the terms on which it will conduct its interrogation of the past. As writers of postmodern historical novels, E. L. Doctorow and Ishmael Reed are perhaps more willing than most to let the marks of the present show in their representations of past eras. Reviewers and critics of *Ragtime* have frequently commented upon how the story of Coalhouse Walker is clearly influenced by the black militant protests of the late 1960s. In Reed's *Mumbo Jumbo,* the Harlem Renaissance and the racism of the 1920s are likewise seen through the lens of late 1960s activism and militancy. But in addition to placing the present in dialogue with the past through their choice and treatment of subject matter, Doctorow's *Ragtime* and Reed's *Mumbo Jumbo* share a historical perspective in which their own representations of history must be placed within a particular history of representation. In *Mumbo Jumbo,* the text's pastiche points toward the development of a mass cultural environment in which the values of truth and narrative closure are supplanted by those of performance and narrative openness. In *Ragtime,* performative narrative syntax points to the artificiality of the text's historical constructions while the novel chronicles, in its content, an entire history of artifice, spectacle, and illusion.

In both novels, then, the history of the development of mass cultural forms of representation is also the history of an epistemology. In his essay "False Documents," Doctorow proposes that "there is no fiction or nonfiction as we commonly understand the distinction: there is only narrative" (26). In both Doctorow's *Ragtime* and Reed's *Mumbo Jumbo,* we have seen that spectacular narrative form operates precisely to put the distinction between fiction and nonfiction into question, and to shift the source of narrative authority from "truth" to performativity. In asserting that "there is only narrative," and with his discussion in that essay of *Robinson Crusoe,* Doctorow is seeking to recover something of the indifference to the distinction between fictional and factual discourses that characterized the novel in its early development.[13] Though this link between premodern and postmodern epistemologies is suggestive, we must be careful not to read Doctorow here as making an ahistorical equation between early-eighteenth-century and late-twentieth-century approaches to questions of narrative authority and referentiality. *Ragtime's* careful attention to the technologies of representation, as well as its play with the conventions of literary representation, suggests a highly self-conscious attempt to situate his own questioning of the fact/fiction distinction within a particular historical moment. That moment, for both Doctorow and Reed, is one in which fiction survives in a mass cultural environment at the price of having its narrative representations continually undercut by spectacle. Whatever depth of historical narrative that these two novels achieve is broken into shards and displayed on the brilliant surface of the text's spectacular performance. Narrative continues to be a necessary means of making meaning, constructing self, and grasping history, yet the interruption of narrative by spectacle on the textual level can be seen as a figure for the larger historical and epistemological condition in which we have come to grant our narratives only local and contingent authority. Spectacular form in both mass culture and fiction works to ensure that all our narratives are interrupted in their reach for closure and mastery.

Minimalist Fiction as "Low" Postmodernism

Raymond Carver, Ann Beattie, and Bobbie Ann Mason are the most prominent members of the group of writers whose fiction has attracted the "minimalist" label. Minimalist fiction has had much to do with the moderate resurgence of the short story in this country in the past twenty years; its style is noted for its relative syntactic and lexical simplicity, muted affect, and meticulous, intimate explorations of mundane life in post-Vietnam America.[1] Though considerably popular both with readers and with younger writers coming up through the ranks of the nation's graduate writing programs in the last fifteen years, minimalist fiction has had more than its share of detractors. In a 1988 defense of his own minimalist practice, Frederick Barthelme summarized the charges against himself and the other writers with whom he is associated: "(A) omission of big 'philosophical' ideas, (B) not enough history or historical sense, (C) lack of (or wrong) political posture, (D) insufficient 'depth' of character, (E) common-place description too reliant on brand names, (F) drabness of 'style,' (G) moral poverty" ("On Being Wrong" 1). Though Barthelme fairly represents the substance of his opposition, he does not capture its tone. Frank Lentricchia has described minimalist writing as "the soft humanist underbelly of American literature," while other critics have termed it "anorexic," "anaerobic," "catatonic," and "brutal."[2] Donald Barthelme, the postmodernist older brother against whom the minimalist Frederick rebels, rejects minimalism's willful simplicity while sniffily defending the "difficulty" of his own postmodern writing: "Art is not difficult because it wishes to be difficult, but because it wishes to be art" ("Not-Knowing" 14). There is more at stake here than either sibling rivalry or a writers' squabble over matters of "style." The tone and temper of the attacks on minimalism are fully intelligible only if one understands the extent to which minimalism is a self-conscious attempt to fashion a "low" postmodernism in opposition to the "high" postmodernism of the metafictional, formalist, and parodic writers who rose to prominence in the late 1960s and 1970s.

The charges leveled against minimalist fiction grow out of deep-seated conflicts over the nature of fictional representation, conflicts which have their contemporary parallels within poststructuralist and postmodernist theory. Of particular interest, given the controversy surrounding the term *history* in recent theoretical debates, is the view that minimalism somehow capitulates to mass culture in its historical attitude, trading a knowledge of place and time for a knowledge of brand names, substituting a consumer's consciousness for a more "genuine" historical one. The attack on minimalism can be placed within the larger debate over the relation of mass culture to historical consciousness that we have explored in previous chapters. In what follows, we will see what position a "low" postmodernism can occupy in this debate.

I begin with a critical overview of minimalist practice, offered here because minimalist fiction has received relatively little comprehensive critical treatment. Raymond Carver's fiction merits sustained attention, both because his work is arguably the strongest of the writing gathered under the minimalist rubric and because a retrospective look at his career reveals issues important to the question of the minimalist aesthetic as a whole. Ann Beattie's fiction, while shaped by different talents and sensibilities, nonetheless shows how minimalist attitudes and practices can be extended to writing about characters who occupy distinctly different social worlds from Carver's. Russell Banks's *Continental Drift*, which I argue should not be considered a minimalist text, allows us by way of contrast to distinguish more clearly certain minimalist approaches to narrative voice and perspective. This overview will prepare us for a return to the question of how minimalism, as a "low postmodernism," engages the problem of historical understanding. Both Frederick Barthelme's defense of minimalist practice and his own work as a novelist allow us to examine how one minimalist sensibility grasps the new mass cultural environments of the postmodern era. Bobbie Ann Mason's 1985 novel, *In Country*, proves specially apt for exploring the relation of the Vietnam War to the minimalist sense of history, and the general problem of historical knowledge under postmodern conditions. We will see that the attitudes toward history found in minimalist fiction belong themselves to a particular historical moment, and grow out of minimalist writers' attempts to capture the ethos of a post-Vietnam America. A troublesome feature of this ethos is the feeling that the recovery of traditional historical "depth" is indeed impossible under postmodern conditions. However, rather than relinquish history altogether, minimalist fiction attempts to give mass culture a place in a new "deep surface," a new and problematic historical consciousness.

In Alfredo's Kitchen: The Minimalist Aesthetic

Readers of minimalist fiction, whether friendly or hostile, discover that the question of history in minimalist writing is not one of thematic development only but is raised by the quality of the prose itself. Before returning to the question of how minimalist fiction engages the problem of historical understanding, some attention to that prose is in order. With the 1980s furor having died down, it is possible to offer a more balanced assessment of minimalism's successes and failures. As with most "-isms" that become the object of polemical sport, minimalism has more virtues than admitted by its opponents, more faults than admitted by its defenders. For a brief look at certain common features of minimalist practice, start with the following three passages, found by choosing a page at random from short-story collections by Ann Beattie, Raymond Carver, and Bobbie Ann Mason, respectively:

It is cold in the house. She is making soup and baking a roast for dinner. The dog barks and jumps. Marshall is home from work. He and Edna are talking in the living room. Soon they will go out to ride their snowmobiles; she'll hear them making a circle around the house, will look out the window, cupping her hands so she can see clearly the tracks in the snow. She had been for a ride on the snowmobile with Marshall. She wore scarves on her head, afraid to put on the helmet. There is talk about outlawing snowmobiles. Edna and Marshall are always upset about it. On the television they said people died on snowmobiles, riding them through barbed-wire fences. She rubs her throat, thinking about barbed wire piercing the skin. ("Marshall's Dog" 77)

He went to the refrigerator. He stood in front of the open door and drank tomato juice while he studied everything inside. Cold air blew out at him. He looked at the little packages and the containers of foodstuffs on the shelves, a chicken covered in plastic wrap, the neat, protected exhibits.

He shut the door and spit the last of the juice into the sink. Then he rinsed his mouth and made himself a cup of instant coffee. He carried it into the living room. He sat down in front of the TV and lit a cigarette. He understood that it took only one lunatic and a torch to bring everything to ruin. ("After the Denim" 76–77)

It is a hot summer night, and Larry and I are driving back from Paducah. We went out to eat and then we saw a movie. We are rather careless about being seen together in public. Before we left the house, I brushed my teeth twice and used dental floss. On the way, Larry told me of a patient who was a hemophiliac and couldn't floss. Working on his teeth was very risky. ("Residents and Transients" 129)

In each of these passages one finds a preference for parataxis over subordination that establishes the primacy of sequence over consequence. Simple and compound subject-verb-object sentences predominate. The use of the present tense, as in two of the passages here, is common in minimalist fiction and can heighten the sense that these characters operate in an ever-present from which deep history is banished. (Bobbie Ann Mason has remarked that the minimalists' preference for the present tense "obviously came from television" (CLC 82: 254).)[3] Only two subordinate clauses can be found, both simple time adverbials (Carver's "while he studied everything inside" and Mason's "Before we left the house"). The refusal to subordinate has much to do with how each passage creates the impression of following the train of associations of the characters' minds without submitting it to any unifying discursive order. Far from the stream-of-consciousness constructions of Joyce and Woolf, however, these offer us a series of casual details unleavened by grammatical unorthodoxy or verbal surprise. The plainness of detail and construction of the sentences seconds the domestic settings of the fiction: the kitchen, the living room, and the car are the primary settings for a fiction that explores the intimate, domestic, personal spaces of ordinary lives. Snowmobiles, television, plastic-wrapped chicken, tomato juice, instant coffee, cigarettes, a movie and dinner out, dental floss—the texture of these lives is rendered in myriad tiny acts of consumption, placing these characters in a landscape of mass consumer culture in which the sight of a torch-bearing lunatic on TV can become an emblem for one's life. Finally, note that each of the passages moves toward a moment of threat: the barbed wire, the torch, and the case of hemophilia are hazards faced by others, yet by which the characters register their own vulnerability. Moreover, these dangers have in common a random, terroristic, externalized quality; they are dangers imposed willy-nilly on hapless victims. Far from strong-willed, these are the sort of characters to whom life just "happens."

Though it might seem a fortuitous coincidence of my selection, I think on the contrary that it is typical of this fiction that the calm surface of the prose belies some danger that can be understood only by reference to the larger fictional situation. In Carver's "After the Denim," for example, the man watching the torch-bearing lunatic on TV has just discovered that his wife may have cancer. It is perhaps unfair to quote these passages out of context for just this reason: what tension such stories do develop often depends on the disparity between the blandness of the prose and the seriousness of the conflict whose emotional stress it fails or refuses to register.

It is for just this refusal that such critics as Charles Newman find minimalist fiction wanting: "This is not the minimalism of [Donald] Barthelme, whose omissions are based on the circumspect demonstration that he *knows* what he is leaving out. These are the elisions of inadvertency and circumscription" (93). Newman, who bemoans the "ongoing humiliation" of literature in what he terms an "inflationary culture," describes minimalism as an "obdurate unsurprised and unsurprising plainstyle which takes that famous 'meaning between the lines' to its absurd conclusion." As a "willful underdeployment of resources," minimalism is "the classic conservative response to inflation— underutilization of capacity, reduction of inventory, and verbal joblessness" (93). Michael Gorra describes minimalist prose as "so attenuated that it can't support the weight of a past or a future, but only a bare notation of what happens, now; a 'slice of life' in which the characters are seen without the benefit of antecedents or social context. They rarely have last names" (155).

However frustrating some critics may find it, the studied reticence at the heart of the minimalist aesthetic has won this work its share of readers. Raymond Carver made this reticence the basis of his method and struggled with its consequences throughout his career. In "Menudo," one of his last stories (Carver died in 1988), a man seeks refuge at a friend's house during a bad time in the man's marriage. The friend, Alfredo, is a painter whose kitchen serves as his studio. Of that kitchen, cluttered with paintings, an easel, palette, and crumpled tubes of paint, the narrator says: "I loved the shabby economy of that little room" (347).[4] Alfredo's kitchen seems a fitting analogue for the space of Carver's stories: small, domestic, visited by drunks, with a view of the alley and loud music heard from the next room, seemingly untidy yet well suited to its purposes, which include the making of art. It is a place where people who are overtaken by feelings find that words fail them. Alfredo asks why the narrator has begun to shake uncontrollably, and the narrator tells us blankly: "I couldn't tell him. What could I say?" (347).[5] Carver's characters are often made speechless by loss, failure, and occasionally by wonder, and his special gift is in bringing the reader into stunning intimacy with his characters at such moments.

This is an art that registers an essential humility in the face of life's changes, and calls more for understatement than for shouting. As his career developed, and in his obsessive revision of his stories even after their initial publication, Carver struggled to strike the right balance between inclusion and exclusion, between what gets left in and what gets cut out, between what needs to be named and what can be left unspecified.[6] The signs of this struggle can be seen on several levels: on the lexical level; on the level of "talk," both by the narrator and in dialogue; and on the larger level of the stories' structure.

On the lexical level, Carver's reticence is found in a stubbornly ordinary diction exemplified by the frequently pivotal function of the word *thing*, in his stories as well as in many of his titles: "Nobody Said Anything," "One More Thing," "Little Things," "The Third Thing That Killed My Father Off," "A Small, Good Thing." For all its frustrating generality, its refusal to specify, "thing" serves a number of calculated rhetorical functions in Carver's stories. In Carver's carefully crafted one-of-the-guys idiom, the word is one means by which Carver disarms the reader's defenses, drawing the reader in with seemingly casual talk. The word can carry an ominously general reference, signal a character's lack of self-knowledge or understanding of a situation, or register a character's pugnacious refusal to be specific. The word is so common in Carver's fiction that in the last stage of his career its use became a deliberate mannerism. In "Blackbird Pie," one of Carver's most self-consciously "literary" stories, the use of the word approaches self-parody. In the first line of the letter in which she announces her intention to quit the marriage, the wife of the protagonist writes: "Things are not good. Things, in fact, are bad. Things have gone from bad to worse" (366). Elsewhere the word can take on an eerie, totemic power. At the end of "Vitamins," a man is thwarted in his desire to sleep with one of his wife's colleagues and returns home after a long, drunken night of tawdry adventure to find his wife, asleep with her clothes on, waking out of a bad dream.

I couldn't take any more tonight. "Go back to sleep, honey. I'm looking for something," I said. I knocked some stuff out of the medicine chest. Things rolled into the sink. "Where's the aspirin?" I said. I knocked down some more things. I didn't care. Things kept falling. (196)

A minimal ending, yet one which resonates with the sense of a life blundering on the tender edge of control. The word *things* here could include the vitamins that the man's wife has made her living by selling, those encapsulated tokens of a vitality that no one in the story seems to possess. And "things" certainly gestures toward everything else in the man's life that is falling or bound to fall.

In "A Serious Talk," Burt insists on visiting his ex-wife's house even after ruining the family's Christmas celebration the day before. Though he is ostensibly there to make amends, he ends up sawing through the phone cord while his ex-wife is talking to her new boyfriend. Having severed one conversation, he is unable to start any significant one of his own, and must finally leave when his ex threatens to call the police.

He was not certain, but he thought he had proved something. He hoped he had made something clear. The thing was, they had to have a serious talk soon. There were things that had to be discussed. They'd talk again. Maybe after the holidays were over and things got back to normal. (127)

Readers looking for redeeming moments will not find them in this story, which ends with a character mired in his lack of self-awareness. Here, "things" is a marker, not for some knowledge that Burt refuses to impart, but for his profound ignorance of his own mind and heart, as well as for his own insistence on crude self-assertion despite overwhelming evidence of the destructiveness of such gestures. It is not "nice" to be brought into intimacy with such characters, but while a number of Carver's stories do end by bringing their protagonists through to some sort of redemption (e.g., "Cathedral," "A Small, Good Thing," "Fever," "Elephant"), Carver's fiction at its most bleakly compelling reminds us that to insist on redemptive moments is to restrict fiction to an impossibly narrow moral scope.

For all their concern with inarticulateness and silence, Carver's stories are obsessively talky. Carver's narrators speak as oral storytellers, and the illusion of casual oral form is furthered by the anecdotal quality of many of the stories' key incidents, which often are tied to an arresting central image: the two men wrestling on the lawn in "Bicycles, Muscles, Cigarettes"; the Vietnam veteran dangling his prize Vietcong ear in "Vitamins"; the furniture in the front yard in "Why Don't You Dance?"; the peacock playing with the baby in "Feathers." A number of his stories begin with perfunctory frames in which a storyteller and audience are introduced briefly so that we can get right to the anecdotal material that forms the core of the story. Carver uses this device to good effect when the anecdote gains necessary resonance through its relation to the story's frame. In "Fat," when a waitress tells a friend about serving an obese man, her story becomes a register of her dissatisfaction with her childless marriage. Though the obese man's grotesque figure fascinates the waitress, it is hardly a bust of Apollo, making Carver's ending homage to Rilke both ironic and poignant: "My life is going to change. I feel it" (52).[7]

In "The Calm," a story told in a barbershop about a botched hunting expedition is recalled by a man about whose present circumstances we know nothing, yet when the story returns at the end to its narrative frame, the anecdote is again tied to a change in the narrator's life:

> That was in Crescent City, California, up near the Oregon border. I left soon after. But today I was thinking of that place, of Crescent City, and of how I was trying out a new life there with my wife, and how, in the barber's chair that morning, I had made up my mind to go. I was thinking today about the calm I felt when I closed my eyes and let the barber's fingers move through my hair, the sweetness of those fingers, the hair already starting to grow. (182)

The implication of this ending is that the calm of the remembered moment has not lasted, yet the stately cadence of these lines suggests that the act of telling the story has itself brought a new moment of revivifying calm into a turbulent life. There are other moments in Carver's fiction when talk proves therapeutic and redemptive, as in "A Small, Good Thing," in which the misanthropic baker is redeemed by talking, the grieving couple helped by listening, or in "Fever," in which a man whose wife has abandoned him and his two children at last unburdens himself to his housekeeper, with cathartic effect.

And yet more often talk fails. The problem, usually, is that it's not the right kind of talk. The wife's Dear John letter in "Blackbird Pie" laments, "It's been such a long time now since we've talked. I mean really *talked*" (366). The story "Careful" begins: "After a lot of talking—what his wife, Inez, called *assessment*—Lloyd moved out of the house into his own place" (197). While the talk that has occurred offstage has at least had some effect, the talk presented in the story itself fails utterly. Lloyd's failure to communicate is of a piece with Burt's in "A Serious Talk": "He began thinking of things he ought to say to her. . . . But when she came back into the room, he couldn't say anything" (201). The lack of communication is rendered comically by Lloyd having his ear plugged with wax. "She said something, but he couldn't make out the words. When she stopped talking, he didn't ask her what it was she'd said" (201). Of course, after the wax is removed the situation is no better: "He didn't listen. He didn't want to. He watched her lips move until she'd said what she had to say" (205). In a similar moment in "Fever," the protagonist receives a phone call from the wife who has abandoned him: "He held the receiver out in front of him. He looked at the instrument, from which her voice was issuing" (234). Often estranged from others' speech, Carver's characters just as often find themselves speechless. In "Feathers," the narrator and his wife have been invited to a friend's house for dinner, only to be confronted with the sight of a peacock strutting in the yard: "'Goddamn,' I said. There was nothing else to say" (251). Later in this singularly awkward evening, the inarticulate cry of the peacock on the rooftop brings inarticulate silence to the dinner guests: "Nobody said anything. What was there to say?" (259). The sight of the hosts' baby brings a similar response: "It was so ugly I couldn't say anything. No words would come out of my mouth" (260). The story ends, as many of Carver's do, with a proleptic leap from the central anecdote to the time of its telling, a time identified as "later, after things had changed for us," evidently for the worse. They've had children, and Fran, the narrator's wife, has grown fat. "We don't talk about it. What's to say?" (264). From the perspective of a marriage wound down into silence and resignation ("She and I talk less and less as it is. Mostly it's just the TV" [265]), the night of the peacock appears as an enchanted evening, having kindled not only a night's lust but a sense of togetherness in the face of a strange world.

As with Carver's "things," speechlessness becomes a familiar Carver mannerism. In the late story "Intimacy," after getting chewed out by his ex-wife, the speechless ex-husband is shown the door: "I look outside and, Jesus, there's this white moon hanging in the morning sky. I can't think when I've ever seen anything so remarkable. But I'm afraid to comment on it. I am. I don't know what might happen. I might break into tears even. I might not understand a word I'd say" (337). There is a sense, at this point in Carver's career, that such moments come too easily, and one feels the rightness of Vivian Gornick's complaint that Carver's male characters are trapped in an outmoded romantic sentimentality essentially unchanged since Hemingway. Speechlessness has become a sort of stylistic tic, a way of indulging in what Gornick calls "a wistful longing for an ideal tender connection that never was," instead of joining "the struggle so many women and so many men are waging now to make sense of themselves as they actually are" (32).

For better or worse, such evasions occur at the structural level of Carver's stories as well. Carver complained that the term *minimalist* "smacks of smallness of vision and execution" and explained the shift from the more minimal stories in *What We Talk about When We Talk about Love* (1981) to the more expansive stories in *Cathedral* (1983) by saying, "I knew I'd gone as far the other way as I could or wanted to go, cutting everything down to the marrow, not just to the bone" (*Paris Review* interview 210). The method of "cutting to the marrow" is seen at its most effective in "One More Thing," which Randolph Runyon notes was drastically cut between its original appearance in *The North American Review* in 1981 and its publication the following year as the last story in *What We Talk About*. The story begins when Maxine comes home to find her husband, L.D., drunk and arguing with their fifteen-year-old daughter, Rae. Maxine tells him to get out. The first line of dialogue points to some previous unspecified talk: "Rae said, 'Tell him, Mom, tell him what we talked about'" (110).[8] On her next attempt, Rae gets more specific: "'Tell him, Mom,' Rae said. 'Tell him it's all in his head'" (156). In the original version the "it" is clearly identified as L.D.'s drinking problem: "if he wants to stop drinking, all he has to do is stop. It's all in his head" (28, cit. Runyon 135). In the later version of the story, we never learn what "it" refers to, and we are therefore witness to an argument between father and daughter whose specific referent is never made clear. The cut is a risky move on Carver's part, but it works in this instance because of the story's dramatic immediacy: we are thrown into the midst of a family quarrel whose nature *is* specific enough for us not to need to know precisely what Rae and L.D. are arguing about. Indeed, the payoff of Carver's method here is that what remains unspecified takes on a larger significance than it would otherwise have had: "it" looms as possibly everything—all hurt, all suffering, all knowledge, all belief. With "it" unspecified, the reader can see the ensuing dialogue as a parodic debate over the mind/body problem as L.D. hurls at his daughter his candidates for conditions beyond the mind's reach: diabetes, epilepsy, cancer. The story's pathos is found in the daughter's earnest effort to defeat her father's arguments, as though he could still be redeemed if somehow brought within the circle of rational discourse.

Carver's method of cutting to the marrow is less effective in other instances, such as "The Student's Wife," in which the wife's final plea—"God, will you help us, God?"—gestures toward troubles too ill defined. A similar problem occurs in "What Do You Do in San Francisco?" in which the narrator announces in the first line a problem that the story never quite overcomes: "This has nothing to do with me" (40). The narrator is a mailman who observes at a distance the failure of a marriage in one of the households on his route. But too much of the story occurs off stage, we never learn who these people are and what has happened, and Carver does not manage the trick he pulls successfully elsewhere of having the anecdote resonate meaningfully in the narrator's life.

No fat, no meat, no bone, no marrow, no story. Compare "What Do You Do in San Francisco?" to the brilliant "Neighbors," where Carver gets just right the balance between inclusion and exclusion. In this story a couple is left to care for their neighbors' cat in the apartment across the hall while the neighbors are away, and in their furtive visits to the apartment both the man and the wife separately indulge their fantasies of their neighbors' less constricted and more erotically charged lives. At the point of entering the apartment together for the first time, breathlessly and unreasonably anticipating a new phase of adventure in their marriage, they find themselves stranded in the hallway, stunned with disappointment at having accidentally locked the key inside the neighbors' apartment. The story's ending gets it just right:

> They stayed there. They held each other. They leaned into the door as if into a wind, and braced themselves. (70)

Here we *know,* with a satisfying balance of specificity and generality, what they are bracing themselves against.

Finding this balance was an aesthetic challenge that occupied Carver to the end of his career.[9] William Stull has documented the shift Carver made in re-writing "The Bath" into "A Small, Good Thing," and those of us who read the later version when it first appeared in *Ploughshares* knew we were seeing something new in Carver's career, an approach that Carver called "fuller and more interesting . . . more generous" (*Saturday Review* interview 22).[10] Not only are his narrators more willing to elaborate, to add shading and nuance, but the characters are more likely to experience moments of redemption from lives worn down by meanness and loss. The shift can be seen in the revisions Carver made in the story "So Much Water So Close to Home" for its appearance in *Where I'm Calling From.* What follows is the opening paragraph, with the additions to the earlier version (from *What We Talk About*) in italics:

> My husband eats with good appetite *but he seems tired, edgy.* He chews *slowly,* arms on the table, and stares at something across the room. He looks at me and looks away *again.* He wipes his mouth on the napkin. He shrugs and goes on eating. *Something has come between us though he would like me to believe otherwise.* (160)

Other than the deletion of a comma after "shrugs," Carver's changes to the earlier version are strictly additive. Throughout the story he is more willing to explain, to add details of characters' appearance and gestures (even employing the dreaded adverb), and most important, to give us greater access to the narrator's interior ruminations. The story concerns a woman whose husband has gained notoriety by discovering the body of a young woman, an apparent victim of rape and murder, on the first day of a fishing trip with his friends. Rather than interrupt their trip, the men decided to tie the body to some tree roots so it wouldn't float away, then fished the next two days before hiking out to report their find to the police. The man's wife, the narrator, becomes obsessed with the dead young woman and with the thought of her husband's complicity in the crime, if not directly, then as part of a culture of male indifference toward (and tacit approval of) violence against women. Her husband protests: "Tell me what I did wrong and I'll listen! It's not fair. She was dead, wasn't she?" (160). The wife replies: "That's the point. She was dead. But don't you see? She needed your help" (161). In the later version the exposition is fuller and more clear. We are cued in earlier as to precisely what has taken place. The husband's defense of his actions is fuller, delivered with a greater sense of remorse, and more plausible, making him a more sympathetic character. At the same time, the wife's fearful musings are more fully elaborated, making her at once more sympathetic and more psychologically fragile. On a picnic near a creek with her husband, the wife imagines herself as the dead girl. The earlier version is:

> I look at the creek. I'm right in it, eyes open, face down, staring at the moss on the bottom, dead. (83)

The revised version reads:

> I look at the creek. I float toward the pond, eyes open, face down, staring at the rocks and moss on the creek bottom until I am carried into the lake where I am pushed by the breeze. Nothing will be any different. We will go on and on and on. We will go on even now, as if nothing has happened. I look at him across the picnic table with such intensity that his face drains. (166)

In the later version Carver has made both characters more complex. The husband is gentler, more sensitive to his wife's anguish, which makes his moments of bad temper and suppressed menace even more terrifying. The woman is both closer to the edge psychologically and stronger, more assertive. Just after the moment quoted above, she finds herself slapping her husband's face, the sort of expressive action not granted her in the earlier version. The story is expanded throughout: the couple's son, Dean, is given a role; a disturbing encounter between the woman and a man she meets on the road is considerably more developed. And most significantly, Carver has thrown out the botched ending of the earlier version, in which the wife returns from a trip to the dead woman's funeral to find Dean playing in the backyard and her husband in the kitchen. In the earlier version, when her husband begins to unbutton her blouse, the story ends: "'That's right,' I say, finishing the buttons myself. 'Before

Dean comes. Hurry'" (88). Because nothing in the story prepares us for this reversal in her attitude toward her husband, it is difficult to read this ending as anything other than the most puzzlingly abject gesture of surrender and self-annihilation. In the revision, which is much more in keeping with the woman's character, especially the more assertive character of the later version, the woman refuses his advance: "'Stop, stop, stop,' I say. I stamp on his toes" (176). Here, what began as a good-natured gesture of reconciliation on the husband's part turns sour, and he ends up dumping her on the floor and shouting abuse. The story ends with the situation unresolved, the wife pitying her husband yet unable to shake her fears, understanding that both of them remain in the grip of grim compulsion: "I realize he can't help it, he can't help himself either" (176). Raymond Carver described the rationale for his method in *What We Talk About* as "a theory of omission. If you can take anything out, take it out, as doing so will make the work stronger. Pare and pare and pare some more" (Stull interview 17; cit. CLC 55: 274).[11] Though all of his work retains his distinctive "shabby economy," in the stories from "Cathedral" onward, he shifted the balance from exclusion to inclusion, increasingly confident that more is more.

The later stories are, on the whole, richer, more complex, more generous in their development of character, more willing to leaven the hard loaf of characters' lives with compassion and understanding in the midst of limitation and grief. Still, one does not want to forget the pleasures of the early stories, which remind us that, in the right hands, less can be more, too. In "Bicycles, Muscles, Cigarettes," for example, a story from Carver's first collection, *Will You Please Be Quiet, Please?* (1978), Hamilton is summoned to a neighbor's house to discuss his son's possible involvement in the theft of the neighbor's son's bicycle. We sympathize with the father's awkwardness as he makes a reasonable effort both to find out the truth of the matter and to protect his son from possible false accusation. Then, in a startling and embarrassing failure of self-control, Hamilton ends up fighting on the lawn with another boy's father. As father and son walk home, we feel Hamilton's shame and frustration, his inability to explain what has just happened, and his sore knowledge, even as he tries to assure his son otherwise, that he is unable to protect his son from life's mishap and mayhem:

> "It's hard to say what people will do when they're angry," Hamilton said.
> They started up the walk to their door. His heart moved when Hamilton saw the lighted windows.
> "Let me feel your muscle," his son said.
> "Not now," Hamilton said. (24)

There is Hemingway here, to be sure (one thinks of the ending of "Indian Camp"), but Hemingway with all the heroism—even of the failed, romantic kind—drained out of it. When his father tucks him into bed that night, the boy rambles on in an expression of love and fear of loss: "I wish I'd known you when you were little. . . . It's like I miss you already if I think about it." When the boy asks his father to leave the bedroom door open, the story ends with the sort of small emblematic gesture for which Carver has a sure touch: "Hamilton left the door open, and then he thought better of it and closed it halfway" (25). The story's pathos is in the way it lays bare all a father's desires—to protect, guide, inspire, instruct—and captures that moment at which the possibilities for doing any of these diminish. They are possibilities not closed, but "closed halfway," the sort of subtle demarcation, in lives continually in flux, that Carver's best work makes.

Raymond Carver and Ann Beattie share the minimalist's resistance to conventional narrative closure, the habit of understatement, and a predilection for characters whose lives seem driven by unlucky accidents and more or less irremediable personal failings. Their characters greet their fates with a bleak resignation that in Carver's characters shades into silent stoicism punctuated by fitful and petty violence, and in Beattie's characters, who are better off economically and socially, into hip oddball humor and withering irony. Beattie has three salient talents: dialogue, the complex exposition of her characters' emotional lives, and the use of imagery as a structuring device. Each talent comes with a risk attached.

From her first novel, *Chilly Scenes of Winter* (1976), onward, Beattie has shown her ability to capture in lifelike dialogue the characteristic tone of a generation of Americans, largely upper-middle-class and college-educated, who came of age in the 1960s and whose later lives have become a loosely stitched fabric of botched relationships and careers governed largely by aimlessness and accident. Surveying her life's course, one character concludes that "what happened happened at random" (*Where You'll Find Me* 14), a view that many of Beattie's characters adopt as an appropriate summary of their experience. The risk in deploying her talent for dialogue is that in her zeal to capture the sound of her characters' speech, Beattie lets some of them go on too long. Chapter 7 of *Falling in Place* (1980) is one extended scene in which two teenage girls prepare for a party:

"How can you be so self-assured?"

"Because I look so good," Angela said. "I wouldn't go over there without any make-up, in this baggy pair of jeans, you know. Did you see the

Chemin de Fer jeans my grandmother bought me? I have to lie down to zip them up. Size seven."

"You showed me. They're really beautiful."

"So?" Angela said. "You should get a pair."

"I wouldn't look the way you do. You walk right. I don't know how to walk like that." (69)

The scene is utterly convincing, by turns funny and poignant, and too long by half. I am left with no doubt that this is the way such girls talk, and yet I do not care to read 4,000 words of such talk—divorced from direct bearing on the novel's principal dramatic action—any more than I would care to be in the same room where these words were being spoken. A similar indulgence is found in chapter 13, which features the rambling, incoherent conversation of three people stoned on marijuana (158–69). Again, the dialogue is utterly convincing, and again largely without dramatic import. At her worst, Beattie seems to be trying to see whether, if pushed far enough, banality itself can be made interesting.[12]

At her best, Beattie captures with perfect pitch the pained notes of characters who are aware of their own faults yet seem compelled to display them. The main action of *Falling in Place* concerns a family whose members specialize in tormenting one another: John, who is secretly having an affair and has moved out to live with his mother except on weekends, when he returns home to his distraught wife, Louise; their daughter, Mary, who has trouble in school and spends all her time with her tight-jeans-wearing friend Angela; and their overeating son, John Joel, who joins his sociopathic friend Parker (whose idea of fun is secretly to make a pinhole in his mother's diaphragm) in various unseemly pastimes, and who eventually shoots and seriously injures his sister with a gun that Parker supplies. In one of the novel's best scenes the entire family eats out at a restaurant. After being commanded by her parents to contribute something to the conversation, Mary asks her father how work was that week. Unable to discuss any of the things that are actually weighing on his mind—his lover, her dope-dealing friend, his alcoholic mother—he can respond only by attacking:

"Why do you always have something sarcastic to say about my going to work? Who do you think supports you? It's not that unusual to have a father who goes to work, Mary."

"Angela sleeps with people," John Joel said.

"What did you say?" Louise said.

John Joel lowered his eyes, but he said it again.

"I don't even believe this," Mary said. "Like, she's my best friend, and I'm supposed to sit here and listen to this from the ten-year-old? I don't even believe that he lies the way he does."

"Why did you say that?" John said.

"Because we were talking," John Joel said.

"You and Angela were talking?"

"No. The four of us. She said something about Angela's father, didn't she? So I just said something."

"You are so out of it," Mary said.

"Oh yeah? Parker's cousin works at the garage and he's got a car behind his shed he's restoring, and the door was unlocked, and Angela and Toddie was in there."

"*Were* in there," John said. (76)

John's correction of his son's grammar is one of those funny and sad moments that characterize Beattie's best dialogue. It speaks volumes about his character: peevish, self-concerned, distracted, grasping at trivialities in the face of a larger loss of control. Mary's referring to her brother as "the ten-year-old," John Joel's by-the-numbers approach to family conversation, Louise's stunned disbelief at her ill fortune for being part of such a family: all inform us vividly of the cruel economy within which family life becomes a private hell and show Beattie's talent for dialogue motivated from sharply yet subtly delineated characters.

Beginning with a heavy reliance on dialogue in her first novel (Beattie has said that *Chilly Scenes of Winter* [1976] was "more like a play than a novel" [Interview 7]) and her early stories (collected in *Distortions* [1976]), Beattie makes progressively greater use of exposition as her work develops. Beattie's talent for complex, incisive exposition of her characters' emotional histories gives her characters the sort of richly rendered personal past that Carver often dispenses with. Indulging this talent, Beattie risks loading down her fiction with exposition—especially risky in the short-story form—yet often the payoff is worthwhile. "In the White Night," from her collection *Where You'll Find Me* (1986), is typical in that the opening dramatic incident—a couple leaving a party on a snowy night—is quickly followed by substantial exposition of their past and their relationship with the hosts whose house they have just left. Carol and Vernon, the ones leaving, have lost their daughter to illness some time ago and still find themselves occasionally ambushed by grief. When they arrive at home, Carol hides her tears in the bathroom:

She patted the towel to her eyes again and held her breath. If she couldn't stop crying, Vernon would make love to her. When she was very sad, he sensed that his instinctive optimism wouldn't work; he became tongue-tied, and when he couldn't talk he would reach for her. Through the years, he had knocked over wineglasses shooting his hand across the table to grab hers. She had found herself suddenly hugged from behind in the bathroom; he would even follow her in there if he suspected that she was going to cry—walk in to grab her without even having bothered to knock. (16)

Many of Beattie's stories succeed on the strength of such moments, in which she so effectively conjures the intimate spaces of relationships. Given that her stories are sparsely furnished with dramatic incident, the subtle turnings that pass for endings gain their force by way of reference to the emotional histories that have been so carefully prepared earlier on. That is, whereas Carver's incidents gain resonance proleptically, through their relation to later events, Beattie's incidents resonate analeptically, through relation to the characters' past. "In the White Night" concludes with the wife leaving the bathroom to find her husband asleep on the living-room sofa. Not wanting to leave him, she stretches out to sleep on the floor beside him, musing at the oddness of the arrangement, yet accepting it as she has learned to accept so much else. The story concludes:

> In time, both of them had learned to stop passing judgment on how they coped with the inevitable sadness that set in, always unexpectedly but so real that it was met with the instant acceptance one gave to a snowfall. In the white night world outside, their daughter might be drifting past like an angel, and she would see this tableau, for the second that she hovered, as a necessary small adjustment. (17)

The reference to the snowfall returns us to the story's governing image and ties the concluding action to a past we have come to know only through expository development earlier in the story.

The use of imagery to effect this sort of closure is another hallmark of Beattie's method, which often relies on a concatenation of images, rather than action per se, to hold a story together. The risk in this method is that the story will remain a collection of fragments, as is the case with such stories as "The Big Outside World" and "Skeletons" (both in *Where You'll Find Me*), which simply don't deliver on the promises of the expository sections introducing us to the characters' lives. But elsewhere the method works well, as in "Janus," a quietly assured story unified by the enigmatic image of a ceramic bowl: "In its way, it was perfect: the world cut in half, deep and smoothly empty" (96). The bowl serves as an emblem for the deep and smoothly empty life of a woman unhappy in her marriage and lonely after being abandoned by the lover who had bought the bowl for her.

Beattie's method works brilliantly in the title story of her later collection, *What Was Mine* (1991), a story that is almost entirely exposition and coheres around two sets of images, one for each of the father figures in the narrator's life. The first consists of two photographs of the narrator's true father, who was killed during the narrator's infancy in a freak accident involving a painter falling off a ladder. The second consists of the nautical-motif decorations in a bar, created by the narrator's mother's lover, Herb, who played jazz in the bar on Saturday nights. Herb lived with the narrator and his mother during the narrator's formative years, and we come to learn that it is Herb's death that prompts the telling of the story, years after Herb and his mother split up, with the narrator now grown to adulthood. The two sets of images come together at the end, when we learn that the photographs of the true father were left to the narrator by Herb, in a packet of mementos to be delivered to the narrator upon Herb's death. With both his mother and Herb now dead, and having been advised by a girlfriend that "images would fade," the narrator resists by recalling the image of the underwater ocean scene that Herb had painted on the wall of the bar:

> Herb had painted it exactly the way it really looks. I found this out later when I went snorkeling and saw the world underwater for the first time, with all its spooky irregularities. But how tempting—how reassuring—to offer people the possibility of climbing up from deep water to the surface by moving upward on lovely white nets, gigantic ladders from which no one need ever topple. (176–77)

Having entered the underwater world of childhood memory, with all its "spooky irregularities," the image of the fishing nets that drape the wall of Herb's bar offers a way up and out of that world into the light of the present. The nets are described in terms that recall the circumstances of the narrator's true father's death, so that in the act of climbing out of his own tale and back into the moment of its telling, the narrator is assuring himself that he need not topple as his father did. With this passage the two father figures of the story are brought together in a way that speaks poignantly of the narrator's desire to strengthen a tenuous connection to the past at the same time as he forgives himself for surviving in the present. In such stories we see Beattie's skillful handling of imagery and exposition, and we also see her work developing in a promising direction: toward a more reflective voice given to a broader perspective on events, and toward characters who have learned to give up the cheap thrills of ironic banter for the more enduring satisfactions of substantive dialogue.

Just the same, when we speak of greater "perspective" in Beattie's later work, that term must be understood as a relative one, for it is a hallmark of minimalist fiction not to offer a narrative voice with knowledge or perspective very different from the characters' own. *Continental Drift* (1985) by Russell Banks provides a useful contrast by which we may distinguish this aspect of minimalist practice. Cited as a work of "trailer park realism," *Continental Drift* is often lumped together with minimalist fiction for its gritty and dispiriting depiction of the declining fortunes of a New Hampshire working-class family. The novel's main character is Bob Dubois, an oil burner repairman in a small New Hampshire town, who, dissatisfied with his constricted life, impulsively quits his job and moves with his wife and children to Florida in search of better opportunities. There, in the course of being taken in and exploited by his brother and his best friend in succession, Bob's impulsive and misdirected life follows a downward spiral to a tragic end. From its focus on characters whose lives are commonly thought of as unexceptional and insignificant, and from its willingness to look unflinchingly at the minutiae of an unraveling marriage and an increasingly squalid domestic scene, one might find much in common between this novel and works of minimalist writers such as Beattie, Carver, Mason, and Frederick Barthelme.

But from the opening lines of its "Invocation," *Continental Drift* announces its intentions to be of quite a different sort:

> It's not memory you need for telling this story, the sad story of Robert Raymond Dubois, the story that ends along the back streets and alleys of Miami, Florida, on a February morning in 1981, that begins way to the north in Catamount, New Hampshire, on a cold, snow-flecked afternoon in December 1979 ... (1)

The presence of this self-conscious, grandly posturing authorial voice immediately sets this writing apart from minimalist practice. The emphatic and precise use of dates and place-names announces an intention to root the narrative in place and time, just as the novel's title announces the global, tectonic intentions of the plot, which stages the collision of the southward-migrating Bob Dubois with the northward-moving Haitians whose progress we follow in counterpoint to that of the Dubois family. Dubois and the Haitians are meant to be seen as counterparts among the global class of the dispossessed, and that their encounter ends tragically for both parties seems the necessary consequence not only of universal human greed and desire but of historically situated political and economic forces. To a disempowered individual such as Bob Dubois, a life ruled by such forces seems a life in the grip of inexplicable impulse, as the narrator is unafraid to tell us. Just before Bob jumps into bed with his best friend's wife, the narrator explains:

> It's that he has no conscious plan, no intent—which is to say that he's got no connection between his past and his future, none in mind, that is. When one gives oneself over to forces larger than one's self, like history, say, or God, or the unconscious, it's easy to lose track of the sequence of events. One's narrative life disappears. (252)

While Dubois himself may not have this sort of perspective "in mind," the narrator is more than willing to provide it.

Such a narrator is not to be found in the fiction of Beattie, Carver, Mason, and Barthelme, whose narrators are more closely bound within the limits of the characters' consciousness and thus are unable and or unwilling to provide the historical perspective that their characters lack. Nor are they prepared to announce ambitions for their fictions such as those with which Banks ends his novel:

> Knowledge of the facts of Bob's life and death changes nothing in the world. Our celebrating his life and grieving over his death, however, will. Good cheer and mournfulness over lives other than our own, even wholly invented lives—no, especially wholly invented lives—deprive the world as it is of some of the greed it needs to continue to be itself. Sabotage and subversion, then, are this book's objectives. Go, my book, and help destroy the world as it is. (366)

This sort of moral confidence in the aims and efficacy of the novel is foreign to the work of the minimalists, whose pretensions are far more modest. In a 1983 interview, Raymond Carver said, "I don't believe for a minute in that absurd Shellyian nonsense having to do with poets as the 'unacknowledged legislators' of this world. What an idea! . . . The days are gone, if they were ever with us, when a novel or a play or a book of poems could change people's ideas about the world they live in or even about themselves" (*Paris Review* interview 220). In the same vein, Ann Beattie explains her avoidance of an editorializing narrator by saying, "I don't think I have an overall view of things to express" (Interview 8).

To those critics and readers who expect a writer to have "an overall view of things," Beattie's statement is an admission of failure: of moral vision, perhaps even of intelligence and skill. Beattie's characteristic modesty at times leads her to make admissions many writers would find embarrassing: "I write in those flat simple sentences because that's the way I think. I don't mean to do it as a technique. It might be just that I am incapable of breaking through to the complexities underlying all that sort of simple statement you find in my work" (CA 81–84: 42). At other moments, Beattie claims that her style results not simply from her own limitations but from the nature of the people and situations she writes about, which resist neat climax and denouement (CLC 63: 8). Frederick Barthelme, perhaps the most savvy of the minimalists in defending his own work, said in a 1985 interview, "I don't like being called a minimalist, which I am called I think because my characters don't get up on boxes and shout out their views of the world. This is not because they do not have views of the world, but rather that they recognize that we make views of the world the same way we make cars—we produce a great many, but they're not very reliable. So the characters shut up. This pleases me" (CA 122: 50). For Barthelme, as for the other minimalists, reticence is a virtue in a world where "big ideas" have too often proved unreliable if not outright dangerous.

What is at issue, however, in the minimalist aesthetic is not simply the complexity of perspective that the *characters* have on their world but the degree to which a narrator is able to provide perspective that the characters themselves lack. Bobbie Ann Mason has remarked that when reading fiction written in the present tense "you get the impression [the author] doesn't know any more than you do about what's happening. . . . If the author starts out in the past tense . . . then you assume he has sorted events out, he has a perspective on them. . . . I think the uncertainty of the present tense said a lot about what we were making of the late twentieth century, or were unable to make of it" (Interview; cit. CLC 82: 254). The example of *Continental Drift,* which is also written in present tense, exposes the mimetic fallacy in this remark, which assumes that the technical decision to write in present tense limits the ability to provide a narratorial perspective not restricted to the present awareness of the characters. In Banks's case, it is not only a question of the grandly rhetorical intrusions by the narrator of the sort quoted above but of a traditional narratorial perspective that operates throughout the novel, setting scenes, providing social and psychological commentary, and otherwise guiding the reader's responses to the dramatized action. Early in the novel, Bob Dubois's visit to a tavern after work occasions this comment on the social function of the neighborhood bar as an escape from the home:

In a community closed in by weather and geography, where the men work at jobs and the women work at home and raise children and there's never enough money, the men and the women tend to feel angry toward one another much of the time, especially in the evenings when the work is done and the children are sleeping and nothing seems improved over yesterday. It's an unhappy solution to the problem, that men and women should take pleasure in the absence of their mates, but here it's a necessary one, for otherwise they would beat and maim and kill one another even more than they do. (5)

It is in this register, with its compassionate yet unsentimental insight, its plain-spoken eloquence, that Banks's narrative voice is at its best. (In general, Banks is more effective when less ambitious; the more pretentious intrusions by the narrator are the weakest elements of the book. Perhaps Banks is associated with the minimalists because at his most minimal he is most memorable.) Such a voice, a staple of nineteenth-century realism, appeared in the 1980s as a refreshing oddity amid the clashing currents of endlessly ironic metafiction and stubbornly reticent minimalism, both of which exercise a thoroughgoing skepticism regarding the sort of direct ethical and historical statements Banks's narrator is willing to make.

Low Postmodernism: The Cool, Mean Style

Banks's narrative voice—confident, assertive, yet largely free of playful self-contradiction and undercutting irony—places his fiction outside of the 1980s conflict between the emergent minimalists and the dominant metafictionists. And it is within the context of this conflict that the critical attacks against minimalism during the 1980s are best understood. The critical debate over minimalism is one in which the nature of fictional representation—and with it the possibilities for historical understanding in fiction—is at stake. What few critics have recognized is the extent to which minimalist fiction is a deliberate, self-conscious response to the same cultural conditions that fuel this debate.[13] As a "low" postmodernism, the new minimalism is a countermove against the "high" postmodernism of such American writers as Thomas Pynchon, John Hawkes, John Barth, Robert Coover, William Gass, and Donald Barthelme, whose ambitiously experimental works dominated the American literary scene in the late 1960s and 1970s.

Donald Barthelme, in his essay "Not-Knowing," summarizes what detractors have said of his own work and that of the other "high" postmodernists: "that this kind of writing has turned its back on the world, is in some sense not about the world but about its own processes, that it is masturbatory, certainly chilly, that it excludes readers by design, speaks only to the already tenured, or that it does not speak at all" (13). As a response to the perceived elitism of high postmodernist language, and the formal tail-chasing of postmodern self-reflexivity, minimalists see themselves as seeking a more direct, honest apprehension of life through a self-imposed poverty of means. In a 1986 interview, Raymond Carver remarked: "As for the experimental fiction of the sixties and seventies, much of that work I have a hard time with. I think that literary experiment failed. In trying out different ways of expressing themselves, the experimental writers failed to communicate in the most fundamental and essential way. They got farther and farther away from their audience" (Stull interview; cit. CLC 55: 274). Minimalism by and large abandons the experimentalist ethic of the high postmodernist writers, rejecting linguistic flight and ontological self-questioning in favor of a willed simplicity that honors the ordinary. Minimalism, like the Puritan plain-style movement in early-seventeenth-century England and America, or the Wordsworth of "Preface to the Second Edition of the Lyrical Ballads," or the fiction of Hemingway, is a plain-style response that seeks to grab the moral and epistemological high ground with its claim to more faithful representation of the speech and experience of "ordinary" men and women.

For now, I am arguing only a rather narrow point about perception and influence, so by identifying a small group of (white male) U.S. writers as "high" postmodernists, I mean not to engage in yet another round of canonical gerrymandering but rather to identify the group of writers that the minimalists were most often and most consciously rebelling against. Though the distinction between high and low postmodernism may seem to install the sort of hierarchical relationship that poststructuralist and postmodernist theory have taught us to suspect, it nonetheless captures something essential to the self-perception of a particular group of authors to whom the minimalist label adheres. Frederick Barthelme, for one, explicitly positions his own fiction as a reaction against "the four big guys" (Hawkes, Barth, Gass, and older brother Donald). Jay McInerney describes his first encounter with Carver's "strict observation of real life . . . even if it was lived with a bottle of Heinz ketchup on the table and the television set droning" as refreshing news "at a time when academic metafiction was the regnant mode" (24). Further, the fact that minimalist fiction so often deals with ordinary, working-class and middle-class characters gives it a strongly populist flavor as a fiction "from below."[14] It should also be clear that, though minimalism deliberately occupies what in the history of aesthetics is the "low" position associated with relative formal simplicity and "ordinary" speech, this by no means detracts from the moral seriousness of its aims. On the contrary, as I have already said, the plain-style response is typically a means of claiming the moral and epistemological high ground from a "low" aesthetic position. Finally, the high/low distinction is not a totalizing scheme but represents only two possible positions within the literary-historical context of the past twenty years. We have already seen that Russell Banks employs narrative techniques eschewed by both high and low camps. Much the same could be said for John Updike. Robert Stone, whose political and "theological" concerns are addressed in a Conradian modernist mode, stands outside of the high/low distinction. Though the fiction of Toni Morrison is arguably postmodern, it would serve little purpose to assign it to either high or low postmodernism, as the distinction belongs to a debate to which her work is seemingly indifferent (nor does her work suffer for this indifference). The use of pastiche and the parodic and metafictional impulses in Ishmael Reed's novels do mark his fiction as belonging to high postmodernism, yet this in no way diminishes our need to see that in his case these formal characteristics engage an African American tradition at least as much as an Anglo-American one. The terms *high* and *low* thus do not claim all writers working today, nor do they adequately account for every aspect of the fiction of those writers whom they do distinguish.

What these terms distinguish are two available positions in a debate that goes far beyond issues of "style." In the case of minimalism, what Charles Newman in his more charitable moments might see as misguided technical assumptions are for Alan Wilde the marks of a too narrow moral vision, a failure to suggest human possibility. Wilde terms the minimalist writers "catatonic realists," whose failure of moral vision is registered in a style and tone that express "a pinched and meager resignation, a resentfully cynical acquiescence to things 'as they are' and, so it is implied, must be" (*Middle Grounds* 4–6). Wilde describes Carver's narrative voice as "invariably marked by coolness and distance, lack of comment, a scrupulous, more than Joycean, meanness of style, and a levelness of tone that add up, one senses, to a defense against desire and despair alike" (112). As though in answer to Wilde, Carver quotes Isak Dinesen, who "said that she wrote a little every day, without hope and without despair. I like that" (*Paris Review* interview 220). It would seem that to Carver the defense against desire and despair is necessary in a world where one inevitably leads to the other.

To minimalist writers and their defenders, the cool, mean style is an appropriate response both to the historical moment they find themselves in and to the perceived verbal excesses of the high postmodernists. As a deliberately crafted literary asceticism, minimalism within the American context echoes Hemingway's stylistic program, though it grows out of a decidedly postmodern ethos. Jay McInerney, one of a generation of younger writers influenced by Carver, writes that, although he at first found Carver's language "unmistakably like Hemingway's," he also found that "Carver completely dispensed with the romantic egoism that made the Hemingway idiom such an awkward model for other writers in the late 20th century" (24). Raymond Carver himself cited Hemingway as a major influence, yet his appropriation of Hemingway is mediated by the existentialist, surrealist, and absurdist writers whom he read in college. Despite James Atlas's claim that Carver's style "insists that the writer's responsibility is only to register what is true in a literal, documentary sense" (97), minimalism is far from a naive return to either the nineteenth century or the social realism of Steinbeck and Dos Passos. Whatever one thinks of her style, it would be a mistake to treat Bobbie Ann Mason, who wrote an intelligent doctoral dissertation on Nabokov's *Ada* (published as *Nabokov's Garden*), as a naive artist. On the contrary, minimalism is in its own way a highly self-conscious response to the postmodern critique of representation, one which knowingly simulates a "return" to plain style while remaining properly ironic about the discredited representational conventions on which plain style rests. Minimalism thus makes what Linda Hutcheon sees to be the typically contradictory gesture of postmodernism, which "uses and abuses, installs and then subverts, the very concepts it challenges" (*Poetics* 3).[15]

Of course the high postmodernists, too, have argued that their fiction is appropriate to the historical moment, to the unprecedented conditions of contemporary experience and the exhaustions of literary convention that seem to demand innovations in fictional form.[16] But in their polemical rhetoric, both camps are guilty at times of the mimetic fallacy in which a particular formal approach is said to have anything more than a conventional relation to the "reality" to which it claims to respond. In the debate between the high and low postmodernists, then, the brothers Donald and Frederick Barthelme sometimes talk past each other. In defending the difficulty of high postmodernist writing, Donald Barthelme writes that "however much the writer might long to be, in his work, simple, honest, and straightforward, these virtues are no longer available to him. He discovers that in being simple, honest, and straightforward, nothing much happens: he speaks the speakable, whereas what we are looking for is the as-yet-unspeakable, the as-yet-unspoken" (14). Minimalism seeks precisely to deflate the romantic pretensions behind the rhetorical trope of "speaking the unspeakable."

As we have seen in the work of Raymond Carver, minimalism accepts the unspeakability of some experience, but this acceptance, while perhaps "honest," is something other than "straightforward." As Frederick Barthelme would have it, minimalism is most misunderstood by those who are least postmodern. He argues that much of the attack on minimalism is based on a naive faith in the conventions of a literary realism that is no longer viable: "As a writer you've got to avoid the empty conventions of character and 'style,' you can't 'philosophize' in that too easy way that comes perhaps too easily to literary types, you have to sidestep the made-simple versions of political and moral issues that bad writers and good TV journalists are so fond of, you've got to use the language carefully, so that you get more than just language" ("On Being Wrong" 27). Far from "straightforward," Barthelme wants to claim for minimalist practice the self-consciousness about the conventions of representation brought about by post-modernist literary practice and poststructuralist theory. Yet with his call for "more than just language," Barthelme distances himself from those poststructuralist fabulators who prefer to see the world as text. Growing up in the shadow of the high postmodernists (literally, in Barthelme's case), part of the conversion experience for the minimalist writers of his generation was the realization "that people were more interesting than words." The minimalist project, then, wants to have it both ways, trying to rescue representation from the stifling conventions of an essentially nineteenth-century literary realism, while avoiding the perceived solipsism and "all over irony" of the high postmoderns. As a low post-modernism, minimalism situates itself between the high postmodernism of the Barth-Gass-Hawkes school and the discredited conventions of a realism that has made its way from the nineteenth-century novel into mass-market paper-backs and the daily offerings of television. Minimalism has both a high culture and a low culture opponent in what reduces to a moral polemic: minimalism accuses both Gass's formalist "World within the Word" and television's formu-laic "As the World Turns" of lacking honest engagement with the real.

Just what the terms of such an "honest" engagement might be remains a problem. Frederick Barthelme's own fiction does not always succeed in justify-ing the rhetoric mounted in its defense. His novel *Second Marriage* (1984) fea-tures a laconic main character who rarely speaks directly about the conflicts before him, choosing instead either ironic quip or silence. At one point his wife challenges him:

> "C'mon, Henry," Theo said. "Why don't you ever say what you mean?"
> "I do," I said. "I just don't mean much." (46)

That Henry may be telling the truth here is the novel's most dispiriting pros-pect. While Barthelme succeeds in keeping his characters from mouthing pre-tentious ideas, he perhaps goes too far in the other direction, choosing to show his characters at their most trivial and distracted. On any page of the novel one finds dialogue consisting of numbing banalities, snappy ironic comebacks, and a general evasion of seriousness. Occasionally a more serious issue peeks through the clutter. Here are Henry and his thirteen-year-old stepdaughter, Ra-chel, at Pie Country restaurant:

Rachel was hard at work on the menu, her finger on pie thirty, Pump-kin Cinnamon Escape. "I wish you were my father," she said.

"What do you think I am?" I reached to brush her hair, but she bumped my hand away.

"I saw this show about people going all over trying to find their real parents," she said. "I guess I'm going to have to do that someday."

"You've got a while yet." (19)

But this is as serious as the dialogue gets. Rachel does not pursue the subject, nor does the issue of Rachel's paternity ever figure significantly in the novel. The conversation switches to the observation that a certain kind of pie is no longer listed on the menu, and from there to a discussion of the waitress's per-fume. Like Beattie's dialogue, this is thoroughly credible, but one waits in vain for the characters to push through to more substantive exchange.

The narrator, Henry, and his wife, Theo, are apparently having trouble in their marriage, but Barthelme avoids writing the conventional scene between Henry and Theo that would sharpen our sense of the conflict. Nor does he pro-vide the sort of background exposition that would help us see where the con-flict came from. Events do not unfold so much as topple into the story: Theo spends several days digging a large hole in the backyard, for no discernible pur-pose; Henry's first wife, Clare, strikes up a friendship with Theo and moves in with them; Clare and Theo, who may or may not have become lovers, take a trip to Colorado, then return. Henry moves out, first to a Ramada Inn and later to his own apartment, meets a series of women, some of whom he sleeps with and some of whom he does not, all the while playing as coy with the reader as he does with his stepdaughter:

Rachel said, "So, what's your side of the story?"

"My side? Are there sides?" (93)

Rachel then explains to her friend Kelsey, who is present during this exchange: "It starts this way sometimes. He won't answer the questions. It gets better." But it never really does get much better, and we come to understand that Rachel's de-scription of her father's behavior is more hopeful than accurate. The novel's structure is largely episodic, following Henry through a series of more or less random encounters with characters either vaguely appealing or vaguely un-pleasant.[17] A brief moment in which Henry struggles to hide tears from a woman with whom he has just had a weekend assignation is perhaps the novel's one foray into conventionally rendered pathos (175–76). Having refused to provide the background that would help us understand the reasons for Henry and Theo's breakup, Barthelme likewise refuses to write the obligatory scene of reconciliation when Henry and Theo are reunited at the novel's end. Thus all that would be at the heart of such a novel, conventionally considered, is missing. Instead of a protagonist forced to confront life's changes, we have one whose ethic seems to be "muddling along. You know, handling the shit" (185).

All of this is not, at least in theory, such a bad idea. Barthelme's intent seems not to be to criticize these characters—he is not writing satire—so much as to criticize certain methods of representing character in general.[18] His fiction is a knowing attempt to undermine the conventions of (pre-postmodern) realism while at the same time providing a sort of rigorous verisimilitude not found in the work of the high postmodernists. It is a worthwhile experiment, if not an altogether successful one. What Barthelme seems to aim at is what a character in one of his short stories admires about "the kind of movie Hollywood started making in numbers about five or six years ago, in which ordinary life is made fun of and made mysterious and beautiful at the same time" (*Moon Deluxe* 74). Where Barthelme succeeds best in realizing this aim in *Second Marriage* is in his evocations of the sort of landscape that one finds everywhere in America now. In the following passage Henry stops by the soft-drink machine at the Ramada:

> A chilly wind cut through the breezeway. There was a slight industrial smell to it, greasy and pungent, just enough to taste. The concrete where I was standing was damp, stained. I heard the engines of big trucks on the highway nearby as the drivers went up through the gears. I stayed at the machine for several minutes, jingling my change and thinking about Theo, thinking of fall nights going back ten years—Theo and me in the car going to the grocery or the drugstore, on an evening just after the summer, one of those first nights of fall when the heat evaporates suddenly and you click off the air conditioner, roll down the car windows, and let the air flood in. The air has a peculiar dense fragrance then, it wraps itself around you, chills you even though it isn't cold, freshens things instantly, and the dashboard lights are magic and eerie, glowing through the white speedometer numerals, and the tires on a parked Cadillac you notice are wholesome and pretty, and the stoplight, strung above the intersection on thick, glinting cables, seems to swagger just for you. (108–9)

The writing here is reminiscent of Nicholson Baker's *The Mezzanine*, its dogged lyricism managing to endow our blighted, postindustrial, ex-urban world with a kind of quirky, luminous beauty.

Critics responding to such writing find the metaphor of the surface ready to hand. Margaret Atwood has written that Barthelme has "a many-faceted insect's eye for the surfaces of things" and that his textures "float on an underlying vacancy like mirages" (1; cit. CLC 36: 50). Ron Loewinsohn writes of *Sec-*

ond Marriage that "the book's world of surfaces remains so sterile because it is so rarely penetrated by any kind of authentic experience" (43; cit. CLC 36: 54). Frances Taliaferro has written that reading Barthelme's short stories "is like watching television with the sound turned off: the images have a flat immediacy with no history and no future except what the viewer is moved to infer" (74; cit. CLC 36: 51). This clustering of terms is familiar by now: surface, flatness, mirage, image, television, lack of historical sense. Together they belong to a critique of contemporary culture in which a particular cultural phenomenon—in this case fiction, though it could as well be public education or teen pregnancies or electoral politics—is damned by an association with mass culture that engenders superficiality, thoughtlessness, and lack of historical sense. As descriptions of Frederick Barthelme's work, these descriptions are apt as far as they go. Yet they miss something important about Barthelme's writing at its best, as in the long landscape passage just quoted. (Given Barthelme's early training as a painter, it is tempting to describe his talent as pictorial rather than narrative. For other examples, see 126, 162.) Barthelme evinces a postmodern historical sense in that he is fully aware of the loss of depth, yet refuses to see that loss as tragic. Responding to critics who complain about his use of consumer brand names in his fiction, Barthelme has said, "I suppose I think we have to make the best of what we've got, rather than lamenting what we haven't got" (CA 122: 50). The doting attention Barthelme gives to his landscapes shows him making the best out of what we have, and implies a historical attitude that calls us to attend to something new and important about our time and place.

Minimal Affect: Too Much TV or the Post-Vietnam Syndrome?

It has become a common taunt in the debates surrounding poststructuralist and postmodernist theory to accuse one's opponents and their theories of being insufficiently historical. The "post" of poststructuralism contrived to reintroduce the question of the historicity of structure, only to be accused in turn of lacking historicity by such critics on the political left as Frank Lentricchia and Terry Eagleton.[19] In recent years the debate surrounding minimalist fiction has served much the same function within the writers' community as have the debates over poststructuralist theory within the academic scholarly community. In the debates over the "historicity" of various discourses, it is rarely only history—if it is history at all—that is being discussed. The question of history in fiction becomes a counter in a larger debate over the nature of realism and representation under postmodern conditions, a debate whose terms carry considerable political freight.

Frederick Barthelme's fiction, in which characters eat at a string of fast-food restaurants and discuss brands of perfume, exemplifies the minimalist approach to a realism that accepts and uses the fact that consumer culture shapes the contemporary landscape. The first page of Bobbie Ann Mason's *In Country* contains the following words: Kents, Exxon, Chevron, Sunoco, Country Kitchen, McDonald's, Stuckey's. Sometimes derided as "brand name fiction," minimalism is accused of relying too heavily on references to mass-cultural artifacts such as these, as well as to television programs, movies, popular music, and consumer goods, as a means of providing details of setting, historical context, and characterization. Thus choice and discrimination—traditional determinants of "character," of Aristotelian *ethos*—are often exercised in decisions about what commodities to buy. The statement that "Sam has heard that Stuckey's is terrible and the Country Kitchen is good"(3) serves as a hopeful expression of what passes for worldliness in a teenage girl driving on the interstate, away from home for the first time. When Sam's Uncle Emmett says that he prefers Pertussin to Vicks Nytol because "it's good on ice cream" (73), he is declaring his individuality by subverting the prescribed use of a cough syrup. Yet this subversion, far from signifying his liberation from a commodified environment, marks the pathetic constraints within which he is able to express his idiosyncrasies. Even the choice of friends and mentors, for Aristotle a key act of self-definition, is articulated in the language of consumption: Sam admires the elegance of Anita, a potential girlfriend for Emmett, who "smelled like a store at the mall that had a perfume blower in the doorway" and whose discrimination is registered by her preference for Betty Crocker brownie mix over Duncan Hines (114, 61). The marked presence of mass culture in these texts, in which outward signs of emotion or psychological conflict—Eliot's "objective correlative"—are given as a choice between fast-food outlets or the impulsive decision to buy a ceramic cat at the mall, is seen by some critics as a renunciation both of moral seriousness and the rigors of the novelist's craft. That reliance on mass-cultural allusions makes this fiction "shallow" in its characterization and historical sense is another instance of the complaint that postmodernism sacrifices "depth" for a banal poetics of the "surface." Worse than banal, the reliance on mass culture is seen as an abandonment of the historical awareness necessary to stave off cultural decline. The attacks against "brand name fiction" thus conform to the pattern identified in Patrick Brantlinger's *Bread and Circuses,* in which the very concept of mass culture is tied to theories of social decay associated with the fall of Rome.[20]

There is no doubt that minimalism has provided us with examples of vapid prose and that the ephemera of mass culture at times provide a field of reference whose particularity seems of little significance.[21] Nonetheless, it is important to recognize the attempt that some of these writers—Mason among them—are making to explore the role of mass culture in forming our historical consciousness under postmodern conditions. It is by now beside the point to accuse minimalism of making a sort of capitulation to mass culture, allowing mass culture to provide the idiom and terms of reference within what should be the distinct province of "literary" practice. If postmodernist theory and practice have done anything to alter the relations between "high" art and mass culture, they have shown us that such calls to keep the barbarians outside the gates, if they were ever anything but deluded, are now clearly too late.[22] Whatever judgments one cares to make about the success of particular minimalist works, what should be said of minimalism at its best is that the work takes seriously the presence of mass culture as a determining feature of contemporary consciousness, and attempts to deal sympathetically with both its promise and its dangers. Minimalists have in their own way come to terms with the difficulty—perhaps impossibility—of restoring "depth" to historical consciousness under conditions in which the realm of the image seems to have engulfed reality. Accepting the loss of depth, they instead explore the function of mass culture in a historical imagination of the deep surface.

The world that minimalist fiction creates, according to Frederick Barthelme, is "not a world without, or ignorant of, history, as it's so often accused of being, but a world in which history isn't what it used to be" ("On Being Wrong" 27). If much minimalist fiction refuses historical "depth," the refusal grows out of a perception that contemporary historical conditions themselves resist representation in language that creates the illusion of depth. Such language has, according to the minimalists, become a debased currency, removed from any "gold standard" that might fix its relation to historical events. Toward the end of Bobbie Ann Mason's *In Country,* the traumatized Vietnam veteran Emmett asserts with some force: "You can't learn from the past. The main thing you learn from history is that you can't learn from history. That's what history *is*" (226). It would be too simple merely to say that the difficulty of constructing a coherent history of the Vietnam War soured for a whole generation the idea of coherent history in general, yet the war and the social upheaval at home did provide one generation with a stunning example of history's ability to confuse. Perhaps minimalism's most important contribution is in registering in a distinctive way the tone and feeling of a large part of a generation of Americans for whom the 1960s and early 1970s brought a loss of historical narrative coherence.

The following exchange from Ann Beattie's *Chilly Scenes of Winter* (1976) captures this mid-seventies sentiment:

"Everybody's so pathetic," Sam says. "What is it? Is it just the end of the sixties?"

"J.D. says it's the end of the world."

"It's not," Sam says. "But everything's such a mess." (215)

The main characters in Beattie's novel are underemployed college-educated young adults who lack the foresight required to buy groceries for more than one meal at a time. Their aimlessness and lack of will seem to grow out of their groggy realization that the world *hasn't* ended; their problem is how to conduct themselves in the wake of an apocalypse that never showed up. In Mason's short story "A New-Wave Format," the character Edwin, who drives a bus, "used to think of himself as an adventurer, but now he believes he has gone through life rather blindly, without much pain or sense of loss. . . . Edwin was in the army, but he was never sent to Vietnam, and now he feels that he has bypassed some critical stage in his life: a knowledge of terror" (217). Edwin's experience must be sharply distinguished from that of African Americans who experienced the civil rights movement, or of the wounded and traumatized veterans, or that of the people of Vietnam, Cambodia, and Laos, few of whom were spared the "knowledge of terror" that Edwin feels he has missed. The fiction of such writers as Beattie, Mason, Carver, and Barthelme registers almost exclusively the experience of those who were white, middle-class noncombatants, for whom the apocalypse that the 1960s promised never quite arrived. The much-noted listlessness and enervated humor of minimalist fiction seem to speak for those Americans for whom the Vietnam War and the turmoil of the 1960s provided the strangely attenuated experience of Armageddon-at-a-distance.

Though earlier generations have experienced the sense of being removed from history, and have registered that sense in an ironic distance within their prose, what distinguishes the generation that came of age during the 1960s and 1970s is the unprecedented influence of mass culture. Vietnam was the first television war, and it was television that paradoxically heightened the sense of history-at-a-distance by exposing noncombatants to the images of war while simultaneously marking the viewers' remove from the actual experience. For Edwin of "New-Wave Format," the salient features of his first marriage are that "Lois Ann fed him on a TV tray while he watched the war. It was like a drama series. . . . He feels terrible, remembering his wives by their food, and remembering the war as a TV series" (222).

The sense that one's history and one's own character or *ethos* are mediated by mass culture is responsible for much of the *affect* of minimalist fiction, that characteristic tone and register of feeling that has been a frequent object of critical attention (and despair). The supposed lack of affect in minimalist characters has been described variously as a "terrible blankness," a "spiritual poverty," and "sang-froid," all signs of "an unwillingness to deal with life other than obliquely."[23] Though he writes to praise Carver, Joe David Bellamy echoes the note of misery in describing Carver's characters: "beneath the surface conventionality of his salesmen, waitresses, bookkeepers, or hopeless middle-class 'occupants' lies a morass of inarticulated yearnings and unexamined horrors; repressed violence, the creeping certainty that nothing matters, perverse sexual wishes, the inadmissable evidence of inadequacy."

Responding to this sort of description, Carver replies: "Until I started reading these reviews of my work, praising me, I never felt the people I was writing about were so bad off. . . . The waitress, the bus driver, the mechanic, the hotel keeper. God, the country is filled with these people. They're good people. People doing the best they could" (Weber 48). Carver's response points to a different interpretation of minimalist affect and to the more sympathetic sort of reading that Stanley Elkin provides: "People get it wrong about minimalism. Those characters are anything but affectless. Every little thing sets off their feelings. This is a boom time in American feelings" (12). The problem for characters in minimalist fiction is not lack of affect but the lack of satisfactory historical or social referents with which to understand and express their feelings. Theirs is an alienation from history that manifests as an alienation from the *language* of history. Elkin, a self-professed "maximalist" writer whose characters are as likely to deliver full-blown arias as one-liners, puts it this way: "I'd say that their characters are just as full of themselves and bright as any of mine, they just don't talk as much."

Of course, Raymond Carver's characters do talk, often obsessively, yet not always productively and often more to us, the readers, than to each other. In Carver's story "Whoever Was Using This Bed," a sleepless couple spends the night in meandering talk that eventually circles around the issue of their own mortality. At one point the wife asks the husband to promise that, should she ever become incapacitated, he would pull the plug on her. The husband's difficulty in responding becomes a subject for reflection:

> I don't say anything right away. What am I supposed to say? They haven't written the book on this one yet. I need a minute to think. I know it won't cost me anything to tell her I'll do whatever she wants. It's just words, right? Words are easy. But there's more to it than this; she wants an honest response from me. And I don't know what I feel about it yet. I shouldn't be hasty. I can't say something without thinking about what I'm saying, about consequences, about what she's going to feel when I say it—whatever it is I say. (327)

Stalling for time, the husband as narrator provides an articulate gloss on his own inarticulateness. Frederick Barthelme has explained that his characters don't talk about their thoughts and feelings "because they've noticed that things talked about 1) are often some distance from things felt, and 2) sometimes tend to disappear in all the talk. In other words, they're skeptical about language and its use" (CA 122: 50). Bobbie Ann Mason has argued that her characters are not inarticulate but have an inbred reticence that comes from a distrust of the often empty sophistication of speech: "They don't often know what to say, but that doesn't mean they don't know words. They don't know how to approach the subject or to find the courage to say what they could say, or maybe they don't want to say it because they are stubborn" (Interview; cit. CLC 82: 252). And a character in an Ann Beattie short story says: "We're all so circumspect that now almost nothing gets said" (*Where You'll Find Me* 83).

Rather than attempt to "speak the unspeakable," Bobbie Ann Mason, like others of her minimalist peers, makes it her business to explore the shape and limits of inarticulateness, the silence and awkwardness routinely belied by the hyperromance conventions of television, where "people always had the words to express their feelings, while in real life hardly anyone ever did" (*In Country* 45). When Sam, the protagonist of *In Country*, talks with Vietnam veterans in an attempt to get some "authentic" data on the war experience, she meets with resistance: "You don't want to know all of that, Sam" (54). "You don't want to know how real it was" (95). When they do speak, it is often to repeat clichés: "A war they wouldn't *let* us win. We could have won it and you know it" (113). "The strategies were all wrong. We had the technology to win that war. No question but we *had* the technology" (135). Sam's search for history is a search for an appropriate language of history. It is in just such a search that mass culture asserts its presence. The language that these characters do speak is one in which brand names, television programs, popular songs, and video games provide the terms in which history is understood. What makes Mason's *In Country* of particular interest is that it questions the adequacy of the mass-cultural idiom while remaining sympathetic to its use.

History on TV: Through a Glass, Darkly?

The development of historical consciousness under postmodern conditions is the theme of Bobbie Ann Mason's *In Country*, which throws into high relief the problems for historical understanding raised by both the Vietnam War and mass culture. The novel's main character, Samantha Hughes, struggles to grasp the reality of the Vietnam War, which killed her father in 1966, while she was still in her mother's womb, and which traumatized her Uncle Emmett into a life of fear, joblessness, and "arrested development." Newly graduated from the high-school class of 1984, on the cusp between adolescence and adulthood, Samantha must find her way to adult truths about the war from within a subjectivity whose terms of reference are provided largely by popular music, M*A*S*H reruns, MTV, video games, fast food, and shopping at the Paducah Mall. In Country constructs both a coming-of-age plot and a search-for-the-father plot but sets them within postmodern conditions in which the progress of both plots is tied to Sam's movement through the landscape of the mass-cultural image. While mass culture provides her with her first understanding of the war, her search for the reality of what happened to her father and her uncle ultimately becomes a struggle to construct a historical consciousness that gets beyond the terms provided to her by mass culture. Her search takes her to more traditional sources of historical understanding, such as books, letters, diaries, and oral accounts. Finally, however, mass culture thwarts any effort at transcendence. Rather than arrive at some kind of "authentic" historical understanding in "depth," she learns to place mass culture in a productive if complex relation to other forms of historical understanding, all of which remain within the culture of the deep surface.

Sam's coming of age can be charted according to her relation to the mass-cultural image. In childhood, the death of Colonel Blake on M*A*S*H was "more real to her than the death of her own father" (25), and an evening news broadcast made her feel that "for the first time, Vietnam was an actual place" (51). As a teenager, her relation to mass-cultural imagery becomes more problematic, and Sam's search for the truth about her father's experience in Vietnam is continually articulated as a struggle for the "real." She tells a Vietnam veteran: "I can't believe it was really real." To which he replies: "It was real all right" (95). But just how much of that reality is available to Sam through the lens of mass culture is not clear. At times she seems to gain genuine insight, as when watching Emmett play the "Space Invaders" video game helps her imagine him firing an M-16. Sam had never understood her Uncle Emmett's habit of pausing to listen for something in the distance until she "thought of the way Radar O'Reilly on M*A*S*H could always hear the choppers coming in with wounded before anyone else could" (50). Sam and her Uncle Emmett usually watch two M*A*S*H reruns a day, and throughout the novel the program serves as a trick mirror to which Sam's understanding of the Vietnam War and the world around her is held up. Sam's breakup with her boyfriend Lonnie is articulated in terms of their differing views of the relations between television and reality. Lonnie charges that "all that stuff on TV you and Emmett watch—it's just fantasy. It's not real. It doesn't have anything to do with here" (187). Though Lonnie is perhaps rightfully suspicious of television, we come to see that his loyalty to "here" is a mark of his provinciality and inertia. Though Sam may be obsessed and misled by images of war, she is at least stimulated toward change, and part of her coming of age is in her realization that Lonnie will never leave the small-town world of Hopewell. One can say, in the hopeful phraseology of liberal education, that television has broadened Sam's horizons. This is a novel that wants to acknowledge television's progressive potential even as it explores the limits and dangers of television's power.

The hard truths that Sam does eventually learn must take their place beside the images of war she has manufactured with the aid of mass culture: "She had a morbid imagination, but it had always been like a horror movie, not something real. Now everything seemed suddenly so real it enveloped her" (206). Though mass culture provides the starting points for Sam's search, it eventually comes to signify the absence of satisfactory historical understanding. The idiom of mass culture, like the clichés of the veterans, can take her only so far. Sam's growing sophistication is registered in the awareness that "on *M*A*S*H* sometimes, things were too simple" (83). Sam becomes skeptical of the ease with which the character of Dr. Sydney Freedman gets his patients to talk about their anxieties. Though Sam wishes Emmett could unburden himself in a similar manner, "she knew very well that on TV, people always had the words to express their feelings, while in real life hardly anyone ever did. On TV, they had script writers" (45). Television appears false by a surplus of language that belies Sam's experience with the reticent and inarticulate veterans from whom she tries to extract stories about the war. Not only does Sam find TV lacking in verisimilitude, she becomes increasingly aware of its internal inconsistency. While watching a movie about Vietnam, she becomes confused by the sight of soldiers walking through what appears to be a field of corn: "She did not know if it was there because Americans had planted it—or had given the Vietnamese the seed and shown them how to plant it—or if in fact corn was ever in Vietnam, since the movie was filmed in Mexico. They certainly had corn in Mexico because corn was an Indian plant. Maize. The woman in the Mazola commercial. It bothered her that it was so hard to find out the truth" (70). Here Sam moves associatively through an intertext containing shreds of public-school curriculum and TV-commercial imagery, as she struggles to make sense of the images on the screen. The banal directness of the last sentence gains its pathos from the desperation of Sam's eighteen-year-old mind, confronted with a shabby array of historical data and fragmented interpretive codes. Accustomed to looking to television for knowledge about her world, she feels betrayed upon having television's truth-effects compromised by incoherence.

Sam attempts to supplement the history provided her by mass culture by turning to other sources, and the novel continually gestures toward reinstating depth as a solution to postmodern problems: she reads library books, talks with veterans and family members, and in a striking return to pretelevision sources of novelistic "realism," discovers first letters and then a diary that her father had written during the war. By invoking these more traditional sources of knowledge, Mason might seem to be reinforcing the valuation of mass culture held by many critics of minimalist fiction: to see the world through mass culture is to see as through a glass, darkly, and Sam's rejection of mass culture is her means of putting away childish things. But in the end these gestures toward depth remain oddly vitiated, and the relevance to contemporary conditions of traditional forms of connection to the past remains in doubt.

Despite their promise, the father's war letters prove unsatisfactory, for they are written in the standard idiom of the patriotic soldier and devoted husband who carries his wife's picture "right inside my pocket next to my heart" and writes that "I'm proud to serve my country and I'm doing the best job I can" (180). Like the veterans with whom Sam speaks, her father seems bound by a code of elision and cliché. Though questioned closely by Sam, Sam's mother provides little help: "I hardly even remember him" (167). And when Sam visits her paternal grandparents' farm both to talk with them and to see once again the place where her father grew up, her grandparents provide her mostly with more clichés on the order of those found in the letters: "he was the thoughtfulest son you could ever have" (196).

But Sam's visit to the pretelevision home of the father, the "small and predictable" world of hound dogs and fence posts, is rewarded with another pretelevision text. As a more "authentic" text, the diary at first promises to supplant the suspect text of her father's letters. Sam's grandmother, Mamaw, has shown the diary to no one in eighteen years. Mamaw does not set much store by the diary, claiming that she never read it all because of the bad handwriting. "You can have it, but I don't reckon it'll tell you anything. He just set down troop movements and weapons and things like that. It's not loving, like the letters he wrote back. Those was personal" (200). As a reader of texts, Sam clearly has different purposes and strategies than her grandmother. Where Mamaw reads love in Dwayne's letters, Sam reads superficiality and evasiveness. The diary bears out Sam's suspicion that the letters left much out; it reveals a young man who not only suffers considerable physical and emotional torment but is eager to kill:

"We got two V.C. I think one of 'em's mine, but Jim C. claimed it too. We had a big day, a big deal over whose it was. No letters. Irene seems too far away to be real. But it's all for her and the baby, or else why are we here? Joe's got 5 notches on his machetty. He's a short-timer. I'm sure I'll get one soon" (202). The same text that reveals to Sam her father's zeal for killing also shows the absence of the real to be symmetrical: if the experience of being "in country" is unreal to Sam, the "World" outside of Vietnam became equally unreal to her father. "When I get back to the World, this will be like a dream, but right now the World is a dream" (205). In leaving the World behind, her father entered a brutally primitive place where men hunt other men: "Aug. 14 Big surprise. Face to face with a V.C. and I won. Easier than I thought. But there wasn't time to think. It was so simple. At last" (204). Sam is "humiliated and disgusted" by the father revealed in the diary, even though the diary in a sense fulfills the narrative expectations she developed by reading the letters as inauthentic. She is especially shocked by what she perceives as an absence of feeling: "Her father hadn't said how he felt about killing the V.C. He just reported it, as though it were something he had to do sooner or later, like taking a test at school" (205). Of course, Sam's father actually has revealed his feelings about killing, but they are feelings Sam at first cannot accept. If Mamaw misreads the text of the diary, Sam does so differently, for her father does not suppress feeling so much as make Sam aware, by the very feeling that he does express, of what is unrepresentable in the war experience. If mass-cultural signs have come to signify for Sam the absence of "genuine" understanding of the war, the letters and diary ultimately are problematic as well. The letters and the diary together form an incoherent text, incapable of producing the truth-effects she seeks. Sam is left with no acceptable explanation for how a loving, homesick husband and expectant father can also be a man who in the press for survival has come to enjoy hunting and killing other men.

The novel's climactic gesture toward depth comes when Emmett finally breaks his silence about the war and describes the battle episode that so traumatized him. But Emmett's revelation is anticipated by television, for Sam had hoped that "Emmett was going to come out with some suppressed memories of events as dramatic as that one that caused Hawkeye to crack up in the final episode of *M*A*S*H*" (222). When Emmett finishes telling a story of considerable horror, Sam responds by comparing it to a TV movie she once saw. Emmett answers:

> "This was completely different. It really happened," he said, dragging on his cigarette. "That smell—the smell of death—was everywhere all the

time. Even when you were eating, it was like you were eating death."

"I heard somebody in that documentary we saw say that," Sam said. (223)

Not only is the form of Emmett's revelation anticipated by television, but its very language has been borrowed from a television documentary. Sam's progress away from the mass-cultural image toward some kind of authenticity thus turns back on itself, as Emmett's sincerity of feeling is compromised by the inauthenticity of his speech.

But once again, compromise is not loss: Sam does move forward in her understanding at this moment, and as a result of her investigations the world "seems more real than it has ever been" (7). She experiences her increased understanding of the past as a form of depth:

> The feeling reminds her of her aerobics instructor, Ms. Hotpants—she had some hard-to-pronounce foreign name—when they did the pelvic tilt in gym last year. A row of girls with their asses reaching for heaven. "Squeeze your butt-*ox*. Squeeze tight, girls," she would say, and they would grit their teeth and flex their butts, and hold for a count of five, and then she would say, "Now squeeze one layer deeper." That is what the new feeling is like: you know something as well as you can and then you squeeze one layer deeper and something more is there. (7)

If mass culture provides knowledge of the surface, Sam would like to think that the more traditional sources of history to which she has turned have brought her to a sense of depth. The depth is understood here in terms of the body, and the humor of this passage is the reader's, not Sam's; she takes the mysteries of her body quite seriously as another source of knowledge in depth. Sam's anxieties about war are intimately connected to those about reproduction; pregnancy, like war, is in her experience something unintended, inexplicable, even freakish. Her own conception, like that of her Aunt Donna and her mother's new child, was accidental; from Sam's point of view they all seem like mistakes. Sam has seen enough of the burdens that child-rearing places on unprepared mothers to have an extremely pragmatic, if not jaded, view: "It used to be that getting pregnant when you weren't married ruined your life because of the disgrace; now it just ruined your life, and nobody cared enough for it to be a disgrace" (103). Sam's best friend, Dawn, breaks the news of her pregnancy to Sam in K-Mart, in a conversation Sam sees as "unreal, like a scene in a movie" (81). Sam tries to persuade Dawn to have an abortion, arguing that the fetus is so small as to be "not even real hardly" (177). Once again Sam's idiom reminds us that, for her, truth is always constructed against the background of the mass-cultural image. What one wishes to exclude from one's reality, whether a fetus or an unsettling vision of war, is pushed into the realm of the image, the not real.

Sam sees her own obsession with Vietnam as "her version of Dawn's trouble" (89). In a climactic image, as she stands facing the wall of names at the Vietnam Veterans Memorial, "Sam doesn't understand what she is feeling, but it is something so strong, it is like a tornado moving in her, something massive and over-powering. It feels like giving birth to this wall" (240). If Sam has discovered depth, it is characterized both by the determinism of biological process and by the unpredictability of the moment of conception. She has arrived not at a sense of history proceeding from willed agency or otherwise intelligible causes but only at the certainty that accidents have consequences.

The novel's ending, set at the Vietnam Veterans Memorial in Washington, D.C., is one last compromised gesture toward depth and authenticity. If the turning point for Sam came with her reading the private, "feminine" forms of the letter and the diary, it is as though her feelings at the end must be validated by the traditional public discourse of the war memorial. While it is true that the Vietnam Veterans Memorial is sunken, dark, and thus "feminine" in contrast with the "big white prick" (238) of the Washington Monument, it is nonetheless, as the official site of public memory, complicit with the patriarchal institutions that were responsible for the war in the first place. It would seem as though, with the journey to Washington, Sam's historical understanding is drawn back once again into the circle of official discourse out of which her father's diary was a dangerous excursion. The ending thus frustrates one set of conventional expectations according to which Sam should achieve a greater degree of transcendence and autonomy. To me the ending completes the turn of the spiral: Sam begins as a creature of the corporate and state-produced languages of mass culture, moves toward an ironic consciousness of their limits, but finally ends up bound within them.

On the way to Washington, driving on a U.S. interstate in her first car, outside of her home state for perhaps the first time in her life, Sam remarks: "You can't get lost in the United States. I wish I could, though. I wish I could wake up and not know where I was" (6). The source of Sam's cryptic remark is a conversation with a Vietnam veteran, who offers the standard complaint that "'We should have paved the Ho Chi Minh Trail and made a four-lane interstate out of it. We could have seen where Charlie was hiding and we would have been ready for him. With an interstate, you always know where you're going.' 'The green signs tell you,' Sam said" (134). The Ho Chi Minh Trail represents a kind of freedom denied the traveler on the interstate: the freedom to get lost, to lose oneself beyond the bounds of signs, and thus gain a form of knowledge beyond the realm of the image. Driving on the interstate serves as the paradigm for life lived on the surface of mass culture; we have the illusory freedom of being able to drive anywhere the road goes while never leaving the system. The interstate lacks depth and true surprise precisely because everything is as visible and obvious as the upthrust signs of Amoco and Shell and only as unpredictable as the next innovative billboard advertisement. Sam's desire to be lost is thus a desire for a depth that can't be recovered. As we saw in the fiction of Don DeLillo, the problem with America, with living in a world of the surface, is that everything is *visible* without necessarily being intelligible. In fact, visibility is often purchased at the cost of coherence. The security of not being lost in a system of signs is a fragile one, threatened at each moment by the realization that the signs are part of a system whose history and totality are beyond our grasp.

At the war memorial, there is a moment of genuine connection as Sam touches first her father's name and then that of a soldier with the same name as hers: "SAM A HUGHES" (244).[24] Having done this, Sam looks again at Emmett, and the novel ends with the words: "He is sitting there cross-legged in front of the wall, and slowly his face bursts into a smile like flames" (245). Robert Brinkmeyer reads this moment as a "phoenix-like rebirth" (31), as Emmett's passage through pain to a new beginning. Surely it is that; but there is also the shadow of another image here: the well-known photographs of self-immolation by Buddhist monks in the streets of Saigon, published in *Life* magazine and elsewhere.[25] Mass culture once again. It is perhaps more than mere coincidence that the *M*A*S*H* television series, of which Sam and Emmett watch two or three reruns each day, contains an episode in which Corporal Klinger performs a mock version of the same suicide protest. At the moment where both novelistic convention and the particular emotional pitch of the scene lead us to expect transcendence, the final image comes to us bearing the mark of mass culture.

And yet, we are meant to believe that both Sam and Emmett do achieve some form of historical understanding and connection. The presence of mass culture in these characters' lives is not to be construed entirely as a loss. As she emerges into adulthood, Sam achieves an ironic sense of reality that, though still problematic, allows her to evaluate the contingent and local value of mass culture in relation to other forms of knowing place and time.[26] Though the novel acknowledges the insufficiency of mass culture as a way of knowing history, it refuses to install more traditional forms of historical "depth" in a hierarchical relationship with mass-cultural forms. Whatever historical texts Sam discovers must be interpolated with the texts of mass culture, and vice versa. The result is neither a historical imagination of the surface nor one of depth, but one that takes the paradoxical form of the deep surface. Refusing to establish a hierarchical order among sources of historical understanding, the historical imagination of the deep surface places the various historical discourses available to it on the same intertextual plane.

This refusal to place historical discourses in hierarchical relation marks minimalism as a postmodern genre. As a low postmodernism, minimalism shares with its polemical opponent, high postmodernism, the "incredulity toward metanarratives" that Lyotard names as the defining feature of postmodern modes of knowledge (xxiv). The historical imagination of the deep surface, in which multiple historical narratives are invoked without establishing an order of priority among them, informs such high postmodernist works as Thomas Pynchon's *Gravity's Rainbow,* Ishmael Reed's *Mumbo Jumbo,* Donald Barthelme's *Snow White,* and Don DeLillo's *Libra.* Minimalism is only one form of literary response to a profound and widely shared skepticism about the ability of historical narrative to comprehend and organize the data of contemporary experience. Yet minimalism contributes uniquely to our understanding of how this skepticism toward history is itself a product of its historical moment. Mason's *In Country* makes explicit the importance of the Vietnam War, not only to the generation of writers now in their fifties who by and large comprise the first wave of minimalists, but to all those for whom the war and the social upheaval of the 1960s brought a loss of historical narrative coherence. Further, the sympathy that minimalist writers show toward mass culture allows them to register the characteristic *feeling* of the age of MTV and shopping malls, when life becomes "lifestyle," and when history and the self can seem to be mere projections on a screen. Minimalism domesticates Lyotard's "incredulity toward metanarratives" as the working assumption of the postmodern couch potato, at home with the discontinuous flow of images on the evening news. As a postmodern plain style, minimalist fiction is at times too plain, yet it nonetheless provides as compelling a vision of the postmodern condition as any in our recent literature.

Pynchon: Enlightenment at the Movies, Revolution on the Tube

For the spy Herbert Stencil Sr. in Pynchon's *V.*, intelligence organizations seek to alter the degree to which blind physical forces shape events and determine history. But toward the end of *V.*, Stencil finds himself caught in a web of confusion in Malta, "where all history seemed simultaneously present." Though supposedly working on behalf of British intelligence, Stencil begins to doubt his purpose there, and reflects: "The Situation is always bigger than you, Sidney. It has like God its own logic and its own justification for being, and the best you can do is cope" (455). In seeking to assert control over physics, Intelligence becomes a surrogate metaphysical agency. But denied any vision of the overall shape of the Situation, the spy's existential condition is that of the individual soul pondering an inscrutable Providence. At this remove from the centers of power, human agency is indistinguishable from Divine.[1] But Stencil quickly backs off any suggestion of metaphysical or even human agency: "Don't act as if it were a conscious plot against you. . . . Any Situation takes shape from events much lower than the merely human." From metaphysics we have descended to physics, to the possibility that history is determined by the properties of matter and energy.[2] But this view, too, leads to difficulties: "The inert universe may have a quality we can call logic. But logic is a human attribute after all; so even at that it's a misnomer" (455). Here Stencil returns to the human, and to the skeptic's dilemma that, whether events are shaped from above or below, that "shape" exists only in the human mind.

In this brief passage, we see Pynchon move quickly through three fundamental theories of history in the Western tradition, three sources of verbs out of which historical narrative can be constructed. Each has its own ontology: metaphysical history depends on the realm of spirit, physical history on the realm of matter, while human history belongs to the vexed middle ground between spirit and matter, partaking of both. Pynchon's quick survey of the ontological levels and their corresponding theories of history typifies the restless movement and comprehensive sweep of his historical imagination. To Pynchon, none of the available means of explaining history is either acceptable or avoidable. We are left with the "cold comfort" of ambiguity, as Stencil concludes: "What are real are the cross-purposes" (455).

The gesture toward multiple possibilities for historical causality, along with a refusal to choose between them, is also a feature of *The Crying of Lot 49*, where Oedipa Maas struggles to distinguish between real historical process and paranoid delusion. Toward the end of that novel, Oedipa confronts the "symmetrical four" alternatives for understanding the history of Tristero and the mysterious W.A.S.T.E. postal system: Tristero really exists, and has survived as a vast conspiracy, a secret shadow America behind the real one; Tristero is a hallucination; Tristero is an elaborate hoax perpetrated by Pierce Inverarity; she is hallucinating the hoax (171). *The Crying of Lot 49* entertains the possibility that Tristero survives in America as a conspiracy of the dispossessed (*Gravity's Rainbow* will call them the Preterite), a secret network of the aggrieved beneath the surface of "ordinary" American life so dense that it has become, paradoxically, the country's true substance, like a wooden desk so worm-eaten beneath its veneer as to be mostly air. But the novel's ending suspends us between incompatible alternatives: "Another mode of meaning behind the obvious, or none. Either Oedipa in the orbiting ecstasy of a true paranoia, or a real Tristero. For there either was some Tristero beyond the appearance of the legacy America, or there was just America" (182). Pynchon's fiction continually leads both his characters and his readers into dilemmas of binary thinking that the narrative refuses to resolve. As Thomas Schaub puts it,

Pynchon's fiction thus "aspires to the condition of simultaneity, in which contradictory possibilities coexist" (4).

Such dilemmas find their value not simply in confounding the reader but in calling attention to those limiting habits of mind that reduce multiple possibilities to binary oppositions. Throughout Pynchon's fiction the habits of binary thinking, of viewing reality in terms of irreconcilable opposites, is associated with the sterile, life-denying traditions of Western rational thought. What leads both characters and readers to face such dilemmas is the way that Pynchon's fictions are structured around the problem of meaning itself. Each novel features at least one major character on a quest for knowledge (Herbert Stencil, Oedipa Maas, Tyrone Slothrop, and Prairie Wheeler), and, as many Pynchon critics have noted, in each case the reader's quest to order the meanings of the text in some way parallels the quest of the characters.[3] Thomas Schaub has discussed how both readers and characters must confront the problem that any attempt to impose meaning and order on experience involves us in sterile abstraction. Coherent structures of thought are necessarily removed from the very life experience they would help us understand. On the other hand, remaining in experience, in the flow of time, leaves us lost in a meaningless succession of distinct events (Schaub 92). The effort to connect events in some timeless order finds its extreme expression in paranoia, "the discovery that *everything is connected*" (GR 703, italics in original). Its opposite is what Pynchon's narrator calls "anti-paranoia, where nothing is connected to anything, a condition not many of us can bear for long" (GR 434). If Pynchon's characters are caught between these extremes, so is the reader. As Steven Weisenburger writes, *Gravity's Rainbow* "combines the elegance of a preordained structure and the unintelligibility of pure coincidence. Does it see history as plotted or accidental? Is the rocket descending on the last page the symbol of divinely prefigured salvation or the triumph of an absolute violence? *Gravity's Rainbow* will not say" (11). Schaub argues that Pynchon's texts "establish for the reader an intentional and strict uncertainty" (4).[4]

But *Gravity's Rainbow* also parodies the habit of thought that wants to reduce all possibilities to irreconcilable opposites. Molly Hite has argued that Pynchon holds up the form vs. chaos dichotomy in order to show its inadequacy: "By allowing each of his novels to entertain the polarized theses that the world is either a rigid, preordained order or else a concatenation of random, unrelated details, Pynchon dramatizes the vacuity of conceiving of experience as plotted and of meaning as resulting only from a culminating synthesis" (20). The novel form itself is an example of what Hite calls an "included middle," a form that makes connections "without achieving abstract intellectual closure" (21). The paranoiac's quest for an all-encompassing order must necessarily fail, and instead the novel embodies the absence of insight "as a plenitude of failed revelations" (31).

The question remains what sort of historical understanding emerges from this plenitude of failed revelations. The narrative gesture that suspends us between alternative histories reaches its fullest elaboration in *Gravity's Rainbow*, where Pynchon rewrites the history of World War II and in so doing rewrites the history of modernity itself. In Pynchon's vision, Empire, Lust, Entropy, the Death Wish, Technology, and Control by the spirit world all provide alternative and competing sets of imperatives for the shape of that history. The problem for historical understanding is not only that history is overdetermined by this plurality of imperatives but also that each one is in itself inscrutable. In Pynchon's hands, each is fundamentally irrational or, what amounts epistemologically to the same thing, possesses a logic beyond our grasp. In the preceding chapter we saw how Bobbie Ann Mason's *In Country* constructs a deep surface by refusing to establish a hierarchy among alternative sources of historical understanding. *Gravity's Rainbow* extends this formal skepticism to another level of inquiry, for what is in question are not simply sources of information about the past but entire narratives, entire systems of historical explanation. In *Gravity's Rainbow* such systems of explanation are rendered in fragments, with the narrative refusing to value one historical determinism above another. The result is a deep surface that moves restlessly among alternative "depth" models of historical explanation, simultaneously invoking and undercutting competing forms of historical analysis.

The deep-surface history that Pynchon writes is coherent only at the most general level: in *Gravity's Rainbow*, and throughout his career, he has chronicled Western civilization's self-destruction, victim of its own dark urges and ravaged by the very forces that have driven its development. He has also, if more fleetingly, offered glimpses of the possibilities for redemption, whether in the form of an organized Counterforce opposed to the forces of oppression, in individual acts of selfless generosity, or simply in the playful, disruptive, and comic energy of his prose. But at the level of particular historical events, whether the development of the V-2 rocket or the failure of the radical movements of the 1960s, Pynchon typically refuses explanation as such in favor of the multiplication of possibilities and exploration of the problem of historical understanding itself. The resulting deep surface involves the reader intimately in the process of historical sense-making. It is an involvement by turns exhilarating and harrowing, as one alternates between the thrill of discovered connections and the shudder of paranoia, developing a historical sense enriched by possibility but not constrained by definitive assertion.

Seasoned readers of Pynchon criticism will find that in what follows I have not attempted to stake out new ground (a daunting task given the highly competitive industry that Pynchon criticism has become) so much as to refocus familiar questions more tightly on the issues of film, video, and the historical imagination.[5] We will see that in *Gravity's Rainbow* and *Vineland* film and video are central to Pynchon's construction of history as well as to his exploration of the problems of historical understanding itself. For Pynchon, as for all of the authors discussed in this study, the technologies of film and video not only are influential developments in themselves deserving of a historian's attention but have come unavoidably to mediate our understanding of the recent past. *Gravity's Rainbow* (1973) looks back twenty-five years at World War II from the vantage point of the Nixon era, a retrospective gaze mediated largely by film. *Vineland* (1990) looks back twenty years at the Nixon era from the vantage point of the Reagan-Bush era. Having leap-frogged from one historical perspective to the next, Pynchon lands squarely in the video generation and investigates the historical consciousness of a generation raised on the Tube.[6]

In *Gravity's Rainbow*, film provides a central metaphor for Pynchon's exploration of the problems of historical causality and explanation. Film stands in paradoxical relation to both history and the self: it represents abstract instrumental reason and the principle of cause and effect; it also represents the breakdown of the dualistic model of selfhood on which such reason and causality are based. In *Vineland*, the abandonment of dualistic assumptions seems to be taken for granted. Film and video have so thoroughly saturated the psyches of many of the characters that mass-cultural images have come to be the primary means by which history and the self are constructed. In such a world, Wallace Stevens's modernist view of "the imagination pressing back against the pressure of reality" seems quaintly obsolete. *Vineland* presents the possibility that the construction of both "imagination" and "reality," of both "within" and "without," is governed equally by the imperatives of the Tube. I say *Vineland* presents this as a "possibility" only, for it is typical of Pynchon's historical imagination to gesture self-consciously toward but finally suspend judgment on any ultimate historical causality.[7]

Pynchon's impulses, like those of Don DeLillo, are simultaneously toward both analysis and mystification. *Vineland*'s analysis is of the operations of a repressive state security apparatus during both the Nixon and Reagan administrations. The novel also indicts the 1960s youth generation as collaborators in their own repression, victims of their own "unacknowledged desires" for order and their "need only to stay children forever" (269). The mystification comes at those moments when the novel suggests that history and the self are the product of mass-cultural images that operate essentially without origin or coherent agency behind them. Mystification summons paranoia at the moment when Pynchon, like DeLillo, would caution us that by accepting either of these formulations—that history is run by the State or by the Tube—we may blind ourselves to "higher" or "deeper" levels of causality that may be running the show. Both *Gravity's Rainbow* and *Vineland* offer rich investigations of the problems of the self, historical causality, and historical understanding. But both novels also leave us at the impasse that much of postmodernist thought has come to: having completed the project, begun in certain strains of modernism, of dismantling a concept of causality based upon the sovereign self, postmodernism is left unable to reconceptualize agency and causality in anything but negative terms. In the end *Vineland* leaves us wondering what forms of resistance, if any, are possible in a world in which power is at the same time everywhere and nowhere, directing our lives from the sanctuary of no known address.[8]

Film and the Discontinuous Self:
Enlightenment Problems Revisited

In a novel so richly allusive, so encyclopedic in its sources, and so dense in its symbolic structures, it is difficult to make a case for the centrality of any one source of symbolic, figurative, or thematic material in *Gravity's Rainbow*, unless it is of course the rocket itself, whose parabolic trajectory provides the novel's title. And yet film holds a special place in this novel, which at its ending purports to be a movie itself, leaving us in a darkened theater among "old fans who've always been at the movies (haven't we?)" an instant before the descending rocket crashes through the roof. Charles Clerc has written that it is "quite possible to take the novel itself as a film, an episodic World War II movie showing definite leanings toward the genre of musical comedy" (112). The assertion that "we've always been at the movies" suggests the way in which, for anyone Pynchon's age or younger (he was born in 1937), World War II exists almost entirely through the medium of movies, newsreels, and documentaries.[9] The novel is saturated with references to film (just as the later *Vineland* is saturated with references to television), making an awareness of film an inextricable part of the experience of reading the text. As McHoul and Wills put it, "some sort of reference to cinema underwrites much of what happens in *Gravity's Rainbow*, so much so that one could well ask whether narrative prose is still possible without such reference" (42). Pynchon takes a particular interest in German expressionist film of the 1920s and 1930s. His fictional characters include the filmmaker Gerhardt von Göll, "once an intimate and still the equal of Lang, Pabst, Lubitsch," and Greta Erdmann, one of von Göll's principal actresses.[10] Not only is film present in the novel through characters such as von Göll and Erdmann, but it is also linked metaphorically to certain paradoxical features of Enlightenment rationality. As a rationalized technique for abstracting representations from reality, film would seem to reinforce the Cartesian subject-object separation fundamental to instrumental reason. However, by showing an ability to colonize the psyche and insert its images into reality, the film medium blurs subject-object distinctions, putting in question the Cartesian dualism on which Enlightenment rationality and techniques of abstraction are based. Film becomes one way in which Pynchon challenges the "fictions" of causality and the human subject, and thus undermines the Enlightenment ideal of a "humanized history endowed with reason."

But Pynchon's project is not entirely negative. The breakdown of dualistic modes of thinking, and of a dependence on cause and effect, opens the way toward new, more holistic modes of cognition. The field concepts of modern physics, as N. Katherine Hayles has shown, provide Pynchon with one means of conceptualizing reality and history beyond the dualisms of subject-object and cause-effect (Hayles 168–97). If physics provides the theory for such transcendence, film in Pynchon's novel provides one form of practice, for there are moments when film becomes the medium through which the barriers set up by dualistic thinking are breached. Just the same, the attempt to abolish dualism meets many difficulties, and the implications of film's challenge to Enlightenment epistemology are as disturbing as they are hopeful.

To begin with, though film has the potential to liberate by challenging subject-object distinctions, this same power can be used as merely another technique for mastery. The "dreams of flight" that the socialist, feminist Leni Pökler sees in German expressionist film are perverted to "pornographies of flight" in the mind of her husband, the rocket engineer at work on machines of death. Von Göll's career as a filmmaker, in which his images seemingly have the power to enter reality, is marked by exploitation and violence. But more fundamentally, in the world of *Gravity's Rainbow* it is never clear if one has escaped one confining dualism only to remain trapped within another larger and more powerful one. To celebrate escape may be only to advertise one's ignorance; claims of liberation may be only a sign of political naïveté. The loss of the distinction between subject and object may only disable the historical imagination and make one susceptible to further exploitation. Whatever utopian moments the novel generates seem always to be drawn back to earth under the gravitational pull of one or another historical determinism, and the novel leaves us suspended between hope and despair. The novel's final image, in which a crowded movie theater is about to be struck by a nuclear warhead, suggests that film, even if not an instrument of oppression and false consciousness, may be only a way to keep us laughing until the bomb hits.

A fundamental problem posed by film is to what extent the film medium by its very nature falsifies reality in representing it. There is in Pynchon's novel a version of the position that "the medium is the message" and necessarily imposes its own conditions upon knowledge.[11] As an abstraction from experience, the film image necessarily removes us from experience even as it gives us the illusion of connection. But Pynchon gives the familiar problem of mediation considerable resonance by linking the abstractions of the film medium to the abstractions of rational thought in general and calculus in particular. Pynchon's narrator says that film and calculus are "both pornographies of flight," in which the continuity of movement is broken up into the discrete frames of film, or the incremental delta-x and delta-y of calculus (567). Film and calculus come together when the German rocket scientists make films of their missiles in flight and then analyze them frame by frame. "There has been this strange connection between the German mind and the rapid flashing of successive stills to counterfeit movement, for at least two centuries—since Leibniz, in the process of inventing calculus, used the same approach to break up trajectories of cannonballs through the air" (407). Pynchon connects film, calculus, and the technologies of death, be they Leibniz's cannonballs or von Braun's missiles. Schaub has written that "film is allied therefore with other types of spurious continuity in Pynchon's writing, and is exemplary of an analytic consciousness in the West" (46). Film and calculus are linked by a technique that substitutes discrete elements for a continuous whole—an abstraction from experience that, when extended metaphorically to stand for a general habit of mind, enables the modern machinery of violence and death.

Despite or perhaps because of the techniques of abstraction and analysis that have shaped so much of our world since the Enlightenment, the mind continues to yearn for continuity, longs for unmediated contact with the real. Leibniz himself elevated continuity to what amounted to an a priori principle, expressed by his famous dictum that "nature does not make leaps." For Leibniz, history must be continuous in order to be intelligible: "To my mind everything is interconnected in the universe by virtue of metaphysical reasons so that *the present is always pregnant with the future,* and no given state is explicable naturally without reference to its immediately preceding state" (185). To Pynchon's narrator, longing for continuity, the stair-step shapes of range and height into which the missile's trajectory is broken by calculus are "reminders of impotence and abstraction" (567). The desire for wholeness and continuity would seem to be driven by a generative principle in Enlightenment thought, a desire to overcome the "impotence" of abstracted thought processes and discontinuous means of representation and achieve the "pregnancy" of historical continuity. Whereas Leibniz relied on "metaphysical reasons," finding continuity and connectedness inherent in the idea of a supreme Being, Pynchon's narrator requires a more earthly principle: hence the need for "pornographies of flight," which stimulate one's desire to make of the increments of calculus a continuous curve, and to see in the "rapid flashing of successive stills" a seamless reality.

The technology of film, then, represents for Pynchon a condition of knowledge that has been with us since the Enlightenment. The fall into this condition, into the separation of subject and object, cause and effect, and into the sterility of abstract analytic thought generally, is the West's original sin.[12] Accordingly, the persistence of vision—the physiological phenomenon that explains our ability to see film as continuous—becomes the physical analogue of our longing for lost innocence, of our desire for continuity and unmediated experience. Franz Pökler, whose daughter was taken from him when a small child and is returned to him for brief annual visits at the whim of the SS, is "given proof that these techniques had been extended past images on film, to human lives" (407). Pökler suspects that the Nazis are in fact giving him a different "daughter" each year for their rendezvous at Zwolfkinder, a children's amusement park, and it is only his desire for genuine reunion that allows him to believe, even provisionally, that it is the same Ilse each time:

> So it has gone for the six years since. A daughter a year, each one about a year older, each time taking up nearly from scratch. The only continuity has been her name, and Zwolfkinder, and Pökler's love—love something like the persistence of vision, for They have used it to create for him the moving image of a daughter, flashing him only these summertime frames of her, leaving it to him to build the illusion of a single child. . . . What would the time scale matter, a 24th of a second or a year? (422)

Here the film metaphor works brilliantly to explore the relationship between illusion and desire, and in the process goes to the heart of Enlightenment anxieties about the problem of personal identity.

Recall that just as Leibniz and Newton's calculus broke up motion into discrete elements, so the emerging "empiricist" epistemology of the time broke up experience into a "succession of perceptions." For David Hume, this way of thinking led to serious difficulties in discovering any sound basis for the idea of the stable, continuous identity. In his *Treatise,* Hume argues that among the succession of discrete perceptions that makes up our experience, we never perceive a "self" that is independent of some particular thing that the self is perceiving: "I never can catch *myself* at any time without a perception, and never can observe anything but the perception" (252).[13] Once experience has been broken down into discrete bits, the problem becomes how to put them back together again. Experience, under Hume's skeptical empiricism, suffers the fate of Humpty-Dumpty. For Hume, it is only memory that, like persistence of vision, holds together the disconnected bits of experience to give us the illusion of continuity.[14] The actual existence of a stable, continuous "self" is neither supported by reason nor confirmed by experience and is rather a convenient fiction enabled by memory and sustained by force of habit.

In his own work on Enlightenment thought, Michel Foucault recognized the connection between the desire for continuous history and the anxiety about personal identity, arguing that the construction of the unitary subject provided a site for the construction of continuous and unified history:

> Continuous history is the indispensable correlative of the founding function of the subject: the guarantee that everything that has eluded him may be restored to him; the certainty that time will disperse nothing without restoring it in a reconstituted unity; the promise that one day the subject—in the form of historical consciousness—will once again be able to appropriate, to bring back under his sway, all those things that are kept at a distance by difference, and find in them what might be called his abode. Making historical analysis the discourse of the continuous and making human consciousness the original subject of all historical development and all action are two sides of the same system of thought. (*Archaeology* 12)

Because it belongs to the same system of thought, the idea of continuous history is vulnerable to the same skeptical demolition as the concept of personal identity. Pynchon links the problem of the self to the problem of history in the following passage from *V.*, part of the "Confessions of Fausto Maijstral." Here Maijstral tries to justify writing an apologia for a life that is not yet complete:

> We can justify any apologia simply by calling life a successive rejection of personalities. No apologia is any more than a romance—half a fiction—in which all the successive identities taken on and rejected by the writer as a function of linear time are treated as separate characters. The writing itself even constitutes another rejection, another "character" added to the past. So we do sell our souls: paying them away to history in little installments. It isn't so much to pay for eyes clear enough to see past the fiction of continuity, the fiction of cause and effect, the fiction of a humanized history endowed with "reason." (286)

Here the rejection of the continuous personal identity is linked to the rejection of cause and effect and the Enlightenment ideal of history. Fausto, with a nod to his namesake, sells his soul to history for a chance to live and write in the present, aware that his narrative method depends upon a specious continuity and causality. Self-consciousness both enables writing and undermines the solidity of self and history.

Thus, while Fausto claims "to see past" the Enlightenment fictions of history and the self, he cannot escape fiction entirely. Fausto's self-representation as a series of discrete "personalities" remains "half a fiction," suggesting that such a representation occupies—like film with its series of discrete images—a mediate position between illusion and the real. To speak, to write, to remain cognitively conscious, requires some acceptance of discontinuity, a willingness to form synchronic structures that unavoidably belie their own rootedness in history and change. To reject discontinuity altogether would be to fall on the other horn of the dilemma, for the purely diachronic produces its own form of paralysis: to remain in pure continuity, pure flow, would make writing and representation impossible. Any representation of history or the self requires us to operate somewhere between the extremes of continuity and discontinuity that lie at opposite, equally ineffable ends of the spectrum of our experience.[15] Both ends mark the border of a mode of experience it is traditionally the task of mysticism to enter and describe.

It is this mode of experience, beyond spatiotemporal limits, that Slothrop enters in the fourth part of *Gravity's Rainbow.* Slothrop's "scattering" takes Fausto's "successive rejection of personalities" to extremes, to the point where Slothrop has difficulty remembering what has happened to him from one moment to the next. Slothrop has been snipped into separate frames of film: "Past Slothrops, say averaging one a day, ten thousand of them, some more powerful than others, had been going over every sundown to the furious host" (624). If film produces the illusion of continuity out of what are actually discrete frames, it is as though Slothrop finally leaves the realm of illusion to exist wholly in one frame at a time. In our final glimpse of him, Slothrop recalls a time, now lost to him, in which he could construct a coherent history out of the ephemera of experience: "rusted beer cans, rubbers yellow with preterite seed, Kleenex wadded to brain shapes hiding preterite snot, preterite tears, newspapers, broken glass, pieces of automobile, days when in superstition and fright he could *make it all fit,* seeing clearly in each an entry in a record, a history: his own, his winter's, his country's" (626). Slothrop has escaped the falsifications of history that are motivated by "superstition and fright," but has done so at the cost of both the stability of self and the coherence of history. But Slothrop has also, paradoxically, "in ways deeper than he can explain," moved *beyond* the fiction of continuous history to a more fundamental connectedness. Our final image of him, "crying, not a thing in his head, just feeling natural," conveys a sense of both freedom and connectedness that causes George Levine to describe this moment as "an enactment of the anarchic visionary ideal" (135), and N. Katherine Hayles to claim that "Slothrop has arrived at a transcendent realization of the essential connectedness of all things" (187). This range of critical reaction supports the notion that anarchy and connectedness, discontinuity and continuity, meet at their extremes. Readers have often commented on the ambiguity of Slothrop's fate: his transcendence is also his inability to affect anything in the physical world; his scattering is a fructifying act, recalling the ritual dismemberment of vegetative gods and possibly calling forth the redemptive action of the Counterforce, but is also a painful rending of self.[16] *Gravity's Rainbow* makes clear that the Cartesian *cogito* is refuge as well as confinement, and whatever the benefits of abandoning the continuous self and the dualistic conception of subject and object, they are not without costs.

David Hume was apparently troubled enough by the issue of personal identity to leave it out altogether when he came to rework his ideas in the later *Enquiries*. But Pynchon's postmodern skepticism is more than simply Hume revisited. Despite doubts and difficulties, skepticism never very long disturbs Hume's neoclassical equanimity. It must be remembered that in Hume's view the skeptical demolition of reason was so much brush-clearing before he could establish moral philosophy on what was to him the solid ground of *sentiment*. Rather than reject the customary fictions about continuity, cause and effect, and personal identity, Hume finds his way to an *embrace* of custom, however conflicted and problematic that embrace may be. Left without reason as the basis of knowledge, in Hume's view we must make do with custom as "the great guide of human life" (*Enquiry* 44). To Pynchon, perhaps this would seem the classic conservative response, an insufferable embrace of the status quo. Pynchon uses the film medium metaphorically as one way to deconstruct the key Enlightenment fictions of continuity, cause and effect, and the human subject. But rather than avoid the consequences of this deconstruction, he has Slothrop act them out; in the process, the novel unravels both its protagonist and its own narrative conventions.

Beyond Dualism: What Price Freedom?

The ambiguous value of Slothrop's "transcendence" should caution us against easy optimism about the liberating possibility of overcoming dualistic thinking. Nonetheless, such a liberation remains the utopian possibility within

Gravity's Rainbow. N. Katherine Hayles has shown how the field concepts of modern physics have provided Pynchon with a way of escaping the dualistic models for conceiving reality: "From a field perspective, interfaces are not barriers, but points of exchange, surfaces through which two orders of being can interpenetrate. This raises the possibility of a holistic field that transcends and includes the interface" (181). Hayles applies the field concept to Pynchon's treatment of film, which in its challenge to the distinction between image and reality provides an example of "how an interface might become a permeable membrane." But what is too little commented upon is how these transgressions of the boundary between film image and reality, far from tending toward a holistic vision of connectedness, typically involve exploitation and misogynist violence.[17]

In discussing the interplay of image and reality, the example most often commented on by critics is that of Greta Erdmann, whose rape by several men for the filming of a scene in von Göll's film *Alpdrücken* results in the conception of a real child, Bianca. The consequences of the film scene extend also to the lives of the men who watch it and go home to father children themselves. This is the case of the young rocket engineer Franz Pökler, who "had come out of the Ufa theater on the Friedrichstrasse that night with an erection, thinking like everybody else only about getting home, fucking somebody, fucking her into some submission. . . . God, Erdmann was beautiful. How many other men, shuffling out again into depression Berlin, carried the same image back from *Alpdrücken* to some drab fat excuse for a bride? How many shadow-children would be fathered on Erdmann that night?" (397). Franz does get his wife, Leni, pregnant, producing Ilse, the "shadow child" who will later be transformed by the SS into a "film" shot in frames one year apart. The image/reality boundary is transgressed once more in the passage immediately preceding the one that describes Franz leaving the theater: a dozen years after the filming, Slothrop and Erdmann explore the abandoned film studio and reenact the sadomasochistic sexual episode on the film's original set. While this sequence of events suggests that the distinction between image and reality can be difficult to maintain, it would also seem that von Göll's transgressions only lead to further transgressions and that the image/reality interface becomes a site not of connection but of mastery and exploitation.

With von Göll's career, Pynchon suggests that when film most powerfully challenges the binary oppositions of subject/object and image/reality, it is also most manipulative and morally problematic. As a master black-marketeer under the alias Der Springer, von Göll is willing to buy and sell anything within the anarchic Zone of occupied Europe; as a filmmaker, his skill, his vision, and his politics are for sale. Art and commerce are mutually sustaining for von Göll, who finances his own films with his black-market profits: "Commerce has not taken away von Göll's Touch: these days it has grown more sensitive than ever" (112). Von Göll is too much of a businessman to make any claim to artistic autonomy; on the contrary, he gains a sort of power out of his very dependence on the larger systems of connection that proliferate throughout the world that the novel creates. The key to power is not freedom from connection, but the ability to see the nature of one's connectedness in order to dance with it: "Everything fits. One *sees* how it fits, ja? learns patterns, adjusts to rhythms, one day you are no longer an actor, but free now, over on the other side of the camera. No dramatic call to the front office—just waking up one day, and knowing that Queen, Bishop, and King are only splendid cripples, and pawns, even those that reach the final row, are condemned to creep in two dimensions, and no Tower will ever rise or descend—no: *flight has been given only to the Springer!*" (494). As Der Springer, von Göll becomes a comic-book hero equipped with the chess knight's power of flight. "He is the knight who leaps perpetually [...] across the chessboard of the Zone [...] He could be anyplace. He is everywhere" (376). Though he considers himself one of the Elite, von Göll's ability to act effectively depends on his ability to perceive his connection to the earthbound preterite: "Remember, we define each other. Elite and preterite, we move through a cosmic design of darkness and light, and in all humility, I am one of the very few who can comprehend it *in toto*" (495).[18]

Von Göll's view of the filmmaker's position contrasts with that of another filmmaker in the novel: Dr. Pointsman. Shot by a "secret cameraman" operating upon Pointsman's instructions, the film of Katje Borgesius is made without her knowledge using a hidden camera (92). In one of the novel's more antic plots, the film is used to condition the octopus Grigori in order to set up the incident on the Riviera in which the octopus attacks Katje. When Slothrop witnesses the attack and rescues Katje, he is brought under Pointsman's control. As a Pavlovian, Pointsman requires the strict separation between subject and object necessary to his model of conditioning and control. In contrast with von Göll, Pointsman would reject any notion of connection with the actors on the other side of the camera. He does not shoot the film himself, and Katje is unaware of the camera, rendered purely an object of sight. Thus neither the consciousness of the "subject" (Pointsman) nor of the "object" (Katje) is directly involved in the film's creation. For Pointsman, the objects of his experiments are to be understood as pure mechanism, utterly distinct from his own subjective consciousness. In the end result, however, Pointsman's methods are no more manipulative than von Göll's. Von Göll's challenges to subject/object and image/reality distinctions are doubly vexed. First, even to the extent that von Göll *is* a free agent, we have seen that he is prone to using that agency for malevolent purposes, exploiting the very We/They distinction into which he claims special insight. For all of von Göll's insight into the nature of connectedness, the inseparability of Elect and Preterite, subject and object, von Göll's career remains one of hypocrisy, manipulation, and violence. Second, and more important, Pynchon leads us to wonder whether *any* appearance of free agency is illusion. No claim of privileged insight, including von Göll's, goes unchallenged in *Gravity's Rainbow*. Pynchon's narrator calls von Göll's vision of his own powers an "ecstasy of megalomania," and it becomes clear, as we shall see, that von Göll's power to affect history may be circumscribed within a number of other historical determinisms whose precise influence and extent is unknowable.

It remains an open question, therefore, whether the escape from dualism is a good thing. Once again, the positive and negative valuations of mass culture that we have seen throughout the postmodern fictions studied here are, in *Gravity's Rainbow*, so closely intertwined as to be inseparable. Were we inclined to celebrate a triumph over dualistic thinking enabled by film's transgression of the boundary between image and reality, the novel's ending, at the very least, should give us pause. Captain Blicero's 00000 rocket containing the human sacrifice of Gottfried arcs across history to land in 1970 on a crowded movie theater in Los Angeles. If the rocket represents the apotheosis of instrumental reason, the death-bound conclusion of the rational separation between subject and object, then in this final scene the Enlightenment goes to the Movies. The ending would seem to suggest, on the most obvious level, that film's manipulations may serve only to distract us from more important historical forces at work. The rocket striking the theater seems a final assertion of a material reality outside the realm of the image. But the rocket's arrival is also the completion of a circuit, the end result of Leibniz's play with images of the cannonball's flight. The rocket may not be a messenger from beyond the realm of the image but rather the child of that realm returning, the final consequence of the rationality that made film possible. The Enlightenment hopes for a progressive, "humanized history endowed with reason" are thus bent earthward as reason returns to its own destruction.

Film and Historical Causality

Having seen how Pynchon uses film to revisit certain Enlightenment problems of subjectivity, and to challenge the related distinction between image and reality, we return to the question of how these explorations bear on the problem of historical causality. One of the ways in which Pynchon constructs a "deep surface" is by continually providing alternate historical frames, alternate meta-narrative perspectives, from which to make a given set of events intelligible. A cogent example is found in the events surrounding the propaganda film made by von Göll as part of Operation Black Wing. To say that one frame of reference for understanding these events is "larger" than the one we might initially have perceived is to use a spatial metaphor whose hierarchical nature the novel ultimately rejects. Rather, we are given a plurality of perspectives from which to make history intelligible, ranged in the paradoxical shape of the deep surface.

The secret British propaganda project named Operation Black Wing aims to exploit the racial fears of the German population by forging a film pretending to document the existence of African troops within the German SS, manning the German V-2 rocket sites. The cast consists of some of Pointsman's crew at "the White Visitation" done up "in plausible blackface," plus one Zouave tribesman, on loan from his French army unit fighting in North Africa. Von Göll captures on film "all that the German might find sinister in his blackness" and, "with a straight face, proclaims it to be his greatest work" (112–13). The film is to be smuggled into Holland and planted in the remains of a counterfeit rocket firing site, to be "discovered" and publicized by members of the Dutch resistance. No one making the film could have anticipated that the fictional "Schwarzkommando," as the Operation Black Wing people dubbed them, would turn out apparently to have real-life counterparts in the Southwest African Herero tribesmen that the Nazis had employed at their rocket installations. With the discovery of the Herero in Germany, it would appear that reality had made an end run around the manipulations of the propaganda effort. But later in the novel, von Göll interprets this development as showing that his images have the power to become reality.

> Since discovering that Schwarzkommando are really in the Zone, leading real, paracinematic lives that have nothing to do with him or the phony Schwarzkommando footage he shot last winter in England for Operation Black Wing, Springer has been zooming around in a controlled ecstasy of megalomania. He is convinced that his film has somehow brought them into being. "It is my mission," he announces to Squalidozzi, with the profound humility that only a German movie director can summon, "to sow in the Zone seeds of reality. The historical moment demands this, and I can only be its servant. My images, somehow, have been chosen for incarnation." (388)

Choosing to believe that his films have become a genuine historical force by their power to insert images into reality, he engages with Squalidozzi, one of a group of exiled Argentine anarchists, to make a film version of *Martin Fiero,* a poem that tells of a gaucho rebellion against the centralizing powers of the developing Argentine national government. "What I can do for the Schwarzkommando," he tells Squalidozzi, "I can do for your dream of pampas and sky" (388). Von Göll holds out the possibility that the image of rebellion will translate into real rebellion, and the exiles will be able to return home.

But were we to believe in von Göll's story of images becoming reality, we would be blinded to the possibility of other forces at work. The presence of the Zouave tribesman whom von Göll uses to make his phony Schwarzkommando film and the presence of the Herero people in Nazi Germany are both results of a European colonialism founded on material exploitation of other cultures. The seeming coincidence is therefore merely the eruption into the cultural superstructure of certain contradictions in the material base of imperialism. But lest we think that the coincidence is "explained" by reference to the narrative of empire, we are reminded that such a narrative merely opens another set of explanatory problems. The narrator reminds us that the presence of Africans in Europe is the outcome of "minor acts of surrealism—which, taken in the mass, are an act of suicide, but which in its pathology, in its dreamless version of the real, the Empire commits by the thousands every day, completely unaware of what it's doing" (129). Hence we have not a logic but a pathology of empire driven by some inexplicable and unconscious death wish. For if we had thought the novel's treatment of the formation of industrial cartels was meant as a materialist history of empire, Pynchon's narrator draws a caricature of the "sly old racist" Karl Marx "trying to make believe it's nothing but Cheap Labor and Overseas Markets. . . . Oh, no. Colonies are much, much more. Colonies are the outhouse of the European soul, where a fellow can let his pants down and relax, enjoy the smell of his own shit" (317). In rejecting the vulgar Marxist view, Pynchon's narrator replaces one vulgarity with another. In the process the narrative rejects a historical understanding based on concepts of exploitation and profit in favor of one based on primal urges, violence, and lust.

Even if we thought that the coincidence of the Schwarzkommando had been "explained" by recourse to the "larger" narrative of empire, Pynchon playfully offers another explanation for the appearance of real Schwarzkommando in Germany as the "return of the repressed." According to certain members of the Psi section of "the White Visitation," the Schwarzkommando are a product not of von Göll's film but of *King Kong:* "the legend of the black scapeape we cast down like Lucifer from the tallest erection in the world has come, in the fullness of time, to generate its own children, running around inside Germany even now" (275). The psychoanalyst Treacle argues with his colleagues "that their repressions *had*, in a sense that Europe in the last weary stages of its perversion of magic has lost, *had* incarnated real and living men, likely (according to the best intelligence) in possession of real and living weapons, as the dead father who never slept with you, Penelope, returns night after night to your bed, trying to snuggle in behind you . . . or as your unborn child wakes *you*, crying in the night and you feel its ghost-lips at your breast . . . they are real, they are living, as you pretend to scream inside the Fist of the Ape" (277). To Treacle, that the images of blackness in film should materialize in the real world is not coincidence, but rather follows from the belief that both film image and reality are manifestations of the psyche.

But we are not done "explaining" the coincidence. One last possibility is that the "Higher Levels" who directed Operation Black Wing knew all along of the existence of the Herero and had the film made for reasons of Their own. This possibility will occur to the people who made the film too late to be verified: "By the time it occurs to them to look back through the Most Secret documentation surrounding Operation Black Wing, to try and get some idea of how this all might've happened, they will find, curiously, that certain critical documents are either missing or have been updated past the end of the Operation" (276). Once again, one explanation momentarily supersedes and cancels another. It may be in the interests of the "Higher Levels" to have people *believe* that an ontological distinction between image and reality has been breached. The transgression of the boundary may be only an illusion They have created, part of Their strategy in preserving the more vital boundary between They and We. In the case of the Schwarzkommando, what appears to be the transformation of a boundary into a permeable interface, whether between image and reality, between material base and cultural superstructure, or between repressed and conscious, can always be seen, in the world of *Gravity's Rainbow,* from a point of view in which the interface is nullified or superseded by another, more solid barrier. The precession of explanations for the Schwarzkommando may be farcical in many respects, but the entire episode serves to remind us how investment in one dualism as a primary means of explanation blinds us to other dualisms that may be in control.

One additional frame of reference that complicates this account yet further is Pynchon's satiric method itself. Pynchon's allusions to and parodies of film and other mass-cultural artifacts, both real and invented, are a continual source of ironic deflection and the constant method of his satire. This prompts two observations. First, the fact that much of the novel's comic affirmation is written in the idiom of mass culture must be weighed against the darker claims that this analysis of the film medium has so far made. Against the account of the limited power of the film medium to liberate us from the confines of dualistic thinking, we must pose the satiric humor and anarchic energy that the prose seems to draw from popular culture itself.[19] The second observation is that taking the satiric context into account introduces another fundamental source of uncertainty to our understanding of film's relationship to the historical imagination at work in this novel.

Consider the following exchange, in which Slothrop objects to von Göll's lack of concern for his sidekick Närrisch, whom they have left alone in a gun battle with a squadron of Russian soldiers:

> "Springer, this ain't the fuckin' *movies* now, come on."
> "Not yet. Maybe not quite yet. You'd better enjoy it while you can. Someday, when the film is fast enough, the equipment pocket-size and burdenless and selling at people's prices, the lights and booms no longer necessary, then...then." (527)

Von Göll's vision is of a world made all film, in which everyone sees reality with the filmmaker's eye, as he already does. As we will see in Pynchon's *Vineland*, it is a world that arguably exists now, in the time of the hand-held video camera, the VCR, the instant replay and slo-mo, a world in which technology takes Rousseau's *amour-propre* to absurd lengths, so that we see ourselves not only as others see us but as others see us through the camera's lens, our self-image always projected on the screen.[20]

But more to the point, the world made all film has already been brought into being by the method of Pynchon's narrative. Not only does the entire novel purport to be a movie, but the narrative continually employs cinematic techniques to remind us of the extent to which our understanding of this period is mediated through film. In the passage preceding von Göll's remark, Slothrop and Närrisch's commando-style raid on the Peenemünde rocket station is parodically rendered in the idiom of war-movie heroism—it really *is* the "fuckin' movies." And immediately after von Göll's words, the narrative voice enters with a parody of either a movie voice-over or directorial notes for a screenplay: "We now come in sight of mythical Rügen off our starboard bow" (527). The ironic presence of film here creates instabilities of meaning in the exchange between Slothrop and von Göll. On the one hand, we may regard von Göll's vision as one more instance of his "megalomania," and Slothrop's fear for Närrisch's life as a legitimate assertion of a reality beyond the reach of image. On the other hand, the exchange takes place in a narrative context whose satire invokes the very condition against which Slothrop objects. The irony suggests that the joke may be on Slothrop, that if Närrisch dies according to a code of heroism he learned in the movies, then Slothrop's objection comes too late. By seeing ourselves as others see us through the camera's lens, by making ourselves into screen images, we become subject to the narrative conventions by which those images are controlled. By colonizing our consciousness, image has so permeated reality that it becomes difficult to distinguish between the two; we all become characters in the movies.

Thus it is perhaps the satire itself that destabilizes most radically the related distinctions of reality/image, subject/object, and cause/effect on which any historical understanding in "depth" depends. We are placed in that typically postmodern dilemma of suspecting that our subjectivity and our agency are controlled by "outside" forces, while the operations of image culture destabilize the boundary between "outside" and "inside" necessary to understand those forces. Indeed, "everything within us that desires a realm," in Derrida's phrase, is frustrated by a narrative that continually installs and then subverts such dualistic distinctions, producing a state that the narrator describes as "Outside and Inside interpiercing one another too fast, too finely labyrinthine, for either category to have much hegemony any more" (681). Each explanation of the "coincidence" of the Schwarzkommando invokes a depth model of historical causality: materialist, psychological, conspiratorial, and so on. And each depth model is subverted in at least two ways, first by the presence of a plurality of depth models among which the narrative refuses to choose, and second by a relentless irony that seemingly undercuts any bid for determinate historical understanding. The succession of controlling explanations at work in the case of the Schwarzkommando, and finally the satiric method of the prose itself, constructs a deep surface that obsessively points toward, yet withholds, any "ultimate" understanding of history. The entire episode would seem to demonstrate how our very eagerness to discover "ultimate" causality, a causality based on confining dualistic models, represents a demand for certainty that can never be satisfied in the life-world that we inhabit.

Vineland: *The Whole World Is Watching*

To confirm that the development of image culture is central to Pynchon's conception of recent history, one need only turn to his most recent novel, *Vineland*. The mediation of experience by film, and even more powerfully by television, is at the heart of this novel's vision of a contemporary American culture in which all acts of resistance and oppression alike have been absorbed into a system whose smothering embrace seems to have the force of metaphysical imperative. If Pynchon's first three novels present a series of problematic oppositions—animate and inanimate, visible America and invisible Tristero legacy, elite and preterite, to name only a few—*Vineland* presents an America in which the oppositions of the earlier novels have been dissolved in the hum of computer circuitry and the flickering light of the television screen. The result is a sense of cultural paralysis in which the question of individual or collective agency, together with any ultimate historical causality, is indefinitely suspended. This suspension is embodied in the movement of a narrative that frustrates conventional expectations by interrupting the forward drive of its various plot lines. The novel leaves us with the suggestion that, in an everyday life of family, food, shopping, and plenty of television, we have reached the end of a history in which individual or collective action can be coherently conceived.

The novel's principal characters are the aging hippie Zoyd Wheeler and his former "old lady," the ex-radical-turned-federal-informant Frenesi Gates; in the post-sixties trajectories of their lives we see the desultory ends to which much of sixties radicalism and counterculture have come. Film and television's mediation of this post-sixties history occurs on several levels. First, in a novel that contains at least twenty references to movies, twenty references to actors or characters in film and television, and forty references to television shows, the reader is continually reminded of the extent to which film and television form the very texture of historical memory and self-understanding.[21] More significantly, given Pynchon's continuing concern with forms of cultural and political resistance, film and television are woven into the personal history of Frenesi Gates, in whose family we find a generational history of radical politics and its relation to image culture. Finally, and most disturbingly, Pynchon suggests that television has itself become a potent historical force that, by producing a docile and distracted citizenry, has largely superseded the efforts of the state security apparatus in enforcing an oppressive status quo.

This is a novel in which the products of mass image culture are woven into the very stuff of personal identity. Nearly all the characters understand themselves in film and video terms. Zoyd Wheeler is typical in seeing his life as a television series, a series of events after each of which it is "time to go to commercials and clips of next week's episode" (42). Televisual self-consciousness comes perhaps more naturally to Zoyd than to most, for some of his life really does exist on videotape: each year he leaps through a barroom window to prove his "insanity" so that he can continue collecting his government disability checks; the event is carefully coordinated with the media, who videotape the annual "defenestration" and air it on the evening news as an amusing human-interest story. But Zoyd's television-soaked mind is hardly unusual. In this novel characters give one another Mr. Spock's Vulcan hand salute (11), interrupt one another with game-show buzzer noises (40), think of future plans as "script possibilities" (44), dismiss the recent past as "already old videotape" (190), liken a marital argument to the dynamics of an "alien-invasion" video game (87), provide "color commentary" to one another's recounting of the past (149), signify a menacing distaste with an "Eastwood-style mouth-muscle nuance" (28), follow jokes with a "Grouchoic roll" of the eyes (175), see themselves as characters in a soap opera (16) and as "actors in a brain-transplant movie" (165), refer to the dusk as "just before prime time" (194), and consider murdering an enemy the chance to "cancel his series" (374). In these many small moments Pynchon has had, of course, little need for outright invention: it seems that one hears and sees as much every day. With uncommon precision and thoroughness, *Vineland* captures the way in which, for anyone who came of age in the sixties or later, television has been absorbed into the everyday rhythms of speech and thought.[22]

But in *Vineland* history is more than the changes in the prime-time listings. The novel achieves its historical scope by tracing three generations of radical politics in the family of Frenesi Gates. Frenesi's 1960s radicalism comes with a pedigree. Her maternal grandfather, Jess Traverse, was a Wobblie crippled as a result of his efforts to unionize loggers in the 1930s, while her maternal grandmother, Eula Becker, came from a family of labor activists in the Montana mining industry, and herself pursued a career of labor organizing in California throughout the 1930s. Frenesi's mother, Sasha Gates, the daughter of Jess and Eula, took up the family tradition in Hollywood in the 1950s, where she and her husband, Hub Gates, soon found themselves blacklisted and harassed as a result of their union activities. When her time came, Frenesi Gates took up the camera as a weapon itself, becoming a key member of the radical film collective known as "24fps," whose tactics included traveling to political hot spots to film, close up, the actions of police in suppressing demonstrations.

On the most obvious level, by creating this family Pynchon suggests that oppression and exploitation are constants in American life and that every generation in every place produces its own version of the Counterforce. But the progression here is significant, for in the Traverse and the Becker families we have a sort of myth of origins: theirs was the politics of timber and mining, with the kind of pretelevision authenticity that only raw materials and brute industrial capitalism can provide. In the next generation Hub and Sasha Gates work in an industry dedicated to leisure, entertainment, and the image. Though Frenesi is aware as a young child of her parents' political activities, it is not until later that, when viewing old movies on television with her parents, she becomes aware that behind the "easy conflicts" of the movie plots themselves

> something else, some finer drama the Movies had never considered worth ennobling, had been unfolding all the time. It was a step in her political education. Names listed even in fast-moving credits, meaning nothing to a younger viewer, were enough to provoke from her parents groans of stomach upset, bellows of rage, snorts of contempt, and in extreme cases, switches of channel. "You think I'm gonna sit and watch this piece of scab garbage?" (82)

Not only is the "real" material history of labor struggle hidden behind the images of Hollywood films, but this history is now only something to be argued about in darkened living rooms. History itself has taken on the quality of a bad movie: "'History in this town,' Sasha muttered, 'is no more worthy of respect than the average movie script. . . . By now the Hollywood fifties is this way-over-length, multitude-of-hands rewrite—except there's no sound, of course, nobody talks. It's a silent movie'" (81). Sasha's complaint cautions against assuming that "real" history can be recovered as an unproblematic corrective to the false images of Hollywood films.

It is telling that in moving to the next generation Pynchon chooses a filmmaker as his representative 1960s radical. Frenesi Gates's work with 24fps attempts to reverse the experience of her parents' generation by putting the "real" history of oppression directly on film. It is a naive and, in the end, failed effort to use the technology of images against the powers that be. Mistaking the power of images for the power of physical force, 24fps attempts to take seriously the metaphor of movie camera as weapon: "A camera is a gun. An image taken is a death performed. Images put together are the substructure of an afterlife and a Judgment. We will be the architects of a just Hell for the fascist pig" (197). 24fps disbands after the debacle at College of the Surf, in which Frenesi betrays her cause. She is seduced by and then collaborates with federal prosecutor Brock Vond; at Vond's direction, she falsely accuses campus protest leader Weed Atman of being a "snitch," and then incites another radical named Rex to murder Atman with a gun that Vond has had Frenesi provide. In the aftermath Frenesi realizes the naïveté of the 24fps approach: "Feel like we were running around like little kids with toy weapons, like the camera really was some kind of gun, gave us that kind of power. Shit. How could we lose track like that, about what was real. . . . The minute the guns came out, all that art-of-the-cinema handjob was over" (259). But the failure of 24fps lies not only in their mistaking radical filmmaking for "real" power. Their naïveté consists in the belief that when placed in the right hands the camera delivers "truth" infallibly, and further in the correlative belief that such "truths" of content possess a power uncorrupted by the *form* of the film image as a representation.[23]

But the final irony of this novel is that the camera may, after all, have a greater power than the gun. It is a *kind* of power, however, that neither 24fps nor their Establishment antagonists could have anticipated. In 1970, the same year in which the rocket reaches the movie theater at the end of *Gravity's Rainbow*, Frenesi gives birth to Prairie, whose father is putatively Zoyd Wheeler but may be Brock Vond. The Gates family history is not over yet. Prairie is the thoroughly postmodern child, of the age of shopping malls and video games, for whom the past exists quite literally as the output of computer terminals and images on the video screen. In Prairie's generation we see the end of radical ideology in consumerist distraction and the aggressive pursuit of "lifestyle."

Or do we? As much as she is a child of her time, Prairie's thinking is not confined to the mass-cultural surface only. Instead we find in Prairie's historical consciousness, as in that of Samantha Hughes of *In Country* and of the narrator of *The Mezzanine*, a deep surface, one which grasps the "genuine" material history of her grandparents' and great-grandparents' generations but whose terms of reference are provided by mass culture. In 1984, the novel's present, the fourteen-year-old Prairie has already lived through at least two generations of shopping mall developments, and is a savvy enough customer to critique both the marketing concepts and the security arrangements at the latest malls. Her historical sensibility is suggested by her response to the "Noir Center," a mall "loosely based on crime movies from around World War II and after," where security personnel

> did everything by video camera and computer, a far cry from the malls Prairie'd grown up with, when security was not so mean and lean and went in more for normal polyester Safariland uniforms, where the fountains were real and the plants nonplastic and you could always find somebody your age working in the food courts willing to swap a cheeseburger for a pair of earrings, and there even used to be ice rinks, back when insurance was affordable. (326)

This passage reminds one of Baker's *The Mezzanine*, in which history consists of the generational history of consumer goods, and historical consciousness is fed by a nostalgia for the discontinued products and services of days gone by. But on the other hand, Prairie has inherited enough of a political consciousness from her grandparents to know "how corrupted everything had been from top to bottom" in Hollywood during the film noir era, so that she resents the nostalgic commodification of the past as "an increasingly dumb attempt to cash in on the pseudoromantic mystique of those particular olden days in this town" (326). Further, her attention to matters of "security" and "insurance" suggests an awareness of the material underpinnings of these consumer environments in which she is an enthusiastic but knowing and at times subversive participant. Prairie's most radical activity to date was her involvement in

> the Great South Coast Plaza Eyeshadow Raid, still being talked about in tones of wounded bewilderment at security seminars nationwide, in which two dozen girls, in black T-shirts and jeans, carrying empty backpacks and riding on roller skates, perfectly acquainted with every inch of the terrain, had come precision whirring and ticking into the giant Plaza just before closing time and departed only moments later with the packs stuffed full of eyeshadows, mascaras, lipsticks, earrings, barrettes, bracelets, pantyhose, and fashion shades, all of which they had turned immediately for cash from an older person named Otis, with a panel truck headed for a swap meet far away. (328)

It remains to be seen whether Prairie's political and historical consciousness will ever push her radicalism beyond this sort of consumerist guerrilla warfare. The ability of the consumer economy to contain the threat of radical activity is suggested by a plan, devised by Prairie's boyfriend Isaiah Two Four, to develop a chain of "violence centers, each on the scale, perhaps, of a small theme park, including automatic-weapon firing ranges, paramilitary fantasy adventures, gift shops and food courts, and video game rooms for the kids, for Isaiah envisioned a family clientele. Also part of the concept were a standardized floor plan and logo, for franchising purposes" (19). Isaiah Two Four's plan is the perfect postmodernist enactment of his name, which derives from the Old Testament verse telling us how "they shall beat their swords into plowshares."[24] In this case the swords are not beaten but simulated and are thus contained within a consumer economy devoted not to forms of primary production, such as agriculture, but to service and leisure.

As do Pynchon's earlier novels, *Vineland* practices a studied ambivalence toward the prospects for effective political resistance and for the efficacy of historical memory itself. The future of history, so to speak, belongs to Prairie and Isaiah Two Four, in whose goofball names (another of Prairie's mall-rat friends is named "Ché") are the traces of a generation whose effort to rewrite history and change the system was defeated by the "Nixonian repression." But for all of her media-soaked, consumerist disconnection from what her parents might have wanted to think of as "authenticity" (something more than nonplastic mall plants, presumably), Prairie still represents the hope of youth.²⁵ She is only fourteen, after all, and Pynchon's decision to place the radical heritage of the Becker and Traverse families in the hands of a punky adolescent is a typically mischievous evasion: we do not know, finally, which way Prairie will turn.

We do know which way her mother turned, and much of the novel's plot is structured around Prairie's search for knowledge about her mother, from whom she was separated during infancy to be raised by Zoyd Wheeler in Vineland. Prairie's search for her mother bears comparison to Samantha Hughes's search for knowledge of her father in Mason's *In Country*. Both novels are set in the summer of 1984, and in both cases the search for the lost parent is mediated largely by film, television, and other mass-cultural sources, supplemented by family lore and oral accounts. For Samantha Hughes, television shows such as *M*A*S*H*, war movies, and video games provide important terms of reference for her search, and we come to understand that whatever more "authentic" sources of historical knowledge she discovers—books, letters, diaries, oral accounts—do not supersede the mass-cultural sources, but rather are placed in productive tension with them. Mass culture is not only the starting point for Samantha Hughes's historical quest, it remains a constant source of reference and insight, structuring the deep surface of her historical consciousness.

Pynchon's satiric method in *Vineland* is to literalize the notion that historical consciousness is unavoidably mediated by image and information technologies. Taking refuge with DL, Frenesi's former best friend from their radical days, at the mountainside retreat of the Sisterhood of Kunoichi Attentives ("a sort of Esalen Institute for lady asskickers"), Prairie logs on to the computer in the Ninjette Terminal Center to cruise the data banks for information about her mother.

> The file on Frenesi Gates, whose entries had been accumulating over the years, often haphazardly, from far and wide, reminded Prairie of scrapbooks kept by somebody's eccentric hippie uncle. Some was governmental, legal history with the DMV, letterhead memoranda from the FBI enhanced by Magic Marker, but there were also clippings from "underground" newspapers that had closed down long ago, transcripts of Frenesi's radio interviews on KPFK, and a lot of cross-references to something called 24fps. (114)

It is only the thoroughly postmodern Prairie, of course, who can find in this sort of information system the homey familiarity of a "scrapbook." The system allows her to call up photographic images as well, and in an example of postmodern ekphrasis Prairie uses a photograph of Frenesi and DL together to imagine the conversation that might have passed between them:

It wasn't politics—Prairie could feel in the bright California colors, sharpened up pixel by pixel into deathlessness, the lilt of bodies, the unlined relaxation of faces that didn't have to be put on for each other, liberated from their authorized versions for a free, everyday breath of air. Yeah, Prairie thought at them, go ahead, you guys. Go ahead. (115)

The "deathlessness" of the image repeats a motif in which the image is seen to mediate between life and death. "If mediated lives," another character asks rhetorically, "why not mediated deaths?" (218). Paging through the computer files, Prairie is "a girl in a haunted mansion, led room to room, sheet to sheet, by the peripheral whiteness, the earnest whisper, of her mother's ghost" (114). And later, when she has a chance to view actual 24fps film footage, much of it shot by her mother, Prairie has a chilling moment of intersubjectivity in which she feels as though she is occupying her mother's body. Seeing on the screen what her mother saw through the camera lens over twenty-four years earlier, Prairie feels "as if Frenesi were dead but in a special way, a minimum security arrangement, where limited visits, mediated by projector and screen, were possible" (199).

The footage brings to life "an America of the olden days she'd mostly never seen, except in fast clips on the Tube meant to suggest the era, or distantly implied in reruns like 'Bewitched' or 'The Brady Bunch'" (198). But what is most striking about this central section of the novel is how it constructs for the reader the voyeuristic situation of seeing the 1960s on film. Prairie's viewing of the 24fps film archives becomes the narrative frame for the recounting of the history of 24fps and the story of the student rebellion at the College of the Surf. Pynchon returns us to the narrative frame at intervals infrequent enough for us to forget that we are within a nested narrative, that the story unfolding is supposedly being reconstructed in the mind of Prairie as she watches the film fourteen years later. The narrative method in this section of the novel thus embodies the real historical situation in which the past is so thoroughly mediated by images that we are unaware of the mediation; images are in a sense indistinguishable from memories of actual lived experience. As we saw in DeLillo's fiction, once one is accustomed to thinking of the past as "on film," then all experience, all memory becomes "as seen on film." For someone such as Prairie, the distinction between film and memory loses its significance as film becomes a sort of a priori perceptual category.

This is a development in consciousness, *Vineland* suggests, for which the 1960s radicals were not adequately prepared. What the members of 24fps could not see was how the image itself was overtaking their own generation, outflanking their efforts to use images for political and social change. By the time the

1970s arrived, television had developed from mere entertainment to a way of life, one capable of anticipating and absorbing all oppositions and resistances. As Mark Crispin Miller writes, by the mid-seventies "students no longer felt themselves estranged from TV, but only felt at home with it, as TV itself became a perfect shelter, a dream container, unbreakable, antiseptic and without surprises" (10).[26] Pynchon's narrator, here focalized through Frenesi, observes that in 1984 "nobody thought it peculiar anymore" that police were presented sympathetically by television programs "relentlessly pushing their propaganda message of cops-are-only-human-got-to-do-their-job, turning agents of government repression into sympathetic heroes. Nobody thought it was peculiar anymore, no more than the routine violations of constitutional rights these characters performed week after week, now absorbed into the vernacular of American expectations" (345). Brock Vond was able to see the potential for this change of attitude earlier than most:

> Brock Vond's genius was to have seen in the activities of the sixties left not threats to order but unacknowledged desires for it. While the Tube was proclaiming youth revolution against parents of all kinds and most viewers were accepting the story, Brock saw the deep—if he'd allowed himself to feel it, the sometimes touching—need only to stay children forever, safe inside some extended national Family. (269)

Vond was able to look past the content of television to what sociologists call the "situation" of television viewing,[27] and to see in the docile, distracted, and newly collectivized television audience the potential for a nationalism of the Tube on which the perfect fascist state could be built. Regardless of the particular content of television programming, so long as the citizenry remains fastened to the Tube as if in answer to deep need, the state security apparatus can reserve its forces for the suppression of marginal "criminal" activity and for mopping-up operations, such as the CAMP marijuana eradication program.

It is only from the perspective of the next generation, that of Frenesi's daughter Prairie and Prairie's boyfriend Isaiah Two Four, that the full effects of television can be seen:

> "Whole problem 'th you folks's generation," Isaiah opined, "nothing personal, is you believed in your Revolution, put your lives right out there for it—but you sure didn't understand much about the Tube. Minute the Tube got hold of you folks that was it, that whole alternative America, el deado meato, just like th' Indians, sold it all to your real enemies, and even in 1970 dollars—it was way too cheap."(373)

Pynchon's 24fps represents that hopeful but naive moment when the technologies of the media are conceived as instruments of resistance and subversion. But the essential form of the media denies true reciprocity in communication and unavoidably cancels authenticity and originality. Ultimately the media can function only as instruments of social control, regardless of their content.

This is the view of Jean Baudrillard, whose analysis of the role of the media in the May 1968 rebellion in France is relevant here, both because it touches directly on this issue and because the events of May 1968 inspired the subversive strategies of such American Yippies as Abbie Hoffman and Jerry Rubin, strategies that bear an affinity to those of Pynchon's 24fps. Baudrillard contests the widely held view that the media were for a brief period transformed into instruments of subversion. By broadcasting to the nation news and images of the student protests in Paris, Baudrillard argues, the media extended the idea of the rebellion too rapidly, short-circuiting the rebellion by not allowing it to develop according to its own momentum. Mediation necessarily emphasizes the reproducibility of the event rather than the event itself, thus robbing it of its original power: "Transgression and subversion never get 'on the air' without being subtly negated as they are: transformed into models, neutralized into signs, they are eviscerated of their meaning. There is no model of transgression, prototypical or serial. Hence, there is no better way to reduce it than to administer it a mortal dose of publicity" ("Requiem" 132). True subversion, according to Baudrillard, never proceeds according to models, and because that is all the media can provide, it cannot serve subversion. When protesters outside the 1968 Democratic National Convention in Chicago chanted that "the whole world is watching," they sought to use the media exposure of police brutality to turn public opinion in their favor. They did not suspect that they were also describing the very condition that would doom authentic radical politics in a postmodern America.

Rather than serve subversion, television's main tendency is to serve as a distraction, lulling one to accept images of subversion rather than practice subversion itself. As Baudrillard writes, the real danger of television is not in its potential use as a tool either of brainwashing or of Orwellian surveillance: "It is useless to fantasize about the state projection of police control through TV.... TV, by virtue of its mere presence, is a social control in itself. There is no need to imagine it as a state periscope spying on everyone's private life—the situation as it stands is more efficient than that: it is the *certainty that people are no longer speaking to each other*" ("Requiem" 130). If television's most powerful effect is that it kills conversation, then there is no moment in *Vineland* more chilling than that when one of the members of 24fps, just informed that protest leader

Weed Atman is an FBI informant, turns to the television for escape: "Embarrassed, he reached for the Tube, popped it on, fastened himself to the screen and began to feed" (236). The suckling image reinforces Brock Vond's observation that the fascination with television indicates a desire to remain children forever and suggests that television's most radical effect is to reduce us to wordless dependence, making us infants in the original sense of that word: without speech.

Pynchon and Baudrillard would both agree, of course, that there were "real" material forces at work in the "repression" of 1968–70, forces that are independent of the media and of developments in information technologies, however much these developments are integral to the structuration and deployment of those forces. *Vineland* is consistent with Pynchon's earlier novels in the way that it persistently asks what forms of social control, material or otherwise, lie "behind" or "above" those that are most obvious—in this case, those of the media and mass consumer culture. Even if one accepts the argument, as I think Pynchon implicitly does, that image technology by its nature is an agent of social control, what is even more disturbing is the possibility that as such the media are the agents of no individual or collective will. As Mark Miller writes, "more disquieting even than the old nightmare of conspiracy is the likelihood that no conspiracy is needed" (17). In *Vineland*, as in DeLillo's *White Noise*, we have a vision of a culture in which all knowledge is mediated, yet in which no one and nothing is demonstrably in control of that mediation.

The other force of social control that *Vineland* acknowledges most forthrightly is the brute force of the state security apparatus. If the camera serves as the icon for social control through the media, the icon for physical force is the gun. Part of Brock Vond's strategy in turning Frenesi Gates is to convince her that the gun's power is greater than that of the camera: "Can't you see, the two separate worlds—one always includes a camera somewhere, and the other always includes a gun, one is make-believe, one is real? What if this is some branch point in your life, where you'll have to choose between worlds?" (241). It is typical of Pynchon's imagination that he constructs this choice between forms of control as a choice between ontological levels: the world of the gun has a reality that the world of the camera lacks. And there is much in the novel to suggest that this is the case. The armed assault on the College of the Surf to end the student protest there; Brock Vond's capture of counterculture radicals for "retraining" as federal informants in his secret detention camp; the framing of Zoyd Wheeler on drug charges as a means of bringing him under state control; the military-style CAMP operation of the Reagan administration to destroy marijuana crops in northern California: these are just a few examples of the ways in which "the gun" as a real historical force is present in the novel.

But as in *Gravity's Rainbow,* in *Vineland* one historical imperative quickly unfolds into another. To divide existence into the two ontological levels of the camera and the gun may be to present a false dichotomy, for Vond's gun may be only a surrogate for his penis, and his political ambitions only expressions of more basic libidinal drives. Vond's quest for Frenesi and Prairie in the novel's present (1984) may be driven by motives more personal than political. From the time of her first seduction by Vond, Frenesi was alive to the substitution of pistol for penis: "Men had it so simple. When it wasn't about Sticking It In, it was about Having The Gun, a variation that allowed them to Stick It In from a distance" (241). Despite this awareness, Frenesi is seduced by the logic of the gun; she sets up Weed to be literally shot as a traitor, at the same time planning to "nail him with my Scoopic" (236). She can take most seriously the metaphor of camera as gun only when she has also accepted the metaphor of gun as penis. It is through this chain of substitutions that Frenesi's radical feminist politics is turned in the service of the patriarchal state power.[28]

But it remains an open question just what Brock Vond's ultimate motivations are. Indeed, Pynchon characteristically deflects any search for "ultimate" motivation of any sort, preferring instead to provide competing alternatives among which the novel refuses to choose. After he is shot and in his Thanatoid state ("like death, only different" [170]), Weed Atman dreams of two companions who "argue like theologians over Brock's motives for wanting me, you'd have to say, iced. 'It was all for love,' says one, and 'Bullshit,' the other replies, 'it was political.' . . . 'A rebel cop, with his own deeply personal agenda.' 'Only following the orders of a repressive regime based on death.' So forth" (366). The last explanation of his motives comes when Vond commandeers a helicopter and heads off to find Prairie: "following his penis—what else could it be?—into the night clouds over Vineland" (377). The interjected question here is typical of a narrative that is fussily self-conscious about human motivation, suspended between individualistic, psychological views of behavior and more structural, systemic ones. Pynchon's text is not unusual, of course, in hovering between these two poles, but is unusual in the extent to which this issue is foregrounded by the narrative voice. The interjected question suggests that Vond's behavior is ultimately driven by libido, while coyly acknowledging that such a hypothesis does not serve political analysis.

And the irony of the interjection goes further: there are, in fact, other imperatives that could be driving Vond. *Vineland* follows the pattern set in *Gravity's Rainbow* in which one apparent historical imperative is superseded by another, operating at another level. The camera gives way to the gun, the gun to the penis, but the penis may be ruled by other forms of control. We learn that

Brock Vond's early political ambitions were formed by dreams of power in "the white mother city," where "he'd caught a fatal glimpse of that level where everybody knew everybody else, where however political fortunes below might bloom and die, the same people, the Real Ones, remained year in and year out, keeping what was desirable flowing their way" (276). The language here recalls the "Higher Levels" of *Gravity's Rainbow* and is echoed again when Weed Atman describes for Prairie his intuition of the levels of causality behind and above the moment when he was shot by Rex: "Used to think I was climbing, step by step, right? toward a resolution—first Rex, above him your mother, then Brock Vond, then—but that's when it begins to go dark, and that door at the top I thought I saw isn't there anymore, because the light behind it just went off too" (366). Causality in this novel ultimately retreats behind the veil of unnamed, unseen powers; all that is known for sure about the post-Nixon years is that "the Repression went on, growing wider, deeper, and less visible, regardless of the names in power" (72).

In a narrative that both analyzes and mystifies relations of power, the lives of the major characters are apparently directed at the whim of an unseen government that may only loosely coincide with the legally constituted one. The novel's plot is set into motion when the "Reaganomic ax blades" apparently chop out the budget line that has been paying for Frenesi's salary as undercover agent. "Bumped off the computer to make way for the next generation" (352), she and her companion Flash find themselves suddenly on their own, without cover, "as if they'd been kept safe in some time-free zone all these years but now, at the unreadable whim of something in power, must reenter the clockwork of cause and effect" (90). It is this "something in power" that turns the wheels and cogs of the novel's plot. Zoyd Wheeler's life in Vineland, we eventually learn, has been every bit as much an "arrangement" as has Frenesi's life under cover. In 1984 Zoyd is a dope-smoking thirty-something hippie, father of the fourteen-year-old Prairie, freelance roofer and handyman, former surfer and keyboardist for a surfadelic band, who would like to think of himself as somehow having escaped the maw of conventionality and remained true to his countercultural ideals. But we learn that his annual leap through the barroom window is part of a decade-old agreement with the government by which he avoided imprisonment on drug charges and retained the custody of his daughter in exchange for keeping his whereabouts known and having no contact with Frenesi. His bizarre action is then packaged as an entertaining and harmless human-interest feature for the "kissoff" story at the end of the evening news, showing how television reinforces the government's efforts to contain subversive action. Whatever transgressive potential Zoyd Wheeler's act may have is contained and co-opted twice over.

The climax of the novel takes the idea that governmental whim can suddenly redirect individual lives and extends it as a parodic deus ex machina. In advance of what threatens to be a full-scale military assault on Vineland, the site not only of intensive marijuana production but also of the radical Traverse and Becker annual clan reunion, Brock Vond suspends himself by cable from a helicopter in an attempt to snatch his could-be daughter Prairie. Dangling "within centimeters of the girl's terrified body," Vond is defeated when "some white male far away must have wakened from a dream, and just like that" Brock is winched back up into the helicopter (376). The satire here is broad: Brock Vond is shown literally to be the government's "puppet"; his life, no less than those of his "subjects," Frenesi and Zoyd, is under the control of unseen powers.

Pynchon's studied deferral of the question of historical causality and the sense of cultural paralysis that pervades his vision of postmodern America are embodied in the novel's frustration of narrative expectations. The novel's final sequence is a series of pulled punches. Brock Vond's invasion of Vineland is called off by executive order in Washington. Vond then commandeers a helicopter, which he crashes into a mountainside, finding himself transported "across the river" to join the Thanatoids. The Thanatoids do not, as we are led to think they might, march down the valley seeking the zombie-movie-style revenge by which they can balance their karma and pass deeper into genuine death. The reunion of Prairie and Frenesi, the climax of the search-for-the-mother plot that has occupied most of the narrative, is announced in the past perfect tense in a subordinate clause (366–67). Their initial meeting, mediated by Frenesi's mother Sasha, consists of Sasha trying to get Prairie to sing the theme song from *Gilligan's Island,* and the subsequent mother-daughter conversation is apparently so ordinary as to merit only one sentence of indirect description (368).

Readers of *Gravity's Rainbow,* in which the protagonist disintegrates by the novel's end, should not be surprised that Pynchon has once again chosen to defy narrative conventions. But there is a heightened staginess to the ending of this novel. Drawn from grade-B movies and the conventions of romance and thriller genre fiction, the novel's main plotlines are poised for a cataclysmic convergence in Vineland. Instead of apocalypse we get barbecue:

> The fragrance of barbecue smoke came drifting down from the pits. . . .
> Soon Traverses and Beckers were filling up the benches at the long red-
> wood tables, as the potato salad and bean casseroles and fried chicken
> started to appear, along with pasta dishes and grilled tofu contributed by
> the younger elements, and the eating, which would continue into the
> night, got under way in earnestness. (369)

When they are not eating or playing cards, the Traverses and Beckers and their extended families are watching television. Zoyd and Flash compare notes on Frenesi while watching a sitcom in the back of a pick-up truck, and then Prairie and her half-brother Justin settle in to get acquainted "in front of the Eight O'Clock Movie, Pee-wee Herman in *The Robert Musil Story*" (370). Has the end of ideology truly arrived? In the novel's last lines Prairie's long-lost dog Desmond returns, adding the last dollop of dogs-and-children smarminess to an ending that recalls the "Morning in America" television commercials aired during Reagan's 1984 reelection campaign. The good guys win in this novel, but the victory is unearned, ambiguous, and temporary. The radicalism of the Traverse and Becker clan seems to live on only in the form of sentimental talk, endless ideological quibbling, and the theft of beef cattle for the barbecue. It would seem that the Traverses and Beckers survive, in the long run, on the strength not of political convictions but of "family values." There is no fighting the power, this ending seems to suggest, so one might as well enjoy one's family and watch the Tube.

Vineland leaves us, then, with equal parts analysis and mystification, suspending the question of whether there is still any hope for those who would resist being swallowed up entirely by the system.[29] The vision of human connectedness provided by the family reunion is balanced by the chilling possibility that such forms of collectivity can now be tolerated by a regime whose victory is total. As everywhere in this novel, television provides the imagery for a vision of a culture in which individual or collective resistance to domination is anticipated and forestalled: "Grandfolks could be heard arguing the perennial question of whether the United States still lingered in a prefascist twilight, or whether that darkness had fallen long stupefied years ago, and the light they thought they saw was coming only from millions of Tubes all showing the same bright-colored shadows" (371). This image returns us to Plato's cave, to the condition of not knowing whether what we see is real or only shadows cast on our confining walls.

It is of course unfair to ask that Pynchon be able to do what postmodernism generally has failed to do: reconceive agency and historical causality at a time when the conditions of everyday life in the culture of the image have undermined—more powerfully than the poststructuralist notion of *différance* could ever anticipate or describe—the solidity of both the sovereign self and the collective will. *Vineland* gives us a culture that delivers on the promise made by Gerhardt von Göll of *Gravity's Rainbow* that "someday, when the film is fast enough, the equipment pocket-size and burdenless and selling at people's prices, the lights and booms no longer necessary," the world will be made all film (527). *Vineland* would seem to argue that if von Göll's prophecy has come true, so has his prediction that, in such a world, history would be driven not by individual or collective liberty but by unprecedented mastery and control by the Elite. For all its internal resistances and contradictions, for all the intricate evasions of ultimacy by which it constructs its deep surfaces, Pynchon's history suggests that in becoming people of, by, and for the image we have sealed our fate.

Novels, Thanatoids, and Other Postmodern Survivals

As the culture of television has made its spectacular rise in the past forty years, we have lived through an equally spectacular reign of death: the death of the author, death of the novel, death of the subject, death of the avant-garde, death of art, and death of history have all received notice in the obituary columns of critical discourse. The threat of nuclear war during this period has been invoked as psychological motivation for apocalyptic thinking in all areas of culture, and in general it seems that the excitements of rapid change provide an excuse to harness to one's rhetoric the energies of pending annihilation. But in each of these cases an intellectual crisis, usually accompanied by some demystifying analysis of the corpse in question, has discovered not death but the means of reinvigorating an area of study. So, too, in postmodern fiction we find not the death of history, but new means of engaging the problems of historical understanding.

Indeed, the question at the end of this century is what to do with the discomfiting fact of our survival. We have witnessed in parade the death of these avatars of depth—history, the subject, the novel, and so on—only to see each of them returned to us. They have not been resurrected and glorified, but perhaps like Pynchon's Thanatoids they have experienced something "like death, only different," emerging humbled yet uncannily resilient, changed yet the same. Pynchon's Thanatoids, who "watch a lot of Tube" (*Vineland* 170), are the obverse of DeLillo's Jack Gladney, who while yet alive carries his statistical death within him. And if death is the ultimate realm of depth, the one absolute we thought we could count on, the horizon and limit of mediation, then both Gladney and the Thanatoids are ways of figuring the paradox of the deep surface, the curious death of death itself. If the shape-shifting Madonna of the 1980s announced the death of the old centered self, replaced by the exuberant display of multiple identities served up for consumption and profit, then the Michael Jackson of the 1990s announces the self's Thanatoid return, his ghoulishly transfigured body blurring gender and racial lines while his *History* album (1995) repackages history as a collection of his own earlier hits and the petulant defense of his own life.

While the Thanatoid is one figure for the deep surface—the undead dead— popular culture provides another in the science-fiction cyborg, a creature part human, part machine. As a combination of organic depth with mechanical surface, the cyborg serves as a figure for the decentered postmodern subjectivity invaded and constituted by the images, discourses, and technologies of the mass-cultural environment. As Donna Haraway's provocative thesis has it, in the late twentieth century "we are all chimeras, theorized and fabricated hybrids of machine and organism; in short, we are cyborgs" (191).

Take for example Paul Verhoeven's 1987 film, *Robocop,* in which a policeman killed in the line of duty is reconstructed as a machine with enhanced physical, perceptual, and computational powers. The problem for Robocop is that, despite thorough reprogramming, shreds of his earlier identity as Officer Murphy remain, including fragmentary memories of his wife and the habit of twirling his handgun gunslinger-style before holstering it—a trick with which he used to impress his son. Haunted by fragments of his prior, deep self, the old centered subject, he nonetheless performs his surface-dwelling Robocop identity diligently, proving an effective tool of the newly "privatized" police apparatus under contract to the city of Detroit. The plot thickens when Robocop uses the computer capabilities that are a prosthetic extension of his sensorium to search the police databases for information about his past, until he experiences what we must now see as the quintessential moment of postmodern self-regard: his human face and vital statistics displayed on a screen, accompanied by the designation "Deceased." But instead of causing him to renounce his police function, the knowledge that he has been used in this way merely spurs him to peak efficiency. In the end he kills the bad guys who had murdered his previous incarnated self, exposes the corrupt officials running the police department as an elaborate criminal organization, and reclaims his human name, "Murphy," as a sign of the apparently successful integration of his human and machine identities. The film contains much pointed political and social satire: it mocks inane TV advertisements and personalities, questions the policy of privatizing government services, and offers a news broadcast telling how a certain two former U.S. presidents were killed when a misfiring laser cannon aboard an orbiting Strategic Defense Peace Platform scorched 10,000 acres near Santa Barbara. The film enacts the common political contradictions of postmodernist practice, however, for its critical stance is countered by its submission to the requirements of genre. Satisfying the conventions of both the cops-and-robbers story and the familiar science-fiction story of the machine that outsmarts its creators, *Robocop* finally celebrates a state corporate efficiency built on the strange undeath of the old centered self, promoting a cyborg identity in which private virtue survives as job satisfaction, public virtue as enhanced performance.

To say that depth's un-dying has produced a deep surface is to say that the entire postmodern turn has been both less and more important than we thought. When I began this project in the late 1980s, the term *postmodernism* had already passed out of its mewling youth into something like adolescence: it was gawky, self-conscious, growing in all directions, rebellious, at once idealistic and cynical, fitfully finding itself. It is by now surely in middle age, more confident, thick around the middle, complacent, unsurprised, the discoveries of its youth now diminished with perspective even as its gains have been consolidated, sure of itself yet conscious of how far short of its early promise the trajectory of its career has carried it. This state of affairs has prompted Linda Hutcheon to ask, in a review of three new books on postmodernism: "How many more re-viewings of the same theories and ideas can the topic bear, without the kind of major changes in evaluation or conceptualization that have kept the debates about modernism alive still today?" ("Once Again, from the Top" 164). Both the repetitious "theorizing" and the impatience for a "new, improved" concept of postmodernism say more about the fashionable hyperactivity of academic trendwatchers than it does about the validity of the concept of postmodernism as a descriptor of cultural phenomena.

But if academic theorists are repeating themselves, artists, musicians, archi-tects, and novelists have moved on. In fitting revenge for having learned from Las Vegas, postmodern architecture as a living (or Thanatoid) practice survives largely in the banalities of shopping mall design, and *postmodern* has entered the popular lexicon as a term applied indiscriminately to anything new, hip, cool, or simply weird. Like a stream emptying into a bay, the term has lost force and distinction even as it has contributed to a larger public conversation about contemporary culture. In literature, the wave of serious postmodernist experi-ment had already passed by the mid-1980s. Minimalist fiction had already begun the return, with a difference, to more conventional modes (Thanatoid realism?), while retaining some of the skepticism and savvy of the high post-modernists. As Kim Herzinger has put it, the high postmodernist, metafictional writers "showed their public the tubes and wires of fiction. . . . The Postmodern revelation, once declared, made everything possible, including a return to story, character, and the conventions of representation" (20). The same point is made in regard to Pynchon's *Vineland* by David Cowart, who supposes that Pynchon has conceded that "the postures of literary exhaustion may themselves be ex-hausted" ("Attenuated Postmodernism" 3). While such assessments are valid as far as they go, one wants to add, as I have argued in the foregoing chapters, that the "return" to realism can never be simply that, but always contains within it the mark of its antecedent experiments. To the extent that postmodernism forms the cultural dominant within which literary and other cultural forms must operate, any "return" to depth is necessarily conditioned by the forms and qualities of the surface.

Certainly E. L. Doctorow's career provides a clear example of how the lessons of metafictional experiment can be absorbed and assimilated into a wary return to more conventional forms. After the experimentation of *The Book of Daniel* and *Ragtime*, Doctorow moved on to a more forthright historicism in subse-quent novels. Yet while each of the later novels owes a large debt to genre—to childhood memoir in *World's Fair*, to *bildungsroman* in *Billy Bathgate*, and to the detective story in *The Waterworks* (1994)—Doctorow's writing consistently dis-plays a self-conscious sophistication about both the historiographic enterprise and the question of genre itself. We have already seen how the time capsules in *World's Fair* and the collections of castoffs in *Billy Bathgate* comment upon the novels' historical methods. Set in New York City in 1871, *The Waterworks* is nar-rated by a newspaper editor, McIlvaine, a man who has devoted his career to ve-racious reporting yet who acknowledges that the news is "constructed" and "construed" to create the illusion of "a stable universe" (14), and who admits that "what you remember as having happened and what truly did happen are no less and no more than . . . visions" (59, ellipsis in original). In addition to Doctorow's other concerns—political and corporate corruption in the age of Boss Tweed, the plight of the city's working class and the dispossessed, and always and everywhere the teeming, hallucinatory, and vital decadence of his beloved New York—the novel attends with care to the history of the newspaper itself, documenting the technological and commercial developments that aided its rise during the second half of the nineteenth century. It is with some irony that the novel is narrated with all the marks of an oral production and includes long passages narrated within quotation marks by people whom the editor "interviews" in his search for the missing Martin Pemberton, erstwhile heir to the Pemberton fortune. Several of the quoted passages (see, for example, chapter 13) are full-blown tales, crafted and embellished in a manner rarely achieved by oral storytellers today. Always alive to the history of genres and forms, Doctorow here invokes both the tradition of the well-told tale and the nineteenth-century novel, which so often made use of such storytellers as narrators. Despite its more forthright historicism, then, *The Waterworks* shares with *Ragtime* a concern for the history of representation in which the text itself is implicated. In its form *The Waterworks* documents the highly developed orality that its narrator's profession, and the entire ascendant print culture, was simultaneously rendering obsolete and preserving as an artifact of printed prose.

Striking, too, is the fact that *The Waterworks* provides us with another instance of the Thanatoid. The solution to the mystery plot involves the discovery that Martin Pemberton's father, Augustus Pemberton, had faked his own death in order to join the secret "mortuary fellowship" of wealthy dying men who had signed their lives over to the care of a brilliant doctor able to keep them alive with unconventional techniques. The amoral genius, Dr. Sartorius, uses the men's wealth to build a secret sanatorium and laboratory, where he conducts his research and preserves the men in a near vegetal state: "no life, no death, but something that was a concurrence of both" (225). The scam is, first, the apotheosis of a rampant and corrupt capitalism: these men leave behind destitute widows and children to pursue a dream of immortality in which it *is* possible to die and take it with you. But if we read Doctorow's text as always commenting upon the present as well as the past (as was overtly the case in *The Book of Daniel* and covertly in *Ragtime*), the Thanatoid old men can seem to represent the curious afterlife of so many postmodern survivals. They could, for example, figure the fate of the postmodern subject, surrendering its sovereignty in a bid for life beyond death, contracting to be invaded and reconstituted by the disciplines of "science," all the while coddled and entertained in a humidified false paradise pulsing with eternal dance music. It is not death the subject suffers under such conditions, but something different. As Dr. Sartorius notes, with characteristic detachment: "the interesting truth is in the great losses that human life can sustain—its individuation of character, its speech, its volition—without becoming death" (215). And like the diffuse and bodiless Foucauldian "discourses" that exert their terrible power on real human bodies, Dr. Sartorius is presented as a disinterested man of science who operates on the bodies of his patients yet who vanishes upon capture: "It is the nature of villainy to absent itself, even as it stands before you. You reach for it and close on nothing" (213). Finally, in this text's recovery of the era of Boss Tweed, we find the death and Thanatoid return of political critique. On the one hand, *The Waterworks* is consistent with the traditional left-wing politics of Doctorow's other novels, siding firmly with the exploited workers and the dispossessed (figured most prominently here by the street-urchin newspaper boy) and naming the bad guys among the ranks of capitalists and corrupt politicians. On the other hand, the rendering of Dr. Sartorius evinces a postmodernist skepticism, his impersonality and elusiveness calling into question such traditional analyses of power.

Despite his return to more conventional historical forms, Doctorow remains possessed of his postmodernist wiles. Bobbie Ann Mason's "return" to history is in some ways more striking, first because of her apparent rejection of postmodernist attitudes, and second in that, unlike Doctorow's, all of her prior work through *In Country* and *Love Life* (1989) has been so thoroughly engaged with contemporary characters and subjects. *Feather Crowns* (1993), however, is set in turn-of-the-century Kentucky, and by all appearances is a straightforward attempt at realistic historical fiction. The story concerns a young Kentucky farm woman, Christie Wheeler, who gives birth to quintuplets and must bear the burden of her ensuing celebrity as she struggles to keep her babies alive within the densely impacted world of her husband's extended family. Things do not turn out well: Christie eventually watches her babies die and then, in order to pay off her and her husband's debts to his uncle, agrees to display their preserved bodies in a traveling sideshow. The plot is not a complex one. What the novel does best is render the essential loneliness of farm women, smothered by the demands of family and work, a closeness that forbids the expression of desire. "What I wanted was friends—out there, outside the whole thorny red-haw tree of a family. I needed to find some connections that weren't kin, that weren't threaded into me like quilting stitches" (447). As sad as Christie's story is, the novel's true tragic figure is Amanda, Christie's sister-in-law, unhappy in her marriage, restless with physical desire. She is Christie's only true ally in the fight for some separate sense of self within the Wheeler hive. "Mandy and me were as close as two people could be without being kin, and yet the trouble was we couldn't be close enough because we had too much kin to tend to all the time" (447). Amanda finally takes her freedom by hanging herself in the smokehouse, the scene of an earlier adulterous transgression. Her death is one more confirmation of Christie Wheeler's view that, for women of her time and place, "there's no honor at home" (453). While *In Country* took as its theme the problem of recovering and representing history from within mass culture, *Feather Crowns* leaves aside postmodernist self-questioning in favor of a plenitude of historical texture and detail rendered without apparent self-consciousness. The novel seeks the sort of knowledge of the past that for the characters themselves is a luxury they cannot afford. As Christie explains: "We can't take time to worry about our ancestors, since we don't have to sew for them or feed them" (322).

Nonetheless we find in *Feather Crowns* the residue of the postmodern sensibility, like dust in the cracks of the conventional historical novel. For one thing, in the novel's attention to consumer goods and domestic detail as a way of rendering the texture of lived experience, we have not traveled far from minimalist practice. Once the quintuplets become a national sensation, the Wheelers are bombarded with the sort of attention we now call "direct mail advertising":

> Merchants sent free literature for elixirs, syrups, and powders; one teething powder company promised to make a baby as fat as a pig, and the pamphlet showed a picture of a little pig with a human baby's face. Other merchants and drummers sent actual products: worm-syrup to cure worms; packaged and canned baby foods; baby clothing and diapers; rubber sheeting; lactated milk; special powder-milk foods that supplemented mother's milk; root beer; a silver spoon; a picture frame, some hemstitch frilling, a nursing corset that Christie couldn't fit into. (208)

We find, also, the effort to fix the historical moment with news of technical innovation. For example, the advantages of the "Deere gang plow" over the "Brinley turning plow" or the "Avery batwing middle buster" are the subject of a stilted dialogue that itself might be a sort of ad copy (294). In passages such as these one sees the belts and pulleys of Mason's historical method too plainly and cannot escape the sense of a novel whose air of historical "authenticity" is too earnestly constructed from period newspaper accounts and mail-order catalogs. In an odd way, then, the novel registers a postmodern sensibility in which such records as newspapers and advertisements *are* history. The problem of a too plainly "constructed" authenticity is only compounded by passages of aggressively folksy diction: "Law, I'd feel plumb helpless if I had to depend on strangers for my grub, not knowing who growed it or how it was put up" (309). And at the end of the novel, as the aging Christie Wheeler looks back on the past, telling her story to a tape recorder ("These electric voices are still a mystery to me" [449]), we get the forced attempt to link the events of the story to some larger historical scheme: "Were quintuplets any more of a miracle than the automobile? Or the aeroplane? Her babies were born right at the dawn of a new age of miracles, almost as if they had been a signal of what lay ahead" (422). Christie's attitude is in telling contrast to that of Doctorow's more worldly McIlvaine, who cautions the reader against just this sort of retrospective fallacy: "You may think you are living in modern times, here and now, but that is the necessary illusion of every age. We did not conduct ourselves as if we were preparatory to your time. There was nothing quaint or colorful about us" (11).

Mason's return to history is less successful artistically than is Doctorow's, yet the two cases suggest the quite different ways that, in the work of writers of divergent talents and sensibilities, the postmodern may persist in the midst of a "return" to history. Which leads to the second half of my observation that postmodernism has turned out both less and more important than we thought. In introducing this book I distinguished between a postmodernism conceived in Anglo-American terms as a wave of artistic and cultural production beginning in the 1950s and 1960s, and a postmodernism conceived in Continental terms as a repudiation, beginning early in this century (seminally with Nietzsche), of an entire three-hundred-year history of "modern" thought. As a first order approximation, it is fair to say that, while postmodernism in the former sense has by now lost much of its force, in the latter sense it has become an intellectual orthodoxy. But right away this formulation begs qualification. For I have been arguing that postmodernism in literature and the arts has suffered not a repudiation but rather a broad diffusion, the sort of victory dictated by its own logic as, first, a self-conscious "return" to the modes and styles previously repudiated by modernism and, second, an embrace of both the aesthetic forms and material means of reproduction found within the mass-cultural environment. Postmodernism as a distinct cultural and artistic movement has both triumphed and disappeared, as its characteristic notes—disruption of ontological levels, ironic quotation of past styles, display of fragmented subjectivities, indifference to high culture/low culture distinctions, and so on—have become the unremarkable background music of our time.

Meanwhile, postmodernism seems to have taken firm hold as both a philosophical development and a widely held historical attitude. As much as its detractors have been eager to announce the death of deconstruction in recent years, the general tenets of poststructuralism—that there is no recourse to some ground or referent that would center or stabilize the differential play of meaning in language and that therefore all truth and knowledge can be only contingent, local, and temporary; that the human subject is "constructed" within the various discourses that constitute our social space and that as such the subject can have no essential or fixed identity, and so on—have become the governing assumptions in much if not most research in the humanities and social sciences. It is a measure of how far postmodernism has come that critic Christopher Norris can denounce it as an "ironcast orthodoxy" that has become, oxymoronically, a "dogmatic relativism" (285). In the field of literary study, postmodernism's dominance is felt not just in the explicit application of poststructuralist methodologies but in the extent to which poststructuralist assumptions are by now unspoken, part of what goes without saying in the course of professional practice. To cite one small example, consider the tone with which Alec McHoul and David Wills are able to complain that "with disturbing regularity" critics find it useful to discuss Pynchon's texts as though they were the actual intended product of "some person called Pynchon" (4–5). In this smug presumption of the poststructuralist viewpoint, we find no longer the contentiousness of an insurgent minority but the righteousness of victors.

The expressions of indignation on both sides of the debate are a sign that postmodernism, though well into its maturity, is yet far from doddering old age. As a historical attitude, postmodernism finds its most generalized expression in the discrediting of the myth of progress. Foucault's attack on the Enlightenment is just one highly influential and sophisticated working through of what has become (despite Habermas's objections) the conventional wisdom: the Enlightenment narrative that places us on the path from barbarism to civilization and that sees the project of modernity as the progressive realization of individual liberties is really a sort of fairy tale whose promulgation aids the further subjugation and exploitation of the powerless. As Christopher Norris puts it, summarizing a position with which he disagrees:

> According to Foucault such Whiggish or progressivist notions are really just a species of self-serving fantasy, a means of ignoring the different kinds of violence—the forms of internalized discipline and constraint—that characterize our current sexual mores, social institutions, psychiatric techniques, ideas of justice, projects of penal reform, etc. What we like to think of as "progress" in these areas is really a history of steadily intensifying pressure, a multiplication of the strategies available for constructing the subject in accordance with societal norms and ensuring compliance with this or that mode of acceptable behaviour and belief. (257)

However bleak a view of history Foucault's may be, it meets a receptive audience among those who have increasing difficulty imagining a future that is an improvement on the past. Albert Borgmann takes things a step further, arguing that a sign of our postmodernity is our inability to imagine any future at all: "One indication [that we have reached the end of the modern era] is the difficulty we have in finding the kind of discourse that would help us to chart the passage from the present to the future. The idiom we have favored since the beginning of the modern era fails to inspire conviction or yield insight; the language of those who are proclaiming a new epoch seems merely deconstructive or endlessly prefatory" (2). That we lack a shared language both for imagining the future and for celebrating present civilizing achievements has become a widely acknowledged feature of public discourse. This gloss by Henry Kissinger, in a review of a biography of Winston Churchill, will serve as an example: "Faith in uninterrupted progress and in the essentially benign operation of human intelligence was succeeded by two world wars, ruthless dictatorships and ethnic exterminations. The result has been a growing proclamation of the relativity of all beliefs, and questions about the validity of Western civilization itself" (7). Norris, Borgmann, and Kissinger, writers whose views span the political spectrum, all wish that we still had a viable narrative of progress, their unity on this point a sure sign that they wish in vain.

In today's talk of adjusting to the new political realities of the post–cold war era, of the need for businesses to adapt to global competition, or of the new opportunities presented by communications resources such as the Internet, to take just three examples, one hears more about innovation than improvement, more about adapting to conditions imposed by circumstance than of rationally directing the course of change. In the repeated exhortations on the part of business and political leaders to "keep up" with new developments, we sense the surety that we are already hopelessly "behind." Whatever the excitements of new technological developments—whether in computing capabilities, biotechnology, or high-definition television—it is impossible to imagine a politician of today deploying the rhetoric of progress in the same way as was common just thirty years ago. During the 1992 campaign, presidential candidate Bill Clinton proclaimed that "we must make change our friend," an expedient expression in the face of change that, however stimulating, fails to halt the decline in real personal income, address our pernicious social problems, or otherwise return to us that vision of a prosperous future it is felt we had, once upon a time in that far-off land of the 1950s. As Fredric Jameson has put it, "the word 'new' doesn't seem to have the same resonance for us any longer" (*Postmodernism* 310).

Postmodernism is both less and more important than we thought. Though it may no longer drive radical experimentation in literature and the arts, its philosophical assumptions and historical attitudes are widespread. This study had its first stirrings in a concern for the fate of the novel in the age of television, a concern that has come to seem quaint. Now, in the age of the Internet, the Web, e-mail, interactive cable television, roof-mounted satellite dishes, and multimedia computer technology, television as practiced in the 1950s, '60s and '70s appears antique. It is time, indeed past time, to announce the Death of Television. Doing so allows a fresh perspective on the familiar argument that pits television as the purveyor of surfaces against the novel as the bearer of depth. For if we thought that this opposition was somehow a necessary consequence of the properties of these two forms of representation, we have once again failed to think our way out of the paper bag of the present moment. It may simply be the nature of cultural dominants to appear as the purveyors of surface, while residual forms appear to us as the bearers of depth. After all, it was during the ascendancy of print culture that the novel came under most frequent attack for its superficiality and moral danger. And it is perhaps only at such a high point of oratorical culture as fifth-century Athens that Plato could have Socrates define oratory as a species of "pandering" and a "spurious counterfeit branch of the art of government" (*Gorgias*). Likewise, it is only during the rise of television that Marshall McLuhan's millenarian pronouncements of the 1960s could have made novelists and critics wonder nervously about the fate of the novel in the midst of an epochal shift from print to electronic culture. It may be that television culture, simply by its nature as the always already everywhere of the past four decades, the water in which we have been swimming, has resisted the hermeneutical enterprise by which surfaces are penetrated to reveal the depths within. Residual forms of communication—the printed, bound book among them—come to us with the authority of age, and with something of the curiosity and whiff of scandal that attend all unlikely survivals.

In its engagements with mass culture, then, and in its attempts "to think the present historically in an age that has forgotten how to think historically in the first place," the postmodern novel has embodied a paradox in which depth is brought to account before surface, in which the venerable processes of the novel as it grasps the historical referent are held up to scrutiny in the flickering half-light of the television screen. But this reasoning also suggests that our sense of this paradox will fade as television gives way to its still emergent successor, a point at which the novel and television will no longer be seen as rivals. Having lived through the death of television, one looks for television's return, staggering stiff-armed in that Thanatoid twilight in which all other avatars of depth—history, the novel, the subject, the author—now dwell. And is it impossible to imagine that a century or two from now, television, film, radio, together with the glossy, perfumed pages of *Vogue,* will be regarded soberly and equally with the novel as lost beacons of truth and light in a world made unbearably superficial by the rise to dominance of some new and—to us—unimaginable form of communication?

N O T E S

Introduction

1. I use the term *cultural dominant* in Raymond Williams's sense: at any moment in history, dominant cultural forms coexist with both older residual forms and newer emergent ones. See Williams, *Marxism and Literature* 121–27. As a new cultural form rises to dominance, earlier forms are not abandoned but transformed and incorporated into a new order. Often the result is that residual and emergent forms, rather than maintaining an oppositional character in resistance to the dominant, become incorporated into the structure of the dominant itself: the politician's sound bite and the televangelist's fund-raising pitch are just two of the more obvious examples of how a dominant cultural form—television—transforms and incorporates the older and now residual forms of political and pulpit oratory. In speaking of the novel as a "residual" form, I am placing the current situation of the novel within the larger shift from "print culture" to "electronic culture" described by communications theorists such as Innis, McLuhan, Meyrowitz, and Ong.

Williams's model of the dominant, residual, and emergent is a useful way of think-ing about this shift, for otherwise the terms *print culture* and *electronic culture* be-come abstracted systems of dominance, making it difficult to describe how one system gives way to another. The rise of electronic culture does not mean the aban-donment of print: we have more print today than ever before. But the form and function of print media, the novel included, have been altered by the print media's position within a communications environment dominated by the electronic media.

2. For an example of how Jameson's rhetoric operates, consider his discussion of "geniuses" or "Great Writers," figures whom in modernism we admired for their "innate subjectivity" but whom in postmodernism we admire for their entrepre-neurial skill, for "their capacity to assess the 'current situation'" and devise innova-tive and marketable permutations of the current system of literary production. Jameson considers this shift to be "a properly postmodern revision in biographical historiography, which characteristically substitutes the horizontal for the vertical, space for time, system for depth." Then, beginning a new paragraph, he writes, "But there is a deeper reason for the disappearance of the Great Writer under post-modernism" (307). One can see how it goes: it is Jameson's project to provide, on the level of analysis, a depth that is lacking on the level of everyday experience. The details are not important here, but the "deeper reason" that he provides for the shift in attitudes toward the Great Writer involves the classical Marxist concept of the mode of production. For at its heart Jameson's argument about postmodernism rests on the Marxist depth model, in which the characteristic cultural forms of any historical period are part of a "superstructure" determined, at least "in the last instance," by the corresponding material and economic "base" or mode of produc-tion. Postmodernism, in this model, is the superstructure, or "cultural logic," cor-responding to the current mode of production (which Jameson, following Ernst Mandel, terms "late capitalism").

3. Though the drama is heightened in Jameson's case because he is describing a con-cept that, if its claims were accepted, would seem to challenge the very basis of Jameson's—or anyone's—analysis. That is, in describing postmodernism Jameson is describing conditions of knowledge in which it is presumably impossible ever to "ground" one's analysis in any disinterested point of view that escapes the very in-stabilities of meaning that one is attempting to describe. Therefore, to his critics Jameson is inconsistent if not hypocritical for attempting to "master" a system premised on the refusal of mastery. Jameson constructs a "totalizing" and unified theory of a system that operates through endless differentiation and fragmentation, and therefore in a sense refuses to be a "system" at all. Jameson answers these objec-tions by arguing that "the notion that there is something misguided and contradic-tory about a unified theory of differentiation also rests on a confusion between levels of abstraction: a system that constitutively produces differences remains a system; nor is the idea of such a system supposed to be in kind 'like' the object it

tries to theorize, any more than the concept of dog is supposed to bark or the concept of sugar to taste sweet" (*Postmodernism* 343). I find Jameson's argument persuasive, though it leaves unanswered the charge that, if one truly accepts the postmodernist and poststructuralist claims about the unavoidable instabilities of language, then one should be more rigorously self-conscious about the instabilities at play in one's own writing. In practice, however, it seems that entering into this vortex produces less insight than it does miserably bad prose, as our critical literature of the past twenty years is clotted with passages of obfuscation and cloying self-consciousness committed in the name of just such self-deconstructing "rigor." Few writers other than Jacques Derrida himself seem to possess the wit required to turn such doubts to good account.

4. Of course one can argue that Baudrillard's defeatism, abetted by his mordant wit, is simply part of another rhetorical strategy, similar to Jameson's, that allows him to "do sociology" even as he describes the conditions in which sociological analysis should be disabled.

5. Nor can the relations between the novel and mass culture be seen as those between "serious" and "popular" culture, between high culture and low. First, the novels discussed here range from the best-selling *Ragtime* and the popular *In Country,* both of which were made into movies, to *Gravity's Rainbow,* which though well established in the academic canon is far more widely purchased than read, to the novels of DeLillo, Reed, and Baker, which find their more select readerships. But, beyond the difficulty of assigning a cultural position to these particular texts, there is the more vexed question of how to situate the novel genre as a whole. Whether one regards the historical separation of elite and mass culture as real or illusory, as on the one hand a genuine difference determined by social formation and/or aesthetic qualities, or on the other hand an ideological assertion of a "purity" that high art never in fact achieved, any student of the novel must confront the fact that through most of its history the novel has laid only the most doubtful claim to high cultural status. As it emerged in the eighteenth century, the novel was produced and distributed largely according to the commercial imperatives of a developing market operating independently of aristocratic patronage. Samuel Johnson was not only a brilliant literary mind but the man who said, "Sir, no man but a blockhead ever wrote except for money," and serves as the representative entrepreneurial author of his age. Just as the novel owed its life to the abilities of authors and publishers to figure a market, so it owed much of its form and content to the haphazard amalgamation of the popular discourses in circulation at the time. The novel in the eighteenth century owed as much to the "low" discourses of ballads, criminal trial reports, letters, diaries, and news and journalism of all kinds, as it did to the "high" cultural discourses of the sermon, the hagiography, the spiritual autobiography, and the philosophical essay. For an excellent analysis of the matrix of discourses out of which the novel emerged, see Lennard Davis, *Factual Fictions.* The standard work on the origins of the English novel is Ian Watt, *The Rise of the Novel,* though

Watt's approach has received significant challenges in recent years, most notably from Michael McKeon in *The Origins of the English Novel, 1600-1740*.

6. David Harvey's overview of postmodernism in chapter 3 of his *The Condition of Postmodernity* has the advantages of lucidity, comprehensiveness, and relative brevity. For an overview that better accounts for the complexities and contradictions within postmodernism, and which more thoroughly treats the historical relations between postmodernism, modernism, the avant-garde, and mass culture, see Andreas Huyssen, *After the Great Divide,* especially the chapter titled "Mapping the Postmodern" (reprinted in Nicholson, ed., *Feminism/Postmodernism* 234–77). An influential collection of essays treating postmodernist developments in art, architecture, mass culture, and literary theory is *The Anti-Aesthetic,* edited by Hal Foster. For essays on postmodernism in the visual arts, and on the political dimensions of postmodernism's relations to modernism and mass culture, see Hal Foster's *Recodings.* Helpful introductory essays on postmodernism in a variety of fields, including music, architecture, and literature, can be found in Trachtenberg, ed., *The Postmodern Moment.* The most influential formulation of postmodernism in architecture is that of Charles Jencks, in *Post-Modernism* and *The Language of Post-Modern Architecture.* A ground-breaking study of the possibilities for a new populism in architecture is Robert Venturi, Denise Scott Brown, and Steven Izenour, *Learning from Las Vegas.*

7. For the reader relatively new to the critical literature on postmodernist fiction, I offer the following selected bibliography. Larry McCaffery has edited a useful anthology, *Postmodern Fiction,* which combines a number of introductory essays with brief bio-bibliographical entries on a wide range of postmodernist fiction writers. For an overview of postmodernism as a literary movement of international dimensions, see the collection of essays edited by Douwe Fokkema and Hans Bertens, *Approaching Postmodernism.* The most closely argued and internally consistent account of postmodernism in fiction is that of Brian McHale in *Postmodernist Fiction.* There he argues for a postmodernist fiction characterized by its "ontological poetics" and applies his definition in a series of careful readings informed by narratological concerns. The book's narrow focus on ontological issues is both its strength and its flaw, as McHale admits in his later *Constructing Postmodernism,* in which he both extends and complicates his original argument. With McHale, Alan Wilde is one of the few writers on postmodernist fiction whose broader theories are supported by extended readings of particular texts. Wilde's *Horizons of Assent* is especially helpful for its distinctions between postmodernist and modernist forms of irony. His *Middle Grounds* is also helpful, though it adopts a more polemical stance, championing the practice of a particular group of postmodernist fiction writers. Yet more sweeping, and more polemical (and more wickedly fun), is Charles Newman's *The Post-Modern Aura,* which argues that the oscillation between realist and formalist modes of fiction in recent decades is symptomatic of an inflationary culture in which all literary production is devalued. Though New-

man takes up a broader cultural critique, his acerbic view of contemporary literary culture shares much in tone and intent with Gerald Graff's earlier *Literature against Itself*. Linda Hutcheon's project is not so much polemical as broadly descriptive; though she rarely pauses long enough to pursue careful, extended readings of texts, her *A Poetics of Postmodernism* demonstrates a sweeping command of postmodernist fiction and literary theory. Her work is especially helpful for its international scope and for the links she establishes between the concerns of literary theorists and the practices of postmodernist fiction writers. Her later book, *The Politics of Postmodernism,* argues for the contradictory nature of postmodernism's political stance and concludes with an argument as to why postmodernism cannot be compatible with feminist politics. Such a view runs counter to the efforts of Patricia Waugh, who in *Feminine Fictions* attempts to refashion our understanding of postmodernism in a way that accounts for the work of feminist writers. Marleen S. Barr has argued for the inclusion of feminist science fiction under the rubric of postmodernism in *Feminist Fabulation,* and the question of the relations between feminism and postmodernism has been treated from a variety of philosophical and theoretical perspectives in the collection edited by Linda Nicholson, *Feminism/ Postmodernism.*

8. The event is recounted with dramatic flair by Frank Lentricchia in *After the New Criticism* (157).

9. As one example, consider Catherine Belsey's statement that "both the Holocaust and Hiroshima produced a crisis of confidence in the Enlightenment version of history as a single narrative of the progressive enfranchisement of reason and truth" (261, cit. Norris 285). This may be so, but isn't it just as much a commonplace to say that this "crisis of confidence" was brought about earlier by World War I?

10. Valuable historical work on advertising has been done by Stuart and Elizabeth Ewen. See their essay "Consumption as a Way of Life" in *Channels of Desire*, 23–51. See also Stuart Ewen, "Advertising and the Development of Consumer Society" in *Cultural Politics in Contemporary America,* ed. Ian Angus and Sut Jhally, 82–95.

11. The incident of the Balinese villagers watching *Dallas* was reported by Steven R. Bailey in "Postcards from Home: Personal Reflections on American Popular Culture in Asia," a paper delivered at the Midwest American Culture Association/ Popular Culture Association Conference, Toledo, Ohio, 1990.

12. Mark Poster follows communications theorists such as McLuhan in sketching a history of communication in which each of the successive phases—oral culture, print culture, and electronic culture—produces its characteristic forms of subjectivity: "In the first, oral stage the self is constituted as a position of enunciation through its embeddedness in a totality of face-to-face relations. In the second, print stage the self is constructed as an agent centered in rational/imaginary autonomy. In the third, electronic stage the self is decentered, dispersed, and multiplied in continuous instability" (6). For Fredric Jameson, the postmodern dilemma "in-

volves our insertion as individual subjects into a multidimensional set of radically discontinuous realities, whose frames range from the still surviving spaces of bourgeois private life all the way to the unimaginable decentering of global capital itself. Not even Einsteinian relativity, or the multiple subjective worlds of the older modernists, is capable of giving any kind of adequate figuration to this process" (*Postmodernism* 413). The particular challenges to subjectivity presented by our predominantly *visual* culture are explored in chapter 2 in connection with the fiction of Don DeLillo.

13. Indeed, recent writers continue to push back the boundaries of postmodernism, making postmodernism the lens through which all earlier periods are seen. Patricia Waugh in *Feminine Fictions* wants to read Virginia Woolf as a postmodernist. In *Constructing Postmodernism,* Brian McHale offers up a postmodernist James Joyce. Diane Elam's *Romancing the Postmodern* pushes the postmodern into the nineteenth century, and to some of the contributors to *Shakespeare and the Question of Theory,* edited by Patricia Parker and Geoffrey Hartman, the bard himself takes on a postmodernist mien. The revisionist project is forthrightly pursued by Bill Readings and Bennet Schaber, the editors of *Postmodernity across the Ages: Essays for a Postmodernity That Wasn't Born Yesterday.*

14. See note 3 above. The most thoroughgoing argument on this and related matters has been made by Richard Rorty. From his pragmatic perspective, the poststructuralists' exaggerated fears of "logocentric discourse" are the result of continued attachment to the very metaphysics they so vigorously denounce. In a sense the poststructuralists are the last true believers in language as a vehicle for fixed truth, for they alone continue to feel that this belief is worthy of attack. In the same way, it might now be said, a hundred years after Nietzsche, that only those who live each day with the mysteries and complexities of faith in God can fully reject any simplistic notion of absolute truth.

15. Locke's theory emphasized that the proper effect of words is in their summoning of clear and distinct ideas in the mind; Burke challenged the Lockean (and Cartesian) doctrine of clarity by arguing that the characteristic effect of language is to arouse the passions. See chapter 2.

16. For Alan Wilde, such an attitude is characterized by the use of "suspensive irony," in which disconnectedness is accepted, the quest for paradise abandoned, and thus a sort of peace attained (*Horizons of Assent* 9–10). In itself this passive formulation does not account either for the active, interventionist nature of some postmodernist fictions or for their energetic playfulness. Wilde provides a more active formulation under the heading of "generative irony," which is that positive aspect of suspensive irony in which one finds "the attempt, inspired by the negotiations of self and world, to create, tentatively and provisionally, anironic enclaves of value in the face of—but not in place of—a meaningless universe" (148). The assertion that some postmodernist fiction succeeds in creating "anironic enclaves of value," however tentative and provisional, is certainly debatable, yet is consistent with

Wilde's claim (both here and in *Middle Grounds*) that certain postmodernist practices are compatible with a limited form of self-conscious humanism.

17. This point is made by Thomas Ferraro, in his essay "Whole Families Shopping at Night!" in Lentricchia, ed., *New Essays on* White Noise.

18. Donna Haraway argues that "the political struggle is to see from both perspectives at once because each reveals both dominations and possibilities unimaginable from the other vantage point. Single vision produces worse illusions than double vision or many-headed monsters" (196). In his essay "The End of Mass Culture," Michael Denning provides an excellent summary of the efforts of cultural critics, particularly Fredric Jameson and Stuart Hall, to overcome these inherited dualisms in attitudes toward mass and popular culture. And while Denning is correct in arguing that among left academic theorists these dualisms have largely been overcome, it is worth noting their persistence in the popular press and among neoconservative cultural critics, as well as within contemporary fiction. For key essays in this debate, see Jameson, "Reification and Utopia in Mass Culture," and Hall, "Notes on Deconstructing 'the Popular.'"

1. *Toward the Postmodern Historical Imagination*

1. For Jameson, the modernist perception of rapid change depended on the coexistence of different modes of production: "Modernism must thus be seen as uniquely corresponding to an uneven moment of social development . . . the coexistence of realities from radically different moments of history—handicrafts alongside the great cartels, peasant fields with the Krupp factories or the Ford plant in the distance." See Jameson, *Postmodernism* 307–13, 404–5. We should note, however, that the social development evinced in *The Moviegoer* belongs to a later phase, to suburbanization rather than to the growth of urban industrial centers during the period of monopoly capitalism that Jameson describes. And yet it is also worth observing that because the American South lagged behind the northern states in the process of industrialization, the kinds of changes that Binx Bolling experiences in the Louisiana of the 1950s may resemble those experienced by many northerners and Europeans during the earlier decades of the century. This accounts in part for the modernist character of Percy's novel despite its concern with image culture—a concern that will become a common preoccupation of postmodernist writers, artists, and theorists.

2. For a discussion of the importance of Stoic philosophy to Walker Percy, see Gretlund.

3. Walker Percy's interest in existentialist writers such as Camus and Sartre is well known and widely discussed by Percy critics, as is his most important intellectual debt to Søren Kierkegaard. While acknowledging the similarity between Percy's method in *The Moviegoer* and Camus's method in *L'Etranger*, however, Tony Tanner argues that certain important differences—such as Binx's "search"—also place

Binx Bolling in a particularly American tradition of the questing "outsider" character. See Tanner.

4. The narrator's practice would thus seem to illustrate Fredric Jameson's objection to Jean-François Lyotard's strategy of "paralogism," in which systems of knowledge, science, and power are undermined by the continual invention of rules for new language games. To Jameson, the strategy of inventing new language games simply feeds capitalism's appetite for innovation, and is thus absorbed into the "dynamic of perpetual change" that is inherent to capitalism itself. See Jameson's "Foreword" to Lyotard's *The Postmodern Condition*, p. xx. It is precisely on the question of the need for master historical narratives that Lyotard and Jameson part company: Lyotard rejects them as inherently repressive, while Jameson embraces the Marxist historical narrative as necessary for effective cultural critique and oppositional politics. The narrator of *The Mezzanine*, then, could be seen as a caricature of the result, in Jameson's view, of Lyotard's rejection of master narratives in favor of parology.

5. See chapter 4. For a useful discussion of this shift as it relates to the social class affiliations of the writers themselves, see Hobson 11–23.

6. Cleanth Brooks sees in Percy's "scientific humanism" a version of a secular Gnosticism, which wants to deny man's fundamental alienation from God and regards the world as perfectible through human action. "In all of Percy's novels the hero inherits what amounts to an orthodox Christian view of man and his relation to reality, but the world inhabited by the hero is dominated by ideas that are powerfully twisted away from the orthodox view" (54).

7. In a letter, Nicholson Baker writes that, though he owned a copy, he had not read *The Moviegoer* prior to writing *The Mezzanine* (Nicholson Baker to Philip Simmons 18 March 1993).

8. For one overheated recital of this accusation, see Tom Wolfe's "Stalking the Billion-Footed Beast." John Aldridge in *Talents and Technicians* has also weighed in with his own version of this by now familiar complaint.

9. There are of course exceptions, such as William Gaddis's *JR* and Joseph Heller's *Something Happened*. And in commercial fiction, the era of the corporate takeover and other financial high jinks has given rise to the new genre of "financial thriller."

10. It is telling that Baker's second novel, *Room Temperature* (1990), takes on the domestic setting directly and is less successful as a result. In the framing action of this novel, the narrator feeds his baby daughter with a bottle, and the narrative ranges over his life as father and husband. By turning its obsessive and erudite attention to the minutiae of a domestic scene already perhaps too familiar to readers of contemporary fiction, the novel loses one of the key ironic effects of *The Mezzanine*. Baker returns to form with his best-selling third novel, *Vox* (1992), which presents one long episode of phone sex between strangers who have reached one another through a 900 number. As it explores the intricacies of the kind of no-risk sex and anonymous intimacy made possible by telecommunications technology, the novel speaks to the quality of many human relationships in the 1990s.

11. I term Percy's existentialism "American" both because it belongs to a particular history of American reception of European existentialist philosophy and because of the particular American literary context in which his existentialist thinking is deployed. All this despite Percy's own statement, "I think of myself as being more in the European group than the American or the Southern. I use the fiction form as a vehicle for incarnating ideas, as did Jean-Paul Sartre and Gabriel Marcel. I long ago decided that my philosophy is in the vein of existentialism, as theirs were" (*Conversations* 9; cit. Westarp ix).

12. Among postmodern cultural theorists much of this debate has been played out over the concept of "totality" as it is used in Fredric Jameson's model of postmodernism first presented in his 1984 essay, "Postmodernism, or The Cultural Logic of Late Capitalism," in *New Left Review*. For several essays critical of Jameson's assertion that postmodernism has eliminated the last vestiges of marginality and authenticity, see the collection edited by Kellner. For Jameson's answer to these criticisms, see his *Postmodernism*, esp. 342–43.

2. *Don DeLillo's Invisible Histories*

1. This phenomenon is discussed by Mark Poster. See *The Mode of Information* 9–10.

2. Light and vision also function in the construction of moral discipline and political authority, a fact that is perhaps so obvious as often to escape our notice. Bentham's panoptic prisons of the eighteenth century, described by Foucault, provide only one relatively late example. The central medallion in Hieronymous Bosch's painting *The Seven Deadly Sins and Last Four Things* bears the inscription: "Beware, beware! God sees." And Machiavelli wrote that princes must *appear* princely "for men in general judge more by the eyes than by the hands, for every one can see, but very few have to feel" (94, cit. Meyrowitz 65.)

3. For example, the requirements of clarity and distinctness produced intractable difficulties in Enlightenment moral philosophy and aesthetics, as the sentimental philosophy of Hutcheson and Hume had to contend with the fact that moral and aesthetic perception could never come up to the clarity and distinctness that the analogue of vision required. The word *aesthetics* was brought into modern discourse in 1735 as a way of ascribing value to forms of experience that were inaccessible to the kind of clear moral and intellectual judgment that Cartesian and Lockean epistemology demanded. Baumgarten used the Greek *aestheta*, sensible facts, in opposition to *noeta*, mental objects, and sought to establish the new science of "sensible cognition." To Baumgarten, following Leibniz, the "*petit perceptions*" of aesthetic experience were "confused," and thus lacked the distinctness required for valid intellectual or moral perception. Aesthetic experience, in this early formulation, was a second-class citizen, of doubtful moral status, a source not of knowledge but of potentially dangerous pleasure. For this reason, Croce saw Baumgarten's as a failed attempt to elevate aesthetics to its deserved status. See Croce 212–13.

4. See Fussell 22. That Burke's humanism is in fact an anachronism in the world of increasingly scientific Enlightenment discourse partly accounts for the poignancy of his rhetoric about the French Revolution.

5. For two examples, see Redfield's "Pynchon's Postmodern Sublime" and Ferguson's "The Nuclear Sublime."

6. Putting it in slightly different terms, Baudrillard writes that "it is a question here of a completely new species of uncertainty, which results not from the *lack* of information but from information itself and even from an *excess* of information" (*Selected Writings* 210).

7. See Foucault, "Panopticism," excerpted from *Discipline and Punish* in *The Foucault Reader* 206–13.

8. Mark Poster describes the fate of the postmodern subject in terms that go beyond the effects of film and television to include all forms of electronic communication. Poster argues for a new concept of the "mode of information" that is analogous to the Marxist concept of "mode of production." "In the mode of information," he writes, "the subject is no longer located in a point in absolute time/space, enjoying a physical, fixed vantage point from which rationally to calculate its options. Instead it is multiplied by databases, dispersed by computer messaging and conferencing, decontextualized and reidentified by TV ads, dissolved and materialized continuously in the electronic transmission of symbols" (15). See also 46.

9. For Baudrillard's glum yet incisive take on opinion polls, see "The Masses" in *Selected Writings,* especially 208–14.

10. It should be noted that Foucault's application of the concept of discourse is not intended as a mystification. He insists that the disciplinary practices he describes are not to be read symbolically for "deeper levels" of meaning. On the contrary, according to Foucault the technologies of discipline and surveillance belong to discourses that are transparent and not in need of interpretation. See "Truth and Power" 57, in *The Foucault Reader.*

11. I am indebted to David Cowart for reminding me that DeLillo thus uses the term "aura" in a sense precisely opposite that of Walter Benjamin, for whom the "aura" of the handcrafted original artwork is destroyed when the artwork is mechanically reproduced. See Benjamin, "The Work of Art in the Age of Mechanical Reproduction." This same ironic reversal of Benjamin is made by Charles Newman in the title of his book, *The Post-Modern Aura.*

12. This event has become the locus classicus of media studies, an obligatory reference point in the discussion of how television exposes its viewers to situations and events in ways previously unimaginable. See McLuhan 292, Meyrowitz 43, Ong 316, Jameson 355. But Mark Crispin Miller argues that, by the mid-1970s, television had largely purged itself of such unexpected events to become "a perfect shelter, a dream container, unbreakable, antiseptic and without surprises" (9–10).

13. Ferrie's discussion of coincidence bears striking resemblance to the theories of "synchronicity" developed by Carl Jung. Throughout much of his career, Jung struggled

to develop the concept of "synchronicity" as a balance to the principle of causality, finally publishing "Synchronicity: An Acausal Connecting Principle" in 1952 at age 74. (See Jung, "Synchronizität als ein Prinzip Akausaler Zusammenhänge." In C. G. Jung and W. Pauli, *Naturerklärung und Psyche*. Zurich: Rascher Verlag, 1952. Published in translation as "Synchronicity: An Acausal Connecting Principle." In C. G. Jung and W. Pauli, *The Interpretation of Nature and the Psyche*. New York: Pantheon Books, 1955.) For Jung, "synchronicity comes into consideration only in the case of two or more causal chains running parallel to each other" that are causally independent of one another (cit. Progoff 131). Ferrie's "third line," that which "cuts across time" and "forces a connection" is for Jung generated by the archetypes that, like Ferrie's "dreams, visions, intuitions, prayers" lie at the "deepest levels of the self" and allow for a patterning of experience outside of the causal order. For Jung, synchronicity operates in a "transpersonal macrocosmic field" (Progoff 129) and characterizes events that have a meaningful but noncausal relationship to one another.

3. The Spectacular Fictions of Ishmael Reed and E. L. Doctorow

1. I am indebted to Dana Polan's essay, "Brief Encounters: Mass Culture and the Evacuation of Sense," for his discussion of Eizykman's work, cited above, and for the idea that postmodernism can be characterized by the combination of narrative and spectacle.

2. Critic Gerald Graff argues that the real avant-garde of our time is advanced consumer capitalism, "with its built-in need to destroy all vestiges of tradition, all orthodox ideologies, all continuous and stable forms of reality in order to stimulate higher levels of consumption" (8). Charles Newman takes up Graff's position, arguing that the ceaseless innovations of mass culture have made earlier avant-garde postures untenable: "Crisis becomes not a revolutionary but the ultimate capitalist metaphor" (51).

3. I am indebted to RoseLee Goldberg's *Performance Art* for my sense of twentieth-century performance art as a distinct tradition. The emphasis on the nonnarrative aspect of performance is mine, however, not hers. A significant exception to performance art's antinarrative stance would be the propagandistic works of Russian futurists and constructivists (40–43).

4. See White, *Metahistory* ix–xii, 1–42. See also White, "The Value of Narrativity in the Representation of Reality."

5. In *The Postmodern Condition,* Lyotard shifts between material and linguistic senses of the "performative": conceived as the requirement for material efficiency, for a low input/output ratio, performativity is the imperative that drives the development of a technologically based capitalist system (41–47); toward the end of *The Postmodern Condition,* however, performativity becomes the imperative behind *resistance* to system. In order to make this dialectical move, Lyotard shifts from the material to the linguistic sense of the "performative" and draws upon Wittgen-

stein's notion of language games to outline a strategy of "paralogism" in which systems of knowledge, science, and power are undermined by the continuous invention of new language games (60–67). In this sense, the "performativity" of a language game is valued simply for its ability to enable further performance, further invention and play outside or alongside existing systems of knowledge and power. While John Mowitt rightly identifies Lyotard's slippage from the material to the linguistic sense of the "performative" as a dialectical move, it should also be seen as a species of the utopian impulse within poststructuralist and postmodernist thought generally: the belief that, by conceiving of cultural and political resistance in linguistic and semiotic terms, one can effect a material intervention as well.

6. This passage, and the phenomenon of "zapping" in general, is discussed by Brian McHale in *Constructing Postmodernism* 132–33. McHale's discussion of television is also helpful for distinguishing between the "ontological structures" of television and film. See 126–28.

7. The bibliography contains its own quirks as well. For example, Zora Neale Hurston's 1935 book of folklore, *Mules and Men,* is listed as the 1955 work of "Zoran Hurston."

8. For a general discussion of the importance of vision to the development of the novel in the early eighteenth century, see Konigsberg. For a discussion of how the mid-eighteenth-century novel develops "voyeuristic" narrative techniques as a means of eliciting the intense imaginative participation of its readers, see my article on John Cleland's *Memoirs of a Woman of Pleasure.*

9. The text's parody of historiographic conventions is responsible for Fredric Jameson's conflicted response to the novel. On the one hand, Jameson acknowledges the novel's serious political engagement with the history of working-class experience and radical politics, yet decries the novel's retreat into nostalgia and laments the fact that the postmodern historical novel "can no longer set out to represent the historical past; it can only 'represent' our ideas and stereotypes about that past (which thereby at once becomes 'pop' history)" ("Postmodernism" 71). In answering Jameson, Linda Hutcheon takes a position similar to Dawson's. In *A Poetics of Postmodernism,* Hutcheon names both *Ragtime* and *Mumbo Jumbo* as examples of "historiographic metafiction," which "not only is self-reflexively metafictional and parodic, but also makes a claim to some kind of (newly problematical) historical reference" (40). For Jameson, *Ragtime* exemplifies postmodernism's effacement of the historical referent, whereas for Hutcheon, *Ragtime* "reinstalls historical contexts as significant and even determining, but in so doing, it problematizes the entire notion of historical knowledge" (89). See also Hutcheon, *The Politics of Postmodernism* 95.

10. The correspondences between *Ragtime* and *Michael Kohlhaus* are detailed by John Ditsky.

11. When a university president declares at a convocation ceremony that "the University is now open," one does not evaluate this utterance the way one would the utter-

ance "fund-raising is up from last year." One looks not to its truth as such, but to whether the person making the utterance has the necessary authority, has made the utterance in the appropriate context, and whether certain other actions and utterances follow as a consequence. See Austin 8–9.

12. Those interested in pursuing the importance of transition might look to the eighteenth-century debates over the idea of "method," outlined by Alkon in "Critical and Logical Concepts of Method from Addison to Coleridge." As Alkon explains, eighteenth-century logicians shifted from an emphasis on logical, sequential order to an emphasis on connections between elements. Thus the term "method" came to have less to do with the order in which elements were ranged and more to do with the transitions between them. The heightened emphasis, among critics of poetry and the essay, on the pleasure and power of connections and transitions, was accompanied within logic by a shift of emphasis from deductive to inductive reasoning.

13. For a fuller discussion of this issue, see *Factual Fictions* by Lennard Davis, who sees indifference to the fact/fiction distinction as essential to the development of the novel during the late seventeenth and early eighteenth centuries.

4. *Minimalist Fiction as "Low" Postmodernism*

1. Other writers whom I would include in the minimalist group are Frederick Barthelme, Tobias Wolff, Joy Williams, Mary Robison, and Elizabeth Tallent. An important moment in the formation of a minimalist canon was the introduction of minimalism to British readers, under the name of "dirty realism," by the editors of *Granta* 8 (1983). Also noteworthy is the special section on minimalist fiction in *Mississippi Review* 40/41 (Winter 1985), introduced by a substantial essay by Kim Herzinger. It has been treated as "neo-realism" by Charles Newman (*The Post-Modern Aura*) and as "contemporary realism" by Alan Wilde (*Middle Grounds*), mainly to distinguish it from the realism of such writers as Saul Bellow and John Updike. Writers sometimes treated as minimalists, but about whom I think differently, are Joan Didion, Anne Tyler, and Richard Ford. What sets these writers apart has less to do with style on the sentence level than with different approaches to narrative form. Didion, Tyler, and Ford are more conventional storytellers, concerned with creating more involved plot structures and achieving a greater sense of narrative closure.

2. See Lentricchia, *Introducing Don DeLillo* 6. For "anorexic," see Gorra 155; for "anaerobic," Helprin xxi; for "catatonic," Wilde, *Middle Grounds* 112; for "brutal," Atlas 96.

3. Throughout this chapter the abbreviation CLC denotes *Contemporary Literary Criticism* (Detroit: Gale Research). CA denotes *Contemporary Authors* (Detroit: Gale Research). Original sources are cited in addition wherever possible.

4. Unless otherwise noted, all Carver citations are from *Where I'm Calling From*.

5. Given the pivotal importance of inarticulate silence in Carver's stories, it is fitting that the early story "Nobody Said Anything" is placed first in his final collection, *Where I'm Calling From* (1988).

6. In the 1983 *Paris Review* interview, Carver said, "I sometimes keep [a new story] around the house for months doing this or that to it, taking this out and putting that in. . . . I've done as many as twenty or thirty drafts of a story. Never less than ten or twelve drafts" (209). In his essay "On Writing," Carver wrote, "Evan Connell said once that he knew he was finished with a short story when he found himself going through it and taking out commas and then going through the story again and putting commas back in the same places. I like that way of working on something" (15). Carver's obsessive revising of his stories continued even after they had been published. Randolph Paul Runyon's book on Carver is helpful for noting differences between collected versions of Carver's stories and versions published earlier in magazines. William Stull, in "Beyond Hopelessville," compares "The Bath" (collected in *What We Talk about When We Talk about Love*) with its substantially revised and expanded version, "A Small, Good Thing" (collected in *Cathedral* and *Where I'm Calling From*), showing how the revision marks the shift from Carver's earlier "existential realism" to the more generous and expansive "humanist realism" of the later phase of his career. For a comparison of earlier and later versions of "So Much Water So Close to Home," see below.

7. In the 1983 *Paris Review* interview, Carver mentions reading Rilke while in his twenties (220). For more explicit references to Rilke, see the first sentence of "The Student's Wife" (26) and a passage in "Collectors" (88).

8. Page numbers are from *What We Talk about When We Talk about Love*, although this version of the story is preserved in the later collection, *Where I'm Calling From*.

9. The balancing act is performed with titles as well. For its final appearance in *Where I'm Calling From,* Carver retitled a very brief story (which parodies the story of Solomon proposing to cut a baby in half in order to resolve a maternity dispute) from the grimly jokey "Popular Mechanics" to the more broadly insinuating "Little Things," leaving the body of the story unchanged.

10. See William Stull, "Beyond Hopelessville: Another Side of Raymond Carver," and note 5 above. "A Small, Good Thing" first appeared in *Ploughshares* 8.2&3 (1982): 213–40. Mona Simpson, in her *Paris Review* interview with Carver, suggested that his new stories were longer and more generous, to which Carver replied: "Generous, yes, that's a good word for them" (211–12).

11. Carver's theory echoes that of Hemingway in the autobiographical novel *A Moveable Feast:* "you could omit anything if you knew that you omitted and the omitted part would strengthen the story and make people feel something more than they understood" (75).

12. Some of the flaws in *Falling in Place* perhaps stem from the haste of its composition. Beattie has said that the novel was written in seven weeks (Interview 7). Both of the chapters I have mentioned could have been improved with editing.

13. One exception is Charles Newman, in *The Post-Modern Aura.*

14. The populist nature of minimalist fiction is discussed in Webster 115–34.

15. Randolph Runyon claims that "Carver is in fact a self-reflexive metafictional writer" (4), though the evidence he marshals in support of that claim does not

make the case as strongly as one might wish. Runyon is concerned primarily with the apparently deliberate linkages between stories as they appear in Carver's collections. While such linkages and correspondences do suggest that Carver was aware of common motifs among his stories, and took some care in arranging his collections accordingly, this does not in itself make him a "metafictional" writer of the sort being described here. My argument is more in the spirit of Kim Herzinger's assessment of the minimalists: "Far from collapsing into a kind of journalistic representation of life in our time, they may well be creating literary constructs as formally rigorous and linguistically savvy as their Postmodernist predecessors. They are not, it seems to me, involved in a backbench effort to return to a premodern or pre-Postmodern 'realism'" (20). For "Postmodernist" substitute "high postmodernist," and then Herzinger and I are in agreement.

16. The text that codified this attitude for high postmodernism is John Barth's 1967 essay "The Literature of Exhaustion." Also important are the essays by Leslie Fiedler.

17. The novel follows the pattern established in Barthelme's earlier collection of stories, *Moon Deluxe* (1983), some of which were rewritten and incorporated into *Second Marriage.*

18. In answer to the common reading of his work as social criticism, Barthelme has said that "my business is not to sit around and attack the way we live" (Interview, CA 122: 49).

19. See Lentricchia, *After the New Criticism,* and Eagleton, *Literary Theory.* For a useful overview of this debate, see Bennington and Young.

20. See Brantlinger 34–35, 296, and my introduction, above. In the present instance, critics of minimalism from both the political right and left are united in seeing mass culture as a threat to historical understanding and, at least implicitly, to civilization itself.

21. A chapter of Mason's *In Country* begins: "It was the summer of the Michael Jackson *Victory* tour and the Bruce Springsteen *Born in the U.S.A.* tour, neither of which Sam got to go to" (23). Even to those versed in the pop music scene of the early 1980s, such references allow one to conclude no more than that this was 1984 and that Sam was no different than millions of other American teenagers.

22. See Andreas Huyssen's *After the Great Divide,* which argues, first, that modernism always required mass culture as a necessary other against which to make its claims for purity, austerity, and autonomy, and second, that postmodernism represents the collapse of the historical separation between modernism and mass culture, between high art and low.

23. Alan Wilde labels minimalism "catatonic realism" in response to his sense that Raymond Carver creates characters who, "in the face of frustration and misery, the eroding of pleasure and the all too evident spectacle of the waste of their lives, demonstrate a terrible blankness that suspends the activities of the self and, except in fantasy or violence, betrays its effective lack of control: its inability to do other than mirror what his characters experience as the insensateness of the world" (*Middle Grounds* 112). Michael Gorra defines minimalism as "a mannerist mode in

which the intentional poverty, the anorexia, of the writer's style is mimetic of the spiritual poverty of his or her characters' lives, their disconnection from anything like a traditional community" (155). Helprin extends the charge of spiritual poverty to the writers themselves: the minimalists "observe everything of great moment as if from a distance," and their "sang-froid" is the sign of a "cowardice," an "unwillingness to deal with life other than obliquely" (xxi).

24. For a discussion of the relation between this scene and traditional images of Confederate graveyards in the literature of the southern renascence, particularly Allen Tate's "Ode to the Confederate Dead," see Brinkmeyer.

25. *Life* reported on the self-immolation of the Buddhist monks, protesting the Diem government, in its issues of June 21, August 2, September 6, and November 15, 1963. Photographs of the suicides were published in each issue except that of August 2, with the photo in the June 21 issue being closest to the image that concludes Mason's novel.

26. A similar observation has been made in poststructuralist terms by Barbara Ryan, who argues that by the end of the novel Sam has learned to be a poststructuralist reader. Samantha must surrender her quest for the ultimate authority of the paternal Logos that her father represents, and instead accept her own responsibility for creative intervention in the free play of signification within the various texts she is given.

5. Pynchon

1. Scott Sanders writes that "paranoia is the last retreat of the Puritan imagination," which uses paranoia to compensate for the loss of God, "the original conspiracy theory" (139–40).

2. Not only physics, of course, but chemistry is offered as a candidate for history's motive force, and both disciplines provide Pynchon with a rich field of allusion and metaphor. Chemistry is especially important in *Gravity's Rainbow*. See Schaub 97–98.

3. Schaub's comment on this point is representative: "Pynchon's fictions are built so that the reader is subjected to the same ambiguities which cripple the characters" (16).

4. Exemplified by the work of Schaub and Hite, the mode of Pynchon criticism that emphasizes uncertainty and ambiguity in Pynchon's texts has been challenged by critics such as Kathryn Hume, who argues in *Pynchon's Mythography* that Pynchon's mythographical approach in *Gravity's Rainbow* is consistent and not undermined by irony or contradiction as are so many of his other ordering structures. In a similar fashion, Weisenburger's assertion in *A* Gravity's Rainbow *Companion* that *Gravity's Rainbow* has the circular structure of a mandala goes against the grain of Pynchon criticism that sees this novel's structure as indeterminate and designed to frustrate the readers' expectations of formal closure. For an overview of these conflicting trends in Pynchon criticism, see Duyfhuizen.

5. There are signs that Pynchon criticism has become in its own way a "literature of exhaustion," able to discuss Pynchon's texts in an original way only by demonstrating the impossibility of Pynchon criticism. This self-reflexive turn is found in Alec McHoul and David Wills's *Writing Pynchon*, a book as much about their "very real dissatisfaction with the Pynchon industry" as it is about Pynchon's writing—an approach that by their own admission requires a "tedious typology of Pynchon criticism" (4). Another example is found in Jeffrey T. Nealon's *Double Reading*, which includes a chapter on *Gravity's Rainbow*. His is a double project, both criticism and meta-criticism: "I emphasize the role(s) of the discipline of literary criticism—and, by extension, the roles of the university—in the production and control of meaning, while simultaneously trying to recognize and account for my own status as a literary critic and as a person who teaches and studies literature within an institution" (2). Not surprisingly, Nealon also finds much that is "wrong" with the state of Pynchon criticism (see, for example, his attack on "humanist/pluralist" readings of Pynchon, 112–20). It remains to be seen whether Pynchon criticism will pass through this phase to become a "literature of replenishment."

6. Joseph Slade discusses the shift from film in *Gravity's Rainbow* to television in *Vineland* (69–70). Brian McHale, in *Constructing Postmodernism*, has argued that "TV functions in *Vineland* analogously to the way movies function in *Gravity's Rainbow*" (120). This too simple statement is then helpfully complicated by his discussion of the different ways and degrees to which film and television upset ontological distinctions and serve as "ontological pluralizers" in Pynchon's texts. See especially 125–33.

7. To Molly Hite, such gestures are part of an important pattern in Pynchon's texts, which she calls "Holy Center approaching." The Holy Center, the site of ultimate meaning, is the "unavailable insight" toward which the text is always pointing, yet which it never reaches. Hite uses poststructuralist terms to describe how this absent center "creates a space in which Pynchon can realize multiple possibilities simultaneously" (31).

8. For an excellent overview of the problems that postmodern artists and theorists have in developing coherent and effective approaches to agency and political opposition, see Charles Altieri, who accuses postmodern artists of attempting "to have a politics without specific political loyalties," and of practicing an art of resistance "bound to that art world which recognizes it as a political gesture, an art haunted by the possibility that it is nothing more than gesture" (458–59). Though I think even the most casual reader of Pynchon's work recognizes a broadly left-wing, antiestablishment stance born of the sixties (with Beat antecedents), critics who emphasize Pynchon's postmodernity inevitably make us aware of the sorts of problems Altieri describes.

Among Pynchon critics, Kathryn Hume has made perhaps the most concerted effort to "rescue" Pynchon's texts from those who emphasize their postmodernist, indeterminate aspect. Hume wants to reclaim a common-sense notion of selfhood and action within Pynchon's texts, arguing that "in theory, individuality is problematic on philosophical, psychological, and sociological grounds, but in practice this seldom prevents a member of the human species from trying to save his or her own skin" (192). According to Hume, Pynchon "is dealing with human action, values, and needs, not just with the nature of reality as viewed by science or philosophy" (198). While Hume may be right here, the assumption that science and philosophy are somehow inhuman, or not concerned with "human action, values and needs," should not go without question. Further, simply to label action, values, and needs "human" does not relieve one of the responsibility of explaining what these are. Indeed, philosophy (and psychology, sociology, and other discourses from which Hume wants to distance her own) is a way of describing these actions, values, and needs. What discourse is Hume proposing as an alternative? The mythological, presumably. But Hume's mythological interpretations of Pynchon's text are no more "common sense" or immediate than these others, and are equally dependent on interpretation and specialized, expert knowledge.

Hume's patient uncovering of the many mythological patterns and themes in *Gravity's Rainbow* is a valuable contribution to our understanding of this novel and serves as a needed corrective to those readings that emphasize the novel's indeterminacy and ambiguity. And it does not make me proud of my profession to find such a skilled critic forced into a strained defense of her approach: "Shuffling the deck of postmodernist reality, Pynchon does not seem to have abandoned all frameworks, and this human frame of reference, this concern for ultimate survival if nothing else, is one he has retained, however counter to the spirit of what critics identify as postmodernism" (199). The problem here is with the unexamined term *human,* held up like a cross to ward off the poststructuralist vampires eager to suck the text dry of "human" meaning. The effort does not amount to much if in the end the only untouched value that Hume can assert is that of "survival," of an individual "trying to save his or her own skin." It need hardly be pointed out that mere survival is an *animal* concern as well, and by itself does little to distinguish our humanness. It is a long way from the primitive urge for survival to an adequate understanding of the full range of "human action, values, and needs." That distance is traversed by many discourses, notably mythological ones, but also the literary, philosophical, scientific, psychological, and sociological discourses whose operations Pynchon's text both enacts and calls into question.

9. This point is made by David Cowart, who has thoroughly catalogued and discussed the presence of film in this novel, including its dozens of allusions to particular movies, directors, actors, and actresses (*Thomas Pynchon* 31–62). Issues relating to film in *Gravity's Rainbow* have also received a thorough treatment by Charles Clerc. For a catalogue of the aspects of film treated in the novel, see especially Clerc 104–6. See also McHoul and Wills 38–45.

10. In writing about the importance of film in *Gravity's Rainbow,* Mark Richard Siegel has noted that German expressionist film might have interested Pynchon because of its "subjective" camera techniques and the lack of an objective narrative frame in

such films as the 1920 *The Cabinet of Dr. Caligari* (25–34). Clerc likewise comments that "emphasis on expressionistic fantasies by Pynchon is perfectly suited to his narrative methods and thematic intentions" (113–14).

11. Pynchon's interest in McLuhan during the time in which he was writing *Gravity's Rainbow* is indicated in the letter reproduced in Seed 240–43.

12. A letter Pynchon wrote in 1969 on the subject of the Hereros of southwest Africa illuminates his views on the destructive effects of Western thought on other cultures: "I feel personally that the number done on the Herero head by the Germans is the same number done on the American Indian head by our own colonists and what is now being done on the Buddhist head in Vietnam by the Christian minority in Saigon and their advisors: the imposition of a culture valuing analysis and differentiation on a culture that valued unity and integration." The letter is reproduced in full in Seed 240–43.

13. For Hume, the relevant metaphor for the play of perceptions in our mind is not film but theater: "The mind is a kind of theater, where several perceptions successively make their appearance; pass, re-pass, glide away, and mingle in an infinite variety of postures and situations" (253). But Hume is careful to remove whatever familiar comfort we might have taken in the theater metaphor: "The comparison of the theater must not mislead us. They are the successive perceptions only, that constitute the mind; nor have we the most distant notion of the place, where these scenes are represented, or of the materials, of which it is composed" (253). Writing the verbs "represent" and "compose" in the passive voice, Hume places his theater producers beyond the bounds of knowledge, where they become, like the "producers" of Pökler's daughter Ilse, an unknowable They.

14. Hume argues that the act of the mind by which we consider a succession of related objects or perceptions resembles the act of the mind by which we consider a continuous, unvarying object, and it is through this resemblance that we mistakenly ascribe an identity to what is actually only a succession of discrete perceptions associated with one another through the power of memory. "As memory alone acquaints us with the continuance and extent of this succession of perceptions, 'tis to be considered, upon that account chiefly, as the source of personal identity" (261).

15. Much the same point is made by Molly Hite in her discussion of "included middles." See *Ideas of Order,* especially 13–17.

16. See Siegel 88, and Cowart, *Thomas Pynchon* 47.

17. Stacey Olster has noted Pynchon's awareness of the voyeuristic, fetishistic, and politically repressive potentials of the film medium (119).

18. Von Göll's view of the relationship between Elite and Preterite echoes that of Slothrop's seventeenth-century ancestor, William Slothrop, who in his unorthodox tract *On Preterition* "argued holiness for these 'second Sheep,' without whom there would be no elect" (555). William Slothrop's views, which caused his book to be "not only banned but also ceremonially burned in Boston," are in turn a close satire of those of Thomas Pynchon's ancestor William Pynchon, whose 1650 pamph-

let *The Meritorious Price of Our Redemption* met the same fate. Von Göll's view is therefore as heretical, in the orthodox Puritan view, as it is pretentious. See Mathew Winston, "The Quest for Pynchon" (reprinted in Levine and Leverenz, eds. 251–63). See also Weisenburger 238.

19. See Clerc 120–21 and 130–31.

20. For a brilliant exploration of the implications of home video, see Don DeLillo's short story "Videotape." The subject of filmic and televisual self-consciousness is discussed at length in chapter 2, above.

21. For a thorough catalog of *Vineland*'s references to television, see Brian McHale, *Constructing Postmodernism* 116–18.

22. Joseph Slade has remarked that the pop-cultural artifacts in *Vineland* "appear slight by comparison" to those in *Gravity's Rainbow* (68). David Cowart appears uneasy with the fact that *Vineland* "dispenses with the high-culture allusion almost entirely," in favor of a "density of reference to the ephemera of popular culture [that] is almost numbing" ("Attenuated Postmodernism" 7). Though *Vineland,* according to Cowart, "favors historical surface to historical depth," Pynchon manages through his evocation of myth "to imbue with extraordinary historical resonance a story that ostensibly depicts the vitiation of the historical sense" (6, 12). While Cowart's description is a fair formulation of what I mean by the "deep surface" that this novel constructs, I would disagree that allusions to popular culture by themselves necessarily give the book a "foreshortened historical sense" (11). I would agree on this point with Stacey Olster's conception of "popular culture as having a history of its own" that can contribute significantly to a text's patterns of meaning (133). And yet one wants to add Charles Clerc's caution that, "if placed in unskilled hands," Pynchon's techniques for alluding to popular culture make "for laziness, for shoddiness, for superficiality of response, for shallowness of perception" (149).

23. Stacey Olster shows the parallels between Frenesi's flawed view of film and those of actual New Left filmmakers of the 1960s. See 120–23.

24. The verse in its entirety reads, in the New Revised Standard Version, "He shall judge between the nations, / and shall arbitrate for many peoples; / they shall beat their swords into plowshares, / and their spears into pruning hooks; / nation shall not lift up sword against nation, / neither shall they learn war any more."

25. Brian McHale argues that Prairie's saturation with "TV-modeled desires and expectations" does not in itself disqualify her from being a figure of hope, for he notes that throughout Pynchon's fiction children "are almost inevitably bearers of positive value" (*Constructing Postmodernism* 124).

26. One material reason for this shift is given by Joseph Slade, who points out that from the years 1963 to 1971 the networks broadcast documentaries "of increasing liberality" made by independent filmmakers. Following the controversy over *The Selling of the Pentagon* in 1971, however, the networks refused to air material by independents (70). Bringing the production of news entirely under network control allowed television to become a more nearly seamless hegemonic discourse.

27. See Meyrowitz, *No Sense of Place*. His situationist analysis of the social effects of television is discussed in chapter 2, above.
28. I am indebted for this observation to Douglas Keesey's paper, "Film and Video in Pynchon's *Vineland*," delivered at the Twentieth-Century Literature Conference, Louisville, Kentucky, February 22, 1992.
29. Alan Wilde is disappointed by this ending, calling it a "personal dodge" of moral seriousness that "dissolves the chapter's dissembled closure, along with the novel's intimations of Eros ascendant, in a farrago of pastoral farce" ("Love and Death" 180, 178–79).

WORKS CITED

Aldridge, John. *The American Novel and the Way We Live Now.* New York: Oxford UP, 1983.

————. *Talents and Technicians: Literary Chic and the New Assembly-Line Fiction.* New York: Scribner's, 1992.

Alkon, Paul K. "Critical and Logical Concepts of Method from Addison to Coleridge." *Eighteenth-Century Studies* (1971): 97–121.

Altieri, Charles. "The Powers and Limits of Oppositional Postmodernism." *American Literary History* 2.3 (Fall 1990): 443–81.

Atlas, James. "Less Is Less." Rev. of *What We Talk about When We Talk about Love*, by Raymond Carver. *Atlantic* June 1981: 96–98.

Attridge, Derek, Geoff Bennington, and Robert Young, eds. *Post-structuralism and the Question of History.* Cambridge: Cambridge UP, 1987.

Atwood, Margaret. "Male and Lonely: *Moon DeLuxe.*" Rev. of *Moon Deluxe*, by Frederick Barthelme. *New York Times Book Review* 31 July 1983: 1, 22. Rpt. in *Contemporary Literary Criticism* 36 (1986): 50–51.

Austin, J. L. *How to Do Things with Words*. Cambridge: Harvard UP, 1962.

Bailey, Steven R. "Postcards from Home: Personal Reflections on American Popular Culture in Asia." Midwest American Culture Association/Popular Culture Association Conference. Toledo, Ohio, 5 Oct. 1990.

Baker, Nicholson. *The Mezzanine*. New York: Weidenfield and Nicolson, 1988.

———. *Room Temperature*. New York: Grove Weidenfield, 1990.

———. *Vox*. New York: Random House, 1992.

Banks, Russell. *Continental Drift*. New York: Harper & Row, 1985.

Barr, Marleen S. *Feminist Fabulation: Space/Postmodern Fiction*. Iowa City: U of Iowa P, 1992.

Barth, John. "The Literature of Exhaustion." *Atlantic* Aug. 1967: 29–34.

Barthelme, Donald. "Not-Knowing." *The Best American Essays 1986*. Ed. Elizabeth Hardwick. New York: Ticknor & Fields, 1986. 9–24.

———. *Snow White*. 1967. New York: Atheneum, 1984.

Barthelme, Frederick. Interview. *Contemporary Authors* 122 (1988): 48–51.

———. *Moon Deluxe*. New York: Simon & Schuster, 1983.

———. "On Being Wrong: Convicted Minimalist Spills Bean." *New York Times Book Review* 3 Apr. 1988: 1, 25–27.

———. *Second Marriage*. New York: Simon & Schuster, 1984.

Barthes, Roland. "The Death of the Author." 1968. *Critical Theory Since Plato*. Ed. Hazard Adams. Rev. ed. Fort Worth: Harcourt Brace Jovanovich, 1992. 1130–33.

Baudrillard, Jean. *America*. 1986. Trans. Chris Turner. London: Verso-New Left Books, 1988.

———. "The Ecstasy of Communication." *The Anti-Aesthetic: Essays on Postmodern Culture*. Ed. Hal Foster. Port Townsend, Wash.: Bay Press, 1983. 126–34.

———. *Jean Baudrillard: Selected Writings*. Ed. Mark Poster. Stanford: Stanford UP, 1988.

———. "Requiem for the Media." *For a Critique of the Political Economy of the Sign*. Trans. Charles Levin. St. Louis, Mo.: Telos Press, 1981. 164–84. Rpt. in *Video Culture: A Critical Investigation*. Ed. John G. Hanhardt. Layton, Utah: Peregrine Smith Books, 1990. 124–43.

Beattie, Ann. *Chilly Scenes of Winter*. 1976. New York: Warner, 1983.

———. *Falling in Place*. New York: Fawcett, 1980.

———. Interview. Rpt. from Larry McCaffery and Sinda Gregory, "A Conversation with Ann Beattie," in *Literary Review* (Fairleigh Dickinson University) 27.2 (Winter 1984): 165–77. *Contemporary Literary Criticism* 63 (1991): 5–9.

———. *Love Always*. 1985. New York: Vintage-Random House, 1986.

———. "Marshall's Dog." *Distortions*. 1976. New York: Warner, 1983. 72–86.

———. *What Was Mine*. New York: Random House, 1991.

———. *Where You'll Find Me*. New York: Simon & Schuster, 1986.

Bell, Madison. "Less Is Less: The Dwindling American Short Story." *Harper's* Apr. 1986: 64–69.

Bellamy, Joe David, ed. *The New Fiction: Interviews with Innovative American Writers.* Urbana: U of Illinois P, 1974.

Belsey, Catherine. "Afterword: A Future for Materialist Feminist Criticism?" *The Matter of Difference: Materialist Feminist Criticism of Shakespeare.* Ed. Valerie Wayne. Ithaca: Cornell UP, 1991. 257–70.

Benjamin, Walter. "The Work of Art in the Age of Mechanical Reproduction." *Illuminations.* Ed. Hannah Arendt. New York: Schocken, 1969. 217–51.

Bennington, Geoff, and Robert Young. "Introduction: Posing the Question." *Post-structuralism and the Question of History.* Ed. Derek Attridge, Geoff Bennington, and Robert Young. Cambridge: Cambridge UP, 1987. 1–11.

Bercovitch, Sacvan. *The Puritan Origins of the American Self.* New Haven: Yale UP, 1975.

Bloom, Harold, ed. *Thomas Pynchon's* Gravity's Rainbow: *Modern Critical Interpretations.* New York: Chelsea House, 1986.

Borgmann, Albert. *Crossing the Postmodern Divide.* Chicago: U of Chicago P, 1992.

Brantlinger, Patrick. *Bread and Circuses: Theories of Mass Culture as Social Decay.* Ithaca: Cornell UP, 1983.

Brinkmeyer, Robert H. Jr. "Finding One's History: Bobbie Ann Mason and Contemporary Southern Literature." *Southern Literary Journal* 19.2 (Spring 1987): 22–33.

Brooks, Cleanth. "Walker Percy and Modern Gnosticism." Rpt. from *Southern Review* 13.4 (Oct. 1977). *Walker Percy.* Ed. Harold Bloom. New York: Chelsea House, 1986. 53–62.

Burke, Edmund. *A Philosophical Enquiry into the Origin of Our Ideas of the Sublime and Beautiful.* Ed. James T. Boulton. Notre Dame: U of Notre Dame P, 1968.

Burke, Kenneth. *Attitudes toward History.* 3d ed. Berkeley: U of California P, 1984.

———. *A Grammar of Motives.* 1945. Berkeley: U of California P, 1969.

Calvino, Italo. *If on a winter's night a traveler.* Trans. William Weaver. New York: Harcourt Brace Jovanovich, 1981.

Carlyle, Thomas. "On History." *Critical and Miscellaneous Essays.* Ed. Ralph Waldo Emerson. New York: 1873. 219–23.

Carver, Raymond. "After the Denim." *What We Talk about When We Talk about Love.* 1981. New York: Vintage-Random House, 1982.

———. *Cathedral.* New York: Knopf, 1983.

———. Interview. "The Art of Fiction LXXVI." With Mona Simpson. *Paris Review* 25.88 (Summer 1983): 192–221.

———. Interview. Rpt. from "Matters of Life & Death: An Interview with Raymond Carver," in *Bloomsbury Review* 8.1 (Jan.–Feb. 1988): 14–17. *Contemporary Literary Criticism* 55 (1989): 273–75.

———. "One More Thing." *North American Review* 266.1 (1981): 28–29.

———. "On Writing." *Fires: Essays, Poems, Stories.* New York: Vintage-Random House, 1983. 13–18.

———. *What We Talk about When We Talk about Love.* 1981. New York: Vintage-Random House, 1982.

————. *Where I'm Calling From.* New York: Atlantic Monthly P, 1988.

————. *Will You Please Be Quiet, Please?* New York: McGraw-Hill, 1978.

Clerc, Charles. "Film in *Gravity's Rainbow.*" *Approaches to* Gravity's Rainbow. Ed. Charles Clerc. Columbus: Ohio State UP, 1983. 103–51.

Coover, Robert. "'Nothing but Darkness and Talk?': Writers' Symposium on Traditional Values and Iconoclastic Fiction." *Critique* 31.4 (Summer 1990): 233–55.

Cowart, David. "Attenuated Postmodernism: Pynchon's *Vineland.*" *The Vineland Papers: Critical Takes on Pynchon's Novel.* Ed. Geoffrey Green, Donald J. Greiner, and Larry McCaffery. Normal, Ill.: Dalkey Archive Press, 1994. 3–13.

————. *Thomas Pynchon: The Art of Allusion.* Carbondale: Southern Illinois UP, 1980.

Croce, Benedetto. *Aesthetic.* Trans. Douglas Ainslie. New York: Macmillan, 1922.

Davis, Lennard. *Factual Fictions: The Origins of the English Novel.* New York: Columbia UP, 1983.

Dawson, Anthony B. "*Ragtime* and the Movies: The Aura of the Duplicable." *Mosaic* 16 (Winter–Spring 1983): 205–14.

DeBord, Guy. *Society of the Spectacle.* 1967. Detroit: Black and Red, 1983.

DeLillo, Don. *Americana.* 1971. New York: Viking Penguin, 1989.

————. *Endzone.* 1972. New York: Penguin, 1986.

————. *Great Jones Street.* 1973. New York: Vintage-Random House, 1989.

————. Interview. *Anything Can Happen: Interviews with Contemporary American Novelists.* Ed. Tom LeClair and Larry McCaffery. Urbana: U of Illinois P, 1983. 79–90.

————. *Libra.* New York: Viking, 1988.

————. *Mao II.* New York: Viking, 1991.

————. *The Names.* 1982. New York: Vintage-Random House, 1983.

————. *Players.* 1977. New York: Vintage-Random House, 1984.

————. *Ratner's Star.* 1976. New York: Vintage-Random House, 1989.

————. *Running Dog.* 1978. New York: Vintage-Random House, 1989.

————. "Videotape." Rpt. from *Antaeus,* Autumn 1994. *Harper's* Dec. 1994: 15–17.

————. *White Noise.* 1985. New York: Penguin, 1986.

Denning, Michael. "The End of Mass Culture." *Modernity and Mass Culture.* Ed. James Naremore and Patrick Brantlinger. Bloomington: Indiana UP, 1991. 253–68.

Descartes, René. *Selections.* Ed. Ralph M. Eaton. New York: Scribner's, 1927.

Ditsky, John. "The German Source of *Ragtime:* A Note." *E. L. Doctorow: Essays and Conversations.* Ed. Richard Trenner. Princeton, N.J.: Ontario Review P, 1983. 179–81.

Doctorow, E. L. *Billy Bathgate.* New York: Random House, 1989.

————. *The Book of Daniel.* New York: Fawcett Crest-Ballantine, 1971.

————. "False Documents." *E. L. Doctorow: Essays and Conversations.* Ed. Richard Trenner. Princeton, N.J.: Ontario Review P, 1983. 16–27.

————. Interview. With Larry McCaffery. *E. L. Doctorow: Essays and Conversations.* Ed. Richard Trenner. Princeton, N.J.: Ontario Review P, 1983. 31–47.

————. *Ragtime.* 1975. New York: Bantam, 1976.

————. *The Waterworks*. New York: Random House, 1994.

————. *World's Fair*. New York: Random House, 1985.

Duyfhuizen, Bernard. "Taking Stock: 26 Years since *V.* (Over 26 Books on Pynchon!)." *Novel* 23.1 (Fall 1989): 75–88.

Eagleton, Terry. "Capitalism, Modernism and Postmodernism." *New Left Review* 152 (1985): 60–73.

————. *Literary Theory: An Introduction*. Minneapolis: U of Minnesota P, 1983.

Eizykman, Claudine. *La Jouissance-cinema*. Paris: Union Generale d'Editions, 1976.

Elam, Diane. *Romancing the Postmodern*. New York: Routledge, 1992.

Elkin, Stanley. "An Interview with Stanley Elkin." *AWP Newsletter* 20.3 (Feb./Mar. 1988): 1, 10–14.

Emerson, Ralph Waldo. "History." *Selected Essays, Lectures and Poems of Ralph Waldo Emerson*. Ed. R. E. Spiller. New York: Simon & Schuster, 1965. 221–40.

Ewen, Stuart. "Advertising and the Development of Consumer Society." *Cultural Politics in Contemporary America*. Ed. Ian Angus and Sut Jhally. New York: Routledge, 1989.

Ewen, Stuart, and Elizabeth Ewen. *Channels of Desire: Mass Images and the Shaping of American Consciousness*. 2d ed. Minneapolis: U of Minnesota P, 1992.

Ferguson, Frances. "The Nuclear Sublime." *Diacritics* 14.2 (1984): 4–10.

Fiedler, Leslie. "Cross the Border—Close the Gap" (1970). *The Collected Essays of Leslie Fiedler*. Vol. 2. New York: Stein & Day, 1971. 461–85.

————. "The Death of Avant-Garde Literature" (1964). *The Collected Essays of Leslie Fiedler*. Vol. 2. New York: Stein & Day, 1971. 454–60.

Fiske, John. *Television Culture*. London: Routledge, 1988.

Fokkema, Douwe, and Hans Bertens, eds. *Approaching Postmodernism*. Amsterdam/Philadelphia: John Benjamins, 1986.

Foley, Barbara. "From *U.S.A.* to *Ragtime*: Notes on the Forms of Historical Consciousness in Modern Fiction." *American Literature* 50.1 (Mar. 1978): 85–105. Rpt. in *E. L. Doctorow: Essays and Conversations*. Ed. Richard Trenner. Princeton, N.J.: Ontario Review P, 1983. 158–78.

Foster, Hal. *Recodings: Art, Spectacle, Cultural Politics*. Port Townsend, Wash.: Bay Press, 1985.

————, ed. *The Anti-Aesthetic: Essays on Postmodern Culture*. Port Townsend, Wash.: Bay Press, 1983.

Foucault, Michel. *The Archaeology of Knowledge and the Discourse on Language*. Trans. A. M. Sheridan Smith. New York: Pantheon, 1972.

————. *The Foucault Reader*. Ed. Paul Rabinow. New York: Pantheon, 1984.

————. *The History of Sexuality: Volume I*. 1976. Trans. Robert Hurley. New York: Vintage-Random House, 1980.

Fussell, Paul. *The Rhetorical World of Augustan Humanism*. Oxford: Clarendon Press, 1965.

Gass, William H. "Where East Meets West—to Boogie!" *New York Times Magazine* part 2, 4 Mar. 1990: 63, 66–67.

Gates, Henry Louis Jr. "The blackness of blackness: a critique of the sign and the Signi-fying Monkey." *Black Literature and Literary Theory.* Ed. Gates. New York, London: Methuen, 1984. 285–321.

Goldberg, RoseLee. *Performance Art: From Futurism to the Present.* New York: Abrams, 1988.

Gornick, Vivian. "Tenderhearted Men: Lonesome, Sad and Blue." *New York Times Book Review* 16 Sept. 1990: 1, 32–35.

Gorra, Michael. "Laughter and Bloodshed." *Hudson Review* 37 (Spring 1984): 151–64.

Graff, Gerald. *Literature against Itself: Literary Ideas in Modern Society.* Chicago: U of Chicago P, 1979.

Gretlund, Jan Nordby. "On the Porch with Marcus Aurelius: Walker Percy's Stoicism." *Walker Percy: Novelist and Philosopher.* Ed. Jan Nordby Gretlund and Karl-Heinz Westarp. Jackson: UP of Mississippi, 1991. 74–83.

Grossberg, Lawrence. "Rockin' with Reagan, or the Mainstreaming of Postmodernity." *Cultural Critique* 10 (Fall 1988): 123–49.

Hall, Stuart. "Notes on Deconstructing 'the Popular.'" 1979. *People's History and Socialist Theory.* Ed. Raphael Samuel. London: Routledge and Kegan Paul, 1981.

Haraway, Donna. "A Manifesto for Cyborgs: Science, Technology, and Socialist Femi-nism in the 1980s." Rpt. from *Socialist Review* 15.80 (1985): 65–107. *Feminism/Post-modernism.* Ed. Linda J. Nicholson. New York: Routledge, 1990. 190–233.

Harvey, David. *The Condition of Postmodernity.* Cambridge, Mass.: Basil Blackwell, 1989.

Hayles, N. Katherine. *The Cosmic Web: Scientific Field Models and Literary Strategies in the Twentieth Century.* Ithaca: Cornell UP, 1984.

Hellman, John. *American Myth and the Legacy of Vietnam.* New York: Columbia UP, 1986.

Helprin, Mark. "Introduction: The Canon under Siege." *Best American Short Stories, 1988.* Ed. Mark Helprin and Shannon Ravenel. New York: Ticknor & Fields, 1988. xi–xxxi.

Hemingway, Ernest. *A Moveable Feast.* New York: Macmillan, 1964.

Herr, Michael. *Dispatches.* 1977. New York: Avon, 1978.

Herzinger, Kim A. "Introduction: On the New Fiction." *Mississippi Review* 40/41 (1985): 7–22.

Hite, Molly. *Ideas of Order in the Novels of Thomas Pynchon.* Columbus: Ohio State UP, 1983.

Hobson, Fred. *The Southern Writer in the Postmodern World.* Athens: U of Georgia P, 1991.

Horkheimer, Max, and Theodor W. Adorno. "The Culture Industry: Enlightenment as Mass Deception." *Dialectic of Enlightenment.* 1944. By Horkheimer and Adorno. Trans. John Cumming. New York: Herder and Herder, 1972. 120–67.

Howe, Irving. "Mass Society and Postmodern Fiction" (1959). *Decline of the New.* New York: Harcourt, Brace & World, 1970. 190–207.

Hume, David. *Enquiry Concerning Human Understanding.* Ed. L. A. Selby-Bigge. 3d. ed. P. H. Nidditch. Oxford: Clarendon Press, 1975.

———. *A Treatise of Human Nature.* Ed. L. A. Selby-Bigge. Oxford: Clarendon Press, 1975.

Hume, Kathryn. *Pynchon's Mythography: An Approach to* Gravity's Rainbow. Carbondale: Southern Illinois UP, 1987.

Hutcheon, Linda. "Once Again from the Top: More Pomo Promo." *Contemporary Literature* 36.1 (Spring 1995): 164–72.

———. *A Poetics of Postmodernism: History, Theory, Fiction.* New York: Routledge, 1988.

———. *The Politics of Postmodernism.* London: Routledge, 1989.

Huyssen, Andreas. *After the Great Divide: Modernism, Mass Culture, Postmodernism.* Bloomington: Indiana UP, 1986.

Innis, Harold A. *The Bias of Communication.* Toronto: U of Toronto P, 1951.

Jameson, Fredric. Foreword. *The Postmodern Condition: A Report on Knowledge.* By Jean-François Lyotard. Trans. Geoff Bennington and Brian Massumi. Minneapolis: U of Minnesota P, 1984. vii–xxi.

———. Interview. *Diacritics* 12 (1982): 72–91.

———. "Marxism and Postmodernism." *New Left Review* 178 (1989): 31–45.

———. *The Political Unconscious: Narrative as a Socially Symbolic Act.* Ithaca: Cornell UP, 1981.

———. "Postmodernism and Consumer Society." *Postmodernism and Its Discontents: Theories, Practices.* Ed. E. Ann Kaplan. London: Verso-New Left Books, 1988. 13–29.

———. *Postmodernism, or, The Cultural Logic of Late Capitalism.* Durham, N.C.: Duke UP, 1991.

———. "Postmodernism, or, The Cultural Logic of Late Capitalism." *New Left Review* 146 (1984): 53–92.

———. "Reification and Utopia in Mass Culture." *Social Text* 1 (Winter 1979): 130–48.

Jencks, Charles. *The Language of Post-Modern Architecture.* 5th ed. New York: Rizzoli, 1987.

———. *Post-Modernism: The New Classicism in Art and Architecture.* New York: Rizzoli, 1987.

Keesey, Douglas. "Film and Video in Pynchon's *Vineland.*" University of Louisville Twentieth-Century Literature Conference. Louisville, Ky., 22 Feb. 1992.

Kellner, Douglas, ed. *Postmodernism/Jameson/Critique.* Washington, D.C.: Maisonneuve Press, 1989.

Kingston, Maxine Hong. *The Woman Warrior: Memoirs of a Girlhood among Ghosts.* 1976. New York: Vintage-Random House, 1977.

Kissinger, Henry. "With Faint Praise." Rev. of *Churchill,* by Norman Rose. *New York Times Book Review* 16 July 1995: 7.

Konigsberg, Ira. *Narrative Technique in the English Novel: Defoe to Austen.* Hamden, Conn.: Archon Books, 1985.

Kucich, John. "Postmodern Politics: Don DeLillo and the Plight of the White Male Writer." *Michigan Quarterly Review* 27.2 (Spring 1988): 328–41.

LeClair, Tom, and Larry McCaffery, eds. *Anything Can Happen: Interviews with Contemporary American Novelists.* Urbana: U of Illinois P, 1983.

Leibniz, Gottfried Wilhelm Freiherr. *Leibniz: Selections.* Ed. Philip P. Wiener. New York: Scribner's, 1951.

Lentricchia, Frank. *After the New Criticism.* Chicago: U of Chicago P, 1980.

———. "Don DeLillo." *Raritan* 8.4 (Spring 1987): 1–29.

———, ed. *Introducing Don DeLillo.* Durham, N.C.: Duke UP, 1991.

———, ed. *New Essays on* White Noise. Cambridge: Cambridge UP, 1991.

Levine, George, and David Leverenz, eds. *Mindful Pleasures: Essays on Thomas Pynchon.* Boston: Little, Brown, 1976.

Loewinsohn, Ron. "Looking for Love after Marriage: *Second Marriage.*" Rev. of *Second Marriage,* by Frederick Barthelme. *New York Times Book Review* 30 Sept. 1984: 1, 43. Rpt. in *Contemporary Literary Criticism* 36: 53–54.

Lyotard, Jean François. *The Postmodern Condition: A Report on Knowledge.* Trans. Geoff Bennington and Brian Massumi. Minneapolis: U of Minnesota P, 1984.

Machiavelli, Niccolo. *The Prince.* Trans. Luigi Ricci. New York: New American Library, 1952.

Maryles, Daisy, ed. "Bantam Gets *Ragtime* for $1,850,000, Highest Ever." *Publishers Weekly* 11 Aug. 1975: 55–56.

———. "1975, the Best Sellers." *Publishers Weekly* 9 Feb. 1976: 42.

Mason, Bobbie Ann. *Feather Crowns.* New York: HarperCollins, 1993.

———. *In Country.* New York: Harper & Row, 1985.

———. Interview. With Bonnie Lyons and Bill Oliver. Rpt. from *Contemporary Literature* 32.4 (Winter 1991): 449–70. *Contemporary Literary Criticism* 82 (1984): 250–58.

———. *Love Life.* New York: Harper & Row, 1989.

———. *Nabokov's Garden: A Guide to* Ada. Ann Arbor, Mich.: Ardis, 1974.

———. "A New-Wave Format." *Shiloh and Other Stories.* 1982. New York: Perennial-Harper & Row, 1985. 213–31.

———. "Residents and Transients." *Shiloh and Other Stories.* 1982. New York: Perennial-Harper & Row, 1985.

McCaffery, Larry, ed. *Postmodern Fiction: A Bio-Bibliographical Guide.* New York: Greenwood Press, 1986.

McCaffery, Larry, and Sinda Gregory, eds. *Alive and Writing: Interviews with American Authors of the 1980s.* Urbana: U of Illinois P, 1987.

McHale, Brian. *Constructing Postmodernism.* London: Routledge, 1992.

———. *Postmodernist Fiction.* New York: Methuen, 1987.

McHoul, Alec, and David Wills. *Writing Pynchon: Strategies in Fictional Analysis.* Urbana: U of Illinois P, 1990.

McInerney, Jay. "Raymond Carver: A Still, Small Voice." *New York Times Book Review* 6 Aug. 1989: 1, 24–25.

McKeon, Michael. *The Origins of the English Novel, 1600-1740.* Baltimore: Johns Hopkins UP, 1987.

McLuhan, Marshall. *Understanding Media: The Extensions of Man.* New York: Signet-New American Library, 1964.

Mendelsohn, J. Snackie. *The Ardent Ubermensch: Camp Songs for the Apocalypse.* Nebagomon, Wisc.: Mirage Press, 1980.

Merleau-Ponty, Maurice. *The Essential Writings of Merleau-Ponty.* Ed. Alden L. Fisher. New York: Harcourt, Brace & World, 1969.

Meyrowitz, Joshua. *No Sense of Place: The Impact of Electronic Media on Social Behavior.* New York: Oxford UP, 1985.

Miller, Mark Crispin. *Boxed In: The Culture of TV.* 3d. ed. Evanston, Ill.: Northwestern UP, 1989.

Mowitt, John. "Performance Theory as the Work of Laurie Anderson." *Discourse* 12.2 (Spring–Summer 1990): 48–65.

Mulvey, Laura. "Visual Pleasure and Narrative Cinema." *Screen* 16.3 (Autumn 1975): 6–18.

Nealon, Jeffrey T. *Double Reading: Postmodernism after Deconstruction.* Ithaca: Cornell UP, 1993.

Newman, Charles. *The Post-Modern Aura: The Act of Fiction in an Age of Inflation.* Evanston, Ill.: Northwestern UP, 1985.

Nicholson, Linda J., ed. *Feminism/Postmodernism.* New York: Routledge, 1990.

Norris, Christopher. *The Truth about Postmodernism.* Oxford: Blackwell, 1993.

Olster, Stacey. "When You're a (Nin)jette, You're a (Nin)jette All the Way—or Are You?: Female Filmmaking in *Vineland.*" *The Vineland Papers: Critical Takes on Pynchon's Novel.* Ed. Geoffrey Green, Donald J. Greiner, and Larry McCaffery. Normal, Ill.: Dalkey Archive Press, 1994. 119–34.

Ong, Walter. *Interfaces of the Word: Studies in the Evolution of Consciousness and Culture.* Ithaca: Cornell UP, 1977.

Orwell, George. *1984.* 1949. New York: Signet-New American Library, n.d.

Parker, Patricia, and Geoffrey Hartman. *Shakespeare and the Question of Theory.* New York: Methuen, 1985.

Percy, Walker. *Conversations with Walker Percy.* Ed. Lewis A. Lawson and Victor A. Kramer. Jackson: UP of Mississippi, 1985.

———. *The Moviegoer.* 1961. New York: Popular Library, 1962.

Piercy, Marge. *Woman on the Edge of Time.* New York: Fawcett Crest-Ballantine, 1976.

Polan, Dana. "Brief Encounters: Mass Culture and the Evacuation of Sense." *Studies in Entertainment: Critical Approaches to Mass Culture.* Ed. Tania Modleski. Bloomington: Indiana UP, 1986. 167–87.

Poster, Mark. *The Mode of Information: Poststructuralism and Social Context.* Chicago: U of Chicago P, 1990.

Progoff, Ira. *Jung, Synchronicity, and Human Destiny: C. G. Jung's Theory of Meaningful Coincidence.* New York: Julian Press, 1973.

Pynchon, Thomas. *The Crying of Lot 49.* 1966. New York: Perennial-Harper & Row, 1986.

———. *Gravity's Rainbow.* New York: Viking, 1973.

———. *V.* 1963. Toronto: Bantam, 1964.

———. *Vineland.* Boston: Little, Brown, 1990.

Readings, Bill, and Bennet Schaber, eds. *Postmodernism across the Ages: Essays for a Postmodernity That Wasn't Born Yesterday.* Syracuse: Syracuse UP, 1993.

Redfield, Marc. "Pynchon's Postmodern Sublime." *PMLA* 104.2 (Mar. 1989): 152–62.

Reed, Ishmael. Interview. With John O'Brien. *The New Fiction: Interviews with Innovative American Writers.* Ed. Joe David Bellamy. Urbana: U of Illinois P, 1974. 130–41.

———. *Mumbo Jumbo.* 1972. New York: Atheneum, 1988.

Roberts, Margaret. "'D' Is for Danger—And for Writer Don DeLillo." *Chicago Tribune* 22 May 1992, sec. 5: 1, 5.

Runyon, Randolph Paul. *Reading Raymond Carver.* Syracuse: Syracuse UP, 1992.

Ryan, Barbara T. "Decentered Authority in Bobbie Ann Mason's *In Country.*" *Critique* 31.3 (Spring 1990): 199–211.

Saltzman, Arthur. "The Stylistic Energy of E. L. Doctorow." *E. L. Doctorow: Essays and Conversations.* Ed. Richard Trenner. Princeton, N.J.: Ontario Review P, 1983. 73–108.

Sanders, Scott. "Pynchon's Paranoid History." *Mindful Pleasures: Essays on Thomas Pynchon.* Ed. George Levine and David Leverenz. 139–59.

Schaub, Thomas H. *Pynchon: The Voice of Ambiguity.* Urbana: U of Illinois P, 1981.

Seed, David. *The Fictional Labyrinths of Thomas Pynchon.* Iowa City: U of Iowa P, 1988.

Siegel, Mark Richard. *Pynchon: Creative Paranoia in* Gravity's Rainbow. Port Washington, N.Y.: Kennikat Press, 1978.

Simmons, Philip E. "John Cleland's *Memoirs of a Woman of Pleasure:* Literary Voyeurism and the Techniques of Novelistic Transgression." *Eighteenth-Century Fiction* 3.1 (Oct. 1990): 43–63.

Slade, Joseph. "Communication, Group Theory, and Perception in *Vineland.*" *The Vineland Papers: Critical Takes on Pynchon's Novel.* Ed. Geoffrey Green, Donald J. Greiner, and Larry McCaffery. Normal, Ill.: Dalkey Archive Press, 1994. 68–88.

Spender, Stephen. *Love-Hate Relations: English and American Sensibilities.* New York: Random House, 1974.

Stewart, Susan. *On Longing: Narratives of the Miniature, the Gigantic, the Souvenir, the Collection.* Baltimore: Johns Hopkins UP, 1984.

Stull, William. "Beyond Hopelessville: Another Side of Raymond Carver." *Philological Quarterly* 64 (1985): 1–15.

———. "Matters of Life & Death: An Interview with Raymond Carver." *Bloomsbury Review* 8.1 (Jan.–Feb. 1988): 14–17. Rpt. in *Contemporary Literary Criticism* 55 (1989): 273–75.

Tabbi, Joseph. "Pynchon's Groundward Art." *The Vineland Papers: Critical Takes on Pynchon's Novel.* Ed. Geoffrey Green, Donald J. Greiner, and Larry McCaffery. Normal, Ill.: Dalkey Archive Press, 1994. 89–100.

Taliaferro, Frances. "*Moon Deluxe.*" Rev. of *Moon Deluxe,* by Frederick Barthelme. *Harper's* Sept. 1983: 74–75. Rpt. in *Contemporary Literary Criticism* 36 (1986): 51.

Tanner, Tony. "*The Moviegoer* and American Fiction: Wonder and Alienation." Rpt. from *The Reign of Wonder.* Cambridge: Cambridge UP, 1965. *Walker Percy.* Ed. Harold Bloom. New York: Chelsea House, 1986. 9–19.

Trachtenberg, Stanley, ed. *The Postmodern Moment.* Westport, Conn.: Greenwood Press, 1985.

Venturi, Robert, Denise Scott Brown, and Stephen Izenour. *Learning from Las Vegas: The Forgotten Symbolism of Architectural Form*. Cambridge: MIT Press, 1972.

Watt, Ian. *The Rise of the Novel*. Berkeley: U of California P, 1957.

Waugh, Patricia. *Feminine Fictions: Revisiting the Postmodern*. London: Routledge, 1989.

Weber, Bruce. "Raymond Carver: A Chronicler of Blue-Collar Despair." *New York Times Book Review* 24 June 1984: 36.

Webster, Duncan. *Looka Yonder! The Imaginary America of Populist Culture*. London/ New York: Routledge, 1988.

Weisenburger, Steven. *A Gravity's Rainbow Companion*. Athens: U of Georgia P, 1988.

West, Paul. "In Defense of Purple Prose." *New York Times Book Review* 15 Dec. 1985: 1.

Westarp, Karl-Heinz. "Preface." *Walker Percy: Novelist and Philosopher*. Ed. Jan Nordby Gretlund and Karl-Heinz Westarp. Jackson: UP of Mississippi, 1991. ix–xiv.

White, Hayden. *Metahistory: The Historical Imagination in Nineteenth-Century Europe*. Baltimore: Johns Hopkins UP, 1973.

———. "The Value of Narrativity in the Representation of Reality." *On Narrative*. Ed. W. J. T. Mitchell. Chicago: U of Chicago P, 1981. 1–23.

Wilde, Alan. *Horizons of Assent: Modernism, Postmodernism, and the Ironic Imagination*. Baltimore: Johns Hopkins UP, 1981.

———. "Love and Death in and around Vineland, U.S.A." *Boundary 2* 18.2 (Summer 1991): 166–80.

———. *Middle Grounds: Studies in Contemporary American Fiction*. Philadelphia: U of Pennsylvania P, 1987.

Williams, Raymond. *Marxism and Literature*. Oxford: Oxford UP, 1977.

Winston, Mathew. "The Quest for Pynchon." *Twentieth-Century Literature* 21.3 (Oct. 1975): 278–87.

Wolfe, Tom. "Stalking the Billion-Footed Beast: A Literary Manifesto for the New Social Novel." *Harper's* Nov. 1989: 45–56.

INDEX

Reagan, Ronald, 72, 151, 176, 178, 180
Realism, 46, 85, 86, 95, 103, 126, 129, 130,
    132, 133, 134, 186, 208 (n. 6)
Reed, Ishmael, 1, 4, 81, 89, 104, 128, 197 (n.
    5); *Mumbo Jumbo*, 10, 14, 18, 19–20, 40,
    45, 85, 86, 90–95, 101, 103, 146, 206 (n. 9)
Religion, 13, 24, 40
Richardson, Samuel, 92
Rilke, Rainer Maria, 112, 208 (n. 7)
Robocop (film), 184–85
Romanticism, 12, 13, 48, 129
Rorty, Richard, 200 (n. 14)
Rousseau, Jean-Jacques, 13, 165
Rubin, Jerry, 175

Salinger, J. D., 26
Sartre, Jean-Paul, 201 (n. 2), 203 (n. 11)
Satire, 91, 93, 164–66, 179
Saussurian linguistics, 7, 47
Science, 8, 49, 62, 212 (n. 8)
Science fiction, 17, 184, 199 (n. 7)
"Scientific" humanism, 37, 202 (n. 6)
Self: Cartesian rescue of, 48;
    communication phases and, 199 (n. 12);
    conspiracies and, 69–70; death and, 56;
    destabilization of, 20, 180; display of,
    49; historical continuity and, 156, 157;
    Hume on, 155–56, 213 (n. 14); image
    culture and, 19, 21, 41, 42, 151, 152;
    Jungian archetypes of, 205 (n. 13); loss
    of, 44; rendering of, 158; screen
    projections of, 165, 166, 167. *See also*
    Subjectivity
Selling of the Pentagon, The (film), 214 (n.
    26)
Shelley, Percy Bysshe, 124
Shopping malls, 66–67, 146, 170, 171, 186
Simpsons, The (TV serial), 87
Socrates, 193
Southern states, 24, 26, 27, 33, 36, 37, 201
    (n. 1)
"Space Invaders" (video game), 139

"Spectacular" fiction, 19, 50, 83–104
Stagecoach (film), 32
Steinbeck, John, 129
Sterne, Laurence, 10, 90–94, 101
Stevens, Wallace, 13, 151
Stone, Robert, 51, 128
Structuralism, 7
Subjectivity, 53, 161, 184, 199 (n. 12)
Suburbanization, 24, 26, 33, 40
Summer Stock (film), 83
Supermarkets, 57, 64

Taxi Driver (film), 72
Technology, 192, 193
Television: advertising on, 31, 86, 87;
    blandness of, 204 (n. 12); centrality of,
    46–47; "deaths" and, 183; in DeLillo
    fiction, 44, 65; depth/surface meta-
    phor and, 4; dissociation from, 68;
    distraction by, 175–76; global broad-
    casts of, 9; illusory knowledge from, 67;
    in *In Country*, 138, 139–41, 142–43;
    independent filmmakers and, 214
    (n. 26); knowledge conditions and, 1; in
    Libra, 78, 80; McHale on, 46, 206 (n. 6),
    211 (n. 6); minimalism and, 108, 130;
    Mumbo Jumbo and, 91; narrative
    discontinuity in, 86–88; oratory and,
    195 (n. 1); in *Players*, 68–69, 87;
    polysemy of, 88, 95; postmodernist
    fiction and, 86, 89–90, 193; public
    reception of, 66; self and, 54, 70, 81;
    social control by, 175, 178; Vietnam War
    and, 136; in *Vineland*, 20–21, 152, 166,
    167, 168, 173–74, 180; in *White Noise*, 58,
    59, 68
Thanatoids, 177, 179, 184, 186, 187, 193
Theater, 68, 213 (n. 13)
Third Man, The (film), 32
Thoth, Book of, 90, 92, 94
Tonight Show, The (TV program), 9
Twain, Mark, 57